TERMINAL
VISIONS

BOOKS BY W. WARREN WAGAR

H.G. Wells and the World State

The City of Man: Prophecies of a World Civilization in 20th-
Century Thought

H.G. Wells: Journalism and Prophecy, 1893–1946 (editor)

European Intellectual History since Darwin and Marx (editor)

Science, Faith, and Man: European Thought since 1914 (editor)

The Idea of Progress since the Renaissance (editor)

Building the City of Man: Outlines of a World Civilization

History and the Idea of Mankind (editor)

Good Tidings: The Belief in Progress from Darwin to Marcuse

Books in World History: A Guide for Teachers and Students

World Views: A Study in Comparative History

The Secular Mind: Transformations of Faith in Modern Europe (editor)

Terminal Visions: The Literature of Last Things

W. Warren Wagar

•

TERMINAL VISIONS

The Literature of
Last Things

•

Indiana University Press • *Bloomington*

PN
56
E63 W33

Manufactured in the United States of America

Library of Congress Cataloging in Publication Data
Wagar, W. Warren.
    Terminal visions.
    Bibliography: p
    Includes index.
    1. End of the world in literature.   I. Title.
PN56.E63W33   809'.9335   81-48625
ISBN 0-253-35847-7   AACR2
1 2 3 4 5 86 85 84 83 82

TO MY STUDENTS PAST AND PRESENT,
who have taught me most of what I know

CONTENTS

◆

Part Four / The War of the World Views

Part Five / Aftermaths

ACKNOWLEDGMENTS

I TAKE PLEASURE in expressing thanks to all those who have helped me in writing *Terminal Visions*. My most tangible debts are to the Research Foundation of the State University of New York, for two summer grants; to the National Endowment for the Humanities, for a Senior Fellowship; and to the State University of New York at Binghamton, for a sabbatical leave. The time released by these generous awards enabled me to begin, continue, and complete my book. I could not have done the job without such support.

I am also grateful to the many friends who have suggested themes, books, and authors to me over the last several years. More than once they guided me to something of importance that I would very likely have missed. Among those who helped, I would like to mention especially my fellow futurist, Michael Marien, founder and editor of *Future Survey*; Lorenz J. Firsching, a shrewd aficionado of speculative fiction and my doctoral student at the State University of New York at Binghamton; and George Zebrowski. George deserves a sentence or two of his own. Despite a busy schedule as one of the rising writers of his generation, he took the time to give my manuscript a thorough critical reading. I also profited from his invaluable bibliographical suggestions through the years, and from the use of his vast library of speculative fiction. Another much appreciated reader of the manuscript was Pamela Sargent. I hasten to add that neither of these gifted writers bears any responsibility for the various blunders, ill-advised omissions, and misinterpretations that may survive into the pages that follow.

My editors at Indiana University Press have been unfailing in their support and assistance. I thank them for making the production of this, my third Indiana book, such a happy experience.

Various passages in Chapters Nine and Fifteen are borrowed from two essays that I have contributed to *World's End: The Imagination of Catastrophe*, a forthcoming volume of critical studies edited by Eric S. Rabkin and Martin H. Greenberg. To its publishers, Southern Illinois University Press, I am indebted for permission to use these materials.

March 1982   W. WARREN WAGAR

A PERSONAL PREFACE

AT ONE TIME, the time when I first thought of writing *Terminal Visions*, I was on the verge of forty, and growing by degrees into a fair copy of John Wither, the Deputy Director of the National Institute of Co-ordinated Experiments in C.S. Lewis's eschatological romance, *That Hideous Strength.*

The Institute, you may remember, was actually an outpost of Hell, managed by demons, for whom Wither and his colleagues served as front men. In his philosophical progress, Wither "had passed from Hegel into Hume, thence through Pragmatism, and thence through Logical Positivism, and out at last into the complete void. The indicative mood now corresponded to no thought that his mind could entertain."[1] Knowledge wielded no power over the Deputy Director. Every truth, every motive, every value had dissolved in the acids of skeptical inquiry, leaving him as clean as a well-picked bone.

In the universe of academic liberalism, where I have spent all my adult life, fair copies of John Wither abound. In the ten generations since Voltaire, the bourgeois intellectual has taken part in an uninterrupted process of credicide: a killing much more tremendous than deicide. Gods are made to die. But credicide is nothing less than the destruction of the will and the power to believe.

The weapons of credicide are all familiar. Deathly sharp are their blades. The sharpest belong to the various relativisms: historical, cultural, psychological. Relativism makes truth and knowledge the creatures of circumstance. Proposition "A" holds good only for Historical Era "A" or Cultural Configuration "A" or Personality Type "A." In "B" circumstances, bring on "B" propositions.

The philosophers have gone beyond relativism. They affirm that all statements of what is good, beautiful, true, and real are matters of private or social preference; moreover that all words, numbers, logics, grammars, and sciences are games. Perhaps we are constructed, by virtue of our biology, to play certain games and no others. Or perhaps our choices are ultimately arbitrary. The difference is slight. Either way, the result is credicide.

In my own situation, at the beginning of the 1970s, the various surrogates that I had invented for the credenda of the traditional culture had

begun to wear through. I had prescribed, for myself and others, a cosmopolitical variety of humanism that looked forward to the establishment of a new
world civilization as the next stage of world history.[2] I had envisaged for my
City of Man a new, severely demythologized religion of "the service of being,"
located halfway between the nineteenth-century French philosopher Auguste
Comte's "religion of humanity" and the nineteenth-century Chinese philosopher K'ang Yu-wei's "religion of serving heaven."[3] The new civilization
would also be more or less liberal, and more or less socialist. To call it into
existence, a worldwide political movement, a Wellsian open conspiracy of
denationalized thinkers and doers, had to begin popping up almost
immediately.

It failed to pop. Reason warned me that time had grown too short for
such vast undertakings. World disasters, from wars to ecological doomsdays,
were imminent. In any case, who could believe anything, in a credicidal
civilization? How could a rational new religion emerge in such a poisoned
mental climate? If new religions did materialize, would they not rather be
crazy throwbacks to primitivism, panic-stricken responses by unsophisticated
minds to the onrush of catastrophe?

I shared my darkest misgivings with no one. Although I continued to
flay liberal advocates of world order for their excessive optimism,[4] I remained
publicly hopeful of the ultimate triumph of reason. Yet I felt myself slipping.
Forty is a good age for presentiments of extinction. I began to detect a certain
uneasy sympathy with the religious prophets, like Jacques Maritain, who had
long been crying that the modern mind was intrinsically evil. The first
apparently innocent step, of preferring man's reason to God's word, had
perhaps—after all!—started the avalanche, the *dégringolade* from rationalism
through positivism to nihilism.

If I remained too "modern" to scurry into the shelter of some ancestral
faith, the only honest alternative was to step bravely out into the void. If the
jig was up, why not go all the way? Never mind the ersatz illusions of
humanism, or the obsession with an unattainable world order. Why not fill
one's lungs with the vacuum of the outer spaces explored by Nietzsche, Kafka,
and Beckett, and proclaim their truthless truth?

In that case, what better metaphor to install in place of the City of Man
than the Day of Doom? Even in Christianity, the final loosing of Satan
follows the Millennium. A brief, understated, airless volume on secular eschatology from Mary Shelley to Kurt Vonnegut would allow me to discharge
my final responsibilities to the moribund science of intellectual history, scatter whatever cosmopolitical followers survived from the 1960s, and invest my
declining years in the role of cynic-in-residence at my campus in the foggy
woodlands of upstate New York.

I had even begun to smack my lips at the prospect of transmitting bittersweet pictures of the Last Things now surely visible on the human horizon. They would come to me like the final bars of Mahler's Ninth Symphony, plaintive, moist with nostalgia, ripe with a warm and somehow comfortable sorrow. Then into the garden of Epicurus, for a dignified, illusionless old age.

Little of that original mood lingers in the pages that follow. The mood passed, leaving behind only the perception that we do indeed live in an endtime, an era in history marked by the collapse of the traditional civilizations of the non-Western world and by the senescence of the national-bourgeois social order in the West. There have been endtimes aplenty in the six thousand years of recorded history, but none so universal or so dangerous. Only the demon of relativism bars us from full consciousness of our predicament. Be not deceived. Our twentieth-century endtime does surpass, in scope and destructive potential, all others.

At the same time it is ridiculous to repair to one's garden and await the apocalypse with folded hands. The chances are good that some significant portion of humankind will outlast the trials still before us. The "void" into which John Wither stepped exists only in tired minds—minds that have forced themselves to forget the pulse of life, the cries of children, the eyes of lovers, the struggles of peoples everywhere for justice and freedom. What ends is not humankind, or even the sorely abused earth, but only ways of life that no longer serve human needs. Feudalism, capitalism, nationalism, Stalinism—all are mortal, and pass. The supernaturalist religions by which men and women have lived since the dawn of civilization are mortal, and they, too, pass. The people remain. The human pattern remains.

It follows that the subject matter of this book springs from a culturally generated consciousness wholly appropriate to our time. Western visions of the world's end reflect an awareness blooming within the very citadels of power that the modern era of history, which began such a short while ago in the birth-wails of the French and Industrial revolutions, is already approaching its endtime. We seldom know what we are seeing. Rather like John the Evangelist before us, we prefer to transmute our perceptions into great apocalyptic beasts, who are easier to picture than metamorphoses of social orders. But wrapped in metaphor or spoken unadorned, the message is much the same.

The task of *Terminal Visions*, then, is to study one way in which a dying culture—in this case, the national-bourgeois culture of the post-Christian West—has chosen to express the loss or decline of its faith in itself. My evidence is the abundant speculative fiction of Last Things. But the Last of what Things? Far from being over, history has not yet even properly begun. Folly and bad luck can produce almost any disaster, but as a species we remain in our age of First Things.

PART ONE

◆

The Dream of
Last Things

1

◆

The End

THE END! Followers of fashion in popular and serious culture since the mid-1970s have been calling wry attention to the resurgence of interest in Last Things: signs of an approaching end of the world. If scatology was a ruling obsession of the 1960s, liberating us from a false cleanliness, perhaps its place has now been taken by eschatology, liberating us from a false cheeriness. Or is all this modish apocalypticism just another merchandising ploy, a cult of "chic bleak"[1] herding us into bookstores and cinemas and revival meetings to buy the latest wares of the latest self-selected messiahs?

The excitement is real enough, whatever its sources, and no matter how high the profits of the prophets. Eschatology has become, once again, after long neglect, a principal concern of Christians. The doomsday sermons of Hal Lindsey, Jack Van Impe, and Herbert and Garner Ted Armstrong have drawn "Bible prophecy" into a golden commerce. One book alone, Lindsey's *The Late Great Planet Earth*, has sold well over fifteen million copies.[2] A cinematic version of Lindsey's work, directed by Robert Amram and narrated by the same Orson Welles who once convinced Americans to look for Martian invaders in New Jersey, has enjoyed a nearly comparable success at the box office. John Wesley White, a Canadian associate of Billy Graham, knows that World War III will be incited by the Antichrist and will fulfill the prophecy of Armageddon laid down in the sixteenth chapter of Revelation.[3] The glossiest product of the new Christian fervor about Last Things is no doubt William Griffin's compilation of readings and illustrations, *Endtime: The Doomsday Catalog*, published in 1979 by the eminently respectable house of Macmillan. It features everything from *New Yorker* cartoons to Dürer woodcuts, and an array of texts by more than a hundred authors, from Lindsey and

Graham to formidable eschatologists of the likes of Saint Augustine, Jacques Ellul, Romano Guardini, and Pierre Teilhard de Chardin.

But eschatology is much more than a Christian (or Jewish or Muslim) doctrine. There is also a secular eschatology, a worldly study of world's ends that ignores religious belief or puts the old visions to use as metaphors for modern anxiety. Thoughts of a secular *dies irae* have been unusually abundant in recent years. They crop up everywhere. Comprehensive summaries of how the world will end according to the natural sciences have been offered by Gordon Rattray Taylor, Fred Warshofsky, Gerrit L. Verschuur, and Isaac Asimov, embracing a rich variety of astrophysical, geological, climatological, and biological dooms.[4] One science in particular, ecology, has generated an immense literature of catastrophe. Ecologists tell of "the population bomb," the coming "death of the oceans," the "limits to growth," the need for a new "lifeboat ethics."[5] There will soon be great famines, droughts, and—take your choice—a new ice age or the transformation of the earth into one vast suffocating hothouse.[6]

After some years of disobeying Herman Kahn's instructions to think the unthinkable, sober studies of the next world war are also back in vogue. Nigel Calder has published *Nuclear Nightmares*, which led to a television documentary with Peter Ustinov in the role of Orson Welles. From the political scientist Louis René Beres comes *Apocalypse: Nuclear Catastrophe in World Politics*, and from General Sir John Hackett and "other top-ranking NATO generals and advisors" a barely fictional account of *The Third World War: August 1985*. Replete with maps and tables and a 16-page "photo history," Hackett's ample volume is advertised as "a major bestseller on two continents."[7]

A related phenomenon, noted in 1979 by *Time* in a piece on "The Deluge of Disastermania," is the expanding public enthusiasm for calamities of all sorts, whether local or planetary. Bookstores are well stocked with encyclopedias and picture-books devoted to disasters through the ages.[8] The "disaster" film, which is almost always an artistic disaster in the bargain, provided up to one-quarter of the cinematic entertainment available in Our Town in any given week of the late 1970s or early 1980s. Of plagues, earthquakes, shipwrecks, meteors, meltdowns, floods, fires, tribulation in every guise, there was no end. The best film thus far inspired by the American devastation of Vietnam was fittingly entitled *Apocalypse Now*. Public interest has also fastened obsessively on the still more deliberately apocalyptic devastation of Europe by Adolf Hitler's Thousand-Year Reich, in any number of televised "docudramas."

The evidence accumulates. Prominent analysts of the social and mental health of modern civilization, including Roberto Vacca, Robert Heilbroner,

William Irwin Thompson, and Christopher Lasch, fill their books with pre-
monitions of breakdown and ruin.[9] Urban "survivalists" stage evacuation
maneuvers that will enable their families to relocate in the wilderness in the
first few hours of Doomsday.[10] A Virginia clergyman has founded End Time
Foods, Inc., an outlet for dehydrated victuals to help the provident endure
the dislocations sure to come, and a professor of geography at U.C.L.A.
reports that the majority of his students, whom he regularly polls, expect
civilization to last no more than a century or two. In one class of 94 students,
the modal expectation was a scant 25 years.[11]

The end of the world, of course, is a familiar time for writers of science
fiction, and they have visited it often in recent years. An American speciality
of late has been the natural catastrophe, once almost a monopoly of British
fantasists. Novels such as Piers Anthony's *Rings of Ice* (1974), Larry Niven
and Jerry Pournelle's *Lucifer's Hammer* (1977), Arthur Herzog's *Heat* (1977),
Gwyneth Cravens and John S. Marr's *The Black Death* (1977), and Arnold
Federbush's *Ice!* (1978), are fair samples. Persuasive pictures of America after
a general apocalyptic collapse are drawn by Edgar Pangborn in *The Company
of Glory* (1975), Kate Wilhelm in *Where Late the Sweet Birds Sang* (1976),
Robie Macauley in *A Secret History of Time to Come* (1979), and many others.
From the literary mainstream, Gore Vidal has added to his ironic soteriogra-
phy of death-wishing messiahs in *Kalki* (1978) and Doris Lessing has published two major eschatological romances, *The Memoirs of a Survivor* (1974)
and *Shikasta* (1979). A work of extraordinary distinction is Russell Hoban's
cyclic vision of doomsday, *Riddley Walker* (1981).

But the current fascination with scenarios of disaster, especially in
America, is by no means unique either to Americans or to the period since
the mid-1970s. The idea of writing *Terminal Visions* came to me in 1971, and
none of the evidence accumulated during the past decade has made any
crucial difference to the forms and shapes of eschatology in the West, religious
or secular, serious or popular. We have seen it all before, over and over again.
No doubt the current swell of interest has its own special character and
reasons for happening, but it is no more than an episode, and to some degree
only a local episode, in a continuing and—in the main—rising flow of speculative thought.

Terminal Visions explores this flow over a period of some one hundred
and seventy-five years. Our theme is disaster in the highest order of magni-
tude: the idea of the end of the world, not as a restatement or exegesis of
Biblical eschatology, but as a creative act of the secular imagination.

Present-day gloom (mixed, more often than not, with dark rapture)
enjoys a distinguished heritage, far older than the one and three-quarters
centuries of *Terminal Visions*. Mythopoeic man often turned his mind to

thoughts of decline, winter, the iron age, calamity, the end. Every primitive and traditional culture has its eschatology, although some take more interest in Last Things than others. The Norse myth of Ragnarök, the Hindu doctrine of the *Kali Yuga,* and the Stoic prophecy of a universal conflagration at the close of the world-cycle are three examples. Nowhere does eschatology figure so centrally as in Christianity, the mother-faith of modern Western civilization. Nearly all the classics of Christian culture, from the New Testament and *The City of God* to *The Divine Comedy,* are steeped in eschatological foretelling.

Studies of eschatology in this original sense of religious teaching about Last Things are plentiful, and they will help us explore the pre-modern sources of our theme in Part Two. Not so plentiful are studies of the eschatological dimension of modern prophetic thought. Most treatments of the secular prophetic mind have touched only marginally on visions of ending. They explore ideas of the future, utopia and dystopia, the belief in progress, cyclical theories of history, millennialism, the sense of decadence.[12] But *Terminal Visions* belongs to eschatology, the science of Last Things. Eschatology seeks and analyzes answers to the question of what will happen at the end—the end of time, the end of man, the end of civilization. The Christian model, clearly, encompassed all three ends, preceded by a chain of disasters (itemized in Revelation 6-20) of singular frightfulness.

Eschatological visions differ from other varieties of prophetic thought in their preoccupation with the end as something supremely important. The end becomes, paradoxically, the center, the axis, the focal point of human experience. Even if the end is not literally final, but will be followed by renewal or salvation, the eschatological vision is principally concerned to depict the end, with all events before and after the end earning only incidental notice. What holds the prophet in thrall is the thought of life's finitude, extending beyond the individual to civilization, to mankind, even to time itself.

Of the related studies of modern prophetic thought mentioned above, none is quite the same as eschatology. "Ideas of the future" include terminal images, but many others as well, and the emphasis patently falls on the future as such. "Utopias and dystopias" are, in modern times, secularized heavens and hells, metaphors of eternity rather than mortality. The "belief in progress" measures the movement toward utopia, and "cyclical theories" are concerned no less with beginnings and rises than with falls and endings.

Of "millennialism" and "the sense of decadence," more should be said. A millennial vision, in the Christian model, prophesies a pre-heavenly utopia, a foretaste of eternal bliss coming just before the end of history. Disasters may usher it in, and take it away again, but the millennium is always a just age, when the good rule and when evil, although well-known and not necessarily vanquished, is held in check. Millennialist studies direct their attention to anticipations of this great commonwealth, and the calamities and revolutions required to achieve it, but they are not end-centered. By the same token, although eschatology may include millennial visions, it views the millennium only as an incident in the endtime, of secondary value relative to the end itself.

Studies of the sense of decadence, or cultural despair, explore ideas of the future as a time of inexorably mounting failure, pointing toward, without necessarily pointing out, the end. Such presentiments may be general enough to constitute a doctrine of retrogression, the antithesis of the belief in progress. They approach eschatology more closely than ideas of progress since the decay, if projected far enough into the future, may lead to death: the end of the human order. Clearly a sense of decadence can be part of any eschatological vision, but it need not be eschatological in and of itself. The decisive point is the extent to which the end is foretold or implied in a given prophet's prognosis. If to his forecast of a decadent future he adds the firm expectation of a still more distant end of the human order, then he may belong to eschatology.

But our theme in *Terminal Visions* is exactly what the two words of the title denote: images of the end, conceived as a public end, the termination of a world-order. Of all the symptoms of disenchantment in our culture, visions of the end are the bluntest and the most powerful. They bear witness, gladly or reluctantly as the case may be, to what Herbert Marcuse has called "the Great Refusal."[13] Through their images, Western man expresses disbelief that his civilization can endure, in anything like its present form. He becomes a nay-sayer, and his nay-saying helps prepare the way for a better or at least a different world.

One peculiarity of the endtime, not shared by "progress" or "decadence" or most of the other large concepts in speculative philosophy of history, is its embarrassing concreteness. It happens in a certain way, at a certain point, for certain reasons. Often it is imagined to come on a single day, even at a single hour. The majority of Jewish and Christian prophets through the ages have been careful to avoid fixing the date of the Last Things. Modern philosophers and ideologists and social scientists have been still more skittish on the subject. From their number only a few unusually brave or unusually foolish thinkers have undertaken the hazardous work of hypothesizing just when, where, and how the end will come. They make an ill-assorted and unrepresentative group, ranging from Schopenhauer's long-forgotten disciple Eduard von Hartmann to Dennis Meadows and his band of world-modelers computing a twenty-first-century doomsday in *The Limits to Growth*.

But one coherent and substantial body of source material does exist, for the student of terminal visions in modern Western secular thought. If he is willing to step outside of formal thought altogether and invade the world of imaginative literature, he will find hundreds of ingenious scenarios of the endtime, whose authors are not in the least embarrassed by the concreteness of Last Things—for whom, indeed, such concreteness is a welcome challenge and even a delight. In *Terminal Visions*, we shall be studying literary sources exclusively, although, as will soon enough be obvious, not from the perspectives of literary criticism. Every fiction is a work of thought, as well as art, and the first aspect is just as legitimate a target for scholarly investigation as the second.

In any event, where the endtime is concerned, the logic and traditions of imaginative literature ensure that it will bear deposits of the richest possible ore. The playwright, tale-teller, and novelist is free to push much further than the philosopher or the social scientist. For that matter, the dramatic conventions established by his Greek forerunners leave him little choice. He must invent protagonists caught in the toils of destiny; he must imagine real troubles and dangers; he must, somehow or other, bring his adventures to an end—happy, tragic, or enigmatic. Nor is he hobbled, like the philosopher, by the demands of scientific prudence. If a writer of fictions elects to blow everything up, he can. Never mind the odds.

The dream of Last Things in imaginative literature summons all the powers of prophecy. It must stretch far. Although modern eschatological fictions do not wield such vast control over our lives as myths of the endtime wielded over the lives of ancient and medieval people, they are no less graphic, no less awful, no less strongly conceived and imagined. I am prepared to match the best of H. G. Wells, Karel Čapek, James Blish, or J. G. Ballard against any mythic vision of antiquity.

My choice of names, however, suggests that the modern rivals of Isaiah and John the Evangelist are to be drawn primarily from the producers of what is known, often with a pejorative sniff, as "science fiction." It may seem at first glance an uneven contest, pitting some of the greatest of ancient prophets against some of the sleaziest of modern writers, but such is not the case.

A word, first, about science fiction, and its relationship to the literary mainstream. The usual practice of critics is to set up an invidious distinction between the two based, at least in part, on subject matter. Whereas the art of the mainstream is an art of life in the round, science fiction supposedly limits itself to one fragment of life, the interaction of science and society, chiefly if not exclusively in the near or far future of mankind. But under even casual inspection, this distinction quickly falls apart. Many mainstream writers, like Henry James, do not treat life in the round at all. Many writers of science fiction, like John Brunner, do. Many mainstream writers, like Aldous Huxley, have produced fictions as sharply focused on the interaction of science and society as the hardest of hard-core science-fictionists. Many writers of science fiction, like J. G. Ballard, have only a peripheral interest in such matters.

There is, to be sure, a literary ghetto of genre fiction tagged as science fiction by its own editors, writers, and fans, a ghetto created more than half a century ago by well-meaning champions like Hugo Gernsback, which occupies a special niche in the literary marketplace.[14] But it is dangerous to build walls in criticism between "real" literature and "genre" literature for which the rationale is a difference of subject matter. It is equally wrongheaded to engage in wholesale condemnation of any sort of fiction because of its relationship to the marketplace. In a capitalist society—and the whole modern world, not excluding the so-called socialist countries, constitutes a single capitalist economic system[15]—every writer who publishes anything becomes entangled to some degree in the forces of the marketplace, the mainstreamer as much as the ghetto-dweller.

Nevertheless, at the core of the concept of a separate literature known as science fiction hides a kernel of truth. The separateness has to do not with subject matter but with mode of inquiry, which in turn leads to differences in setting. Whereas most fictions explore life in the known past or present, some delve into the unknown future, or into past or present worlds alternative to our own. Their jumping-off point is the creation in the mind of a reality beyond the reality of present-day knowledge. For fiction in this mode of inquiry, the best term is "speculative." All of it, in turn, can be conveniently divided into two main varieties, the "realistic"—which extrapolates plausibly from current science and learning—and the "fantastic"—which deliberately ignores or contravenes present-day knowledge. Much of what passes for science fiction clearly fits into the category of "realistic speculation," a phrase once seriously proposed by Robert Heinlein as a replacement for "science fiction."[16] The other term, "fantastic speculation," describes fantasy fiction, although less aptly. Fantasists are not so much "speculating" as reinventing or adapting pre-modern myth and legend.

Be this as it may, we shall use the phrase "speculative literature" in *Terminal Visions* to denote any work of fiction, including drama and narrative poetry, that specializes in plausible speculation about life under changed but rationally conceivable circumstances, in an alternative past or present, or in the future. Nearly all "science fiction" adheres to this definition. So do many works of the mainstream, from Mary Shelley's *Frankenstein* and Bernard Shaw's *Back to Methuselah* to Hermann Hesse's *Das Glasperlenspiel* and Kurt Vonnegut's *The Sirens of Titan*. The mention of a work like *The Sirens of Titan* is not, incidentally, a slip of the pen. Satire and fabling also have their place in the games of speculation, although they play the speculative game at deeper levels than those of formal waking consciousness, and plausibility is achieved by somewhat different criteria—those of behavioral, rather than social or natural, science or those of metaphysics, rather than physics.

It follows from all the foregoing that our sources in *Terminal Visions* are not confined to "the sleaziest of modern writers." Of the some three hundred titles consulted, and listed at the end of this book, more than one-third are by authors generally regarded as men and women of the literary mainstream. Of the rest, the majority exhibit qualities of craftsmanship, human understanding, and artistic integrity equal to what one typically finds in the mainstream. All the titles consulted, no matter by whom, meet the definition of speculative literature offered above. Such literature is entirely serious in its purposes and methods, traveling in regions of the imagination just as important to the vitality of culture as any other, and yielding—from time to time—masterpieces suitable for shelving with *Candide*, *Madame Bovary*, and *The Magic Mountain*—or The Book of Revelation.

It is even possible to join forces with several critics of recent decades, such as Frank Kermode, and discover in apocalypticism the key to an understanding of most or all of modern mainstream literature. In *The Sense of an Ending*, Kermode suggests that modern fiction and drama is nothing less than a secularized and immanentized version of ancient apocalyptic prophecy. Just as modern theology (by which Kermode means Rudolf Bultmann) has elaborated a demythologized eschatology that wipes out any expectation of a literal end, but makes the end something present or potential in every moment of our lives, so modern literature transforms the end into "a predicament of the individual." The process began, he contends, in the literature of the Renaissance, which saw "the terrors of apocalypse . . . absorbed by tragedy," and culminates in contemporary absurdist literature, which disengages itself even from the notion of tragedy, and leaves the individual human atom stranded in howling chaos.[17]

Kermode deals almost exclusively with works of the mainstream, by Yeats, Eliot, Beckett, Sartre, and others. He makes clear that modern man rejects the "naive" apocalypticism of antiquity because he has lost faith in his power to know and predict the future. The result is a "sophisticated" apocalypticism that confronts ignorance and unbelief and still manages, even in absurdist fictions, to give us a sense of moving through time and a sense of beginnings and endings. Our psychic thirst for the orientation supplied by the traditional apocalyptic paradigms, is quenched.

John R. May in *Toward a New Earth* furnishes a comparable analysis of

American literature in its relationship to the apocalyptic imagination. May defines a vision as apocalyptic if it possesses at least two of the specific symbolisms of the traditional apocalypse: catastrophic change and a norm of judgment.[18] By these criteria Herman Melville's *Moby-Dick* and *The Confidence-Man* and Nathanael West's *The Day of the Locust* and *Miss Lonelyhearts* rank as classic examples of secular apocalyptic fiction. A literal end of the world is not required, and seldom provided, although it may be foreshadowed. Almost all serious contemporary American fiction, May concludes, qualifies as apocalyptic in this radically immanentized sense.

Ironically enough, Kermode and May and various other critics who have dealt with the apocalyptic dimension of modern fiction (such as R. W. B. Lewis and Northrop Frye) make their case with scant reference to the overt doomsdays of speculative literature. For Kermode, in fact, a good deal of speculative literature is perhaps no more than an anachronistic nuisance, a throwback to the "naive" apocalypticism of antiquity. It comes as a relief to encounter one major critical study, David Ketterer's provocative *New Worlds for Old*, that devotes more than half its pages to studies of literal apocalypses in fiction, pleading even that the apocalyptic imagination "finds its purest outlet in science fiction."[19]

Ketterer makes a further point that, I think, is absolutely decisive. Whether or not the rest of modern fiction should be marshaled under the rubric of secular eschatology (a question that lies beyond the scope of the present study), the doomsdays of speculative fiction tend to hold what Ketterer terms both a "negative" and a "positive" charge. They destroy old worlds; most of them, although not all, create new ones, too. "The fulfillment of the apocalyptic imagination," as Ketterer writes, "demands that the destructive chaos give way finally to a new order."[20] The prototype is John in Revelation, and as we shall learn in Chapter Sixteen, most world's ends in speculative fiction, like the vision of John, transcend cultural fatigue and despair.

To come, then, to a summing-up: our province in this book is the fiction of public endtimes, literal ends of the world of modern man. Such cataclysms range in scale from the death of the universe or the destruction of earth or its biosphere, to the end of man's life as a species or the collapse of his civilization. The fiction may be a fiction in the ordinary sense of the word, or a "fabulation," Robert Scholes's term for a post-realist, self-consciously fabling tale in the manner of John Barth.[21] The endtime may be intended, in whole or in part, to represent something other than the end of the world. It may be intended to represent nothing more, and yet may succeed in reaching other levels of meaning in spite of itself. In the narrative structure, the end may precede or follow the time of the storytelling, or may occur at any point within it. The endtime may be final, or mankind may win a reprieve or a new life. It may be set in the far future, or on the day after tomorrow. It may be gradual or sudden, good or evil, natural or man-made. All we ask is that it be expressed in a secular fiction centrally concerned with the public end of the world of modern man.

2

•

A Short History of Doomsday

ANOTHER WAY to define the task of *Terminal Visions* is to take an obscenely rapid journey through the texts of eschatological fiction, in more or less chronological order, winnowing our wheat from our chaff, before settling down in later chapters to analysis of the texts themselves. For those who are thoroughly at home in the world of speculative literature, this overview may prove a little wearisome. For those less familiar, it will furnish a map to all that follows. For anyone, it may help bring alive the all too abstract definitions of our theme in Chapter One. I am not enough of a historist to agree with Nietzsche's maxim that only that which has no history can be defined. But no definition is complete unless it clothes the bones of logic with the corruptible flesh of history.

One book deserves somewhat more leisurely treatment, even here, because it marks such a critical breaking point between traditional and secular eschatology in Western thought. It is also a model, of sorts, for many of the texts written in the generations that followed its first publication in 1826. Brian Aldiss, in his *Billion Year Spree*, describes Mary Shelley's *Frankenstein* as the first authentic work of modern science fiction, a pioneering effort to bring man and the science and technology of his modern world into significant confrontation.[1] But it is not *Frankenstein* that concerns us now. What Shelley published in 1826, eight years after *Frankenstein*, was a large and somewhat turgid romance in three volumes entitled *The Last Man*. If the earlier work founded the genre of science fiction (a sticky point, which I shall not pursue), *The Last Man* has an even stronger claim to consideration as the first major example of secular eschatology in literature.

The place of Shelley's novel at the breaking point between tradition and secularism owes much to her family, her time, and her own Janus-like mind. Born during Year V of the French Revolution, in 1797, she was the daughter of two great liberators, the feminist Mary Wollstonecraft and the philosopher William Godwin, prophet of progress and communitarian anarchism. From her father she learned that mankind was perfectible, and would fulfill its destiny as soon as it replaced the tyranny of political power with the sovereignty of reason. Mary's husband, the archetypal romantic poet Percy Bysshe Shelley, drew much of his own social optimism from Godwin, and a great deal survives of the hopes of both in *The Last Man*. But, as Jane Dunn remarks, the atheism and anarchism that seethed all around her did not touch Mary viscerally. "She was innately conservative, and romantic about religion, believing in a comfortable, anthropomorphic God and life after death." At the same time she was a woman of superior intellect who "dismissed the cant and prejudice of much of religion."[2] How would she go about treating the theme of the world's end? Almost anything might have emerged from such a mix of influences, abilities, and temperaments.

What did emerge was astonishing in many ways, if not always eloquent or gripping. She set her story in the last decade of the twenty-first century. Although by the standards of present-day speculative fiction Shelley's imagination did not stretch far, she clearly intended her future world to seem marvelous by contrast with the age of George IV. In the happy days with which the first volume is concerned, men travel about in balloons. The cutting of canals and the building of bridges occupy engineers. Projects are afoot to abolish poverty and disease once and for all. And why not? "The arts of life, and the discoveries of science had augmented in a ratio which left all calculation behind; food sprung up, so to say, spontaneously—machines existed to supply with facility every want of the population."[3] Adrian, son of England's last king, foresees a universal era of peace, freedom, abundance, and health. "Earth will become a Paradise," he predicts in the bucolic spring of 2093. "The energies of man were before directed to the destruction of his species: they now aim at its liberation and preservation."[4]

But nature soon turns the tables. In the same year a plague originating in the East enters Europe, and by the end of the decade, only one human being remains, the last man, Lionel Verney. Lionel is a bosom friend of Adrian's. He is also a masculine version of Mary herself. The last man was in fact a woman.

For Shelley's *The Last Man* reflected personal tragedy as well as romantic *Weltschmerz*. When she wrote her novel, the year was 1824. Her close friend Byron had just died in Greece, fighting for that country's independence. Percy had drowned two years before in a sailing mishap. She felt abandoned. Hugh J. Luke, Jr., connects her sensibility with Wordsworth's metaphysics of alienation, "his great recurring myth of the Solitary . . . the threat of man's aloneness in an unintelligible universe."[5] Yet Mary's aloneness was more than metaphysical. Her husband and friend had died long before their proper time, and it was only natural for someone of her powers of vision to search for a way of expressing her grief in the codes of literature. The sensitive Adrian is Percy, his robust friend Lord Raymond (who dies in the second volume, during a twenty-first-century Greek conquest of Constantinople) is Byron, and the friend of both of them, Lionel Verney, is Mary.

What concerns us more at this point is the author's decision to enlarge personal tragedy until it embraced the whole world. She gives subjectivity free rein. The end spins out slowly, painfully, and hopelessly. Mob violence, barbarism, and superstitious madness deprive the endtime of most of its dignity, and give the lie to the Godwinian dreams of human reasonableness that had seemed so near to realization earlier in the story. In the confusion Adrian is compelled to lead an English army against a ragtag band of Irish and Scots invaders. A famous scientist, Merrival, loses his sanity after the plague kills his family, and curses God like a character out of the novels of the Marquis de Sade. When the last English survivors flee southward into France, the lower classes among them fall under the power of a raving Methodist evangelist, who calls on everyone to repent.

But the plague continues its work, undermining the preacher's authority, until only four members of the party survive—Adrian, Lionel, and two children. They escape to Italy, finding no one alive. One of the children dies of typhus. Repeating Percy's death, Adrian is drowned in a storm en route to Greece. The other child dies in the same disaster, leaving Lionel alone, beached near Ravenna. He makes his way to Rome, where he lives until early in the year 2100. As the novel comes to a close, he has decided to take to the sea again. He will sail along the coastlines of the world looking for signs of other survivors. But he is not optimistic. "Neither hope nor joy are my pilots—restless despair and fierce desire of change lead me on."[6] The end is not a gateway to a new world, nor a judgment, but simply an end, produced by the cold necessity of natural causes.

The Last Man is thus a more or less pure example of secular eschatology. Shelley's nature goes its own way, indifferent to man and man's hopes and powers. As an "internal voice" tells Lionel, there is no point in' reading backwards "the unchangeable laws of Necessity."[7] To be sure, traces remain of earlier symbologies. Shelley's characters sometimes reflect gloomily on the exhaustion or old age of the earth, in an Epicurean vein.[8] Even more jarring to modern readers is the occasional display of celestial fireworks that accompanies the progress of the plague. A black twin of the sun rises one day in the west, intersecting with the true sun at high noon; unusual storms buffet the earth; three meteors as big as the sun terrify the fleeing Englishmen as they prepare to sail for France. But the novel has no real need for such decorations. They are, as it were, tacked on, in casual obeisance to the traditional vision of the world's end. At its core, *The Last Man* is a secular tale of man's extinction, told not as an act of faith or holy fear, but because it was now easy, in Shelley's day, to imagine a purposeless end self-generated by the world-order. The alienation of romantic heroes such as René or Obermann or Childe Harold is carried a step further: the very existence of humankind becomes problematical, and mother earth is beheld murdering her own children. Of the anthropomorphic God and the life after death in which Shelley, paradoxically, believed, there is hardly a word. They are not expressly excluded; but she does not need them in her story, even though its subject is the end of all human life on earth.

The Last Man will probably never rank as a first-rate work of imaginative literature, and will probably always be overshadowed by *Frankenstein*. But its writing is an event of high significance in the history of secular eschatology, and in the history of the secularization of Western consciousness itself. No such book could have been produced in earlier centuries, or at any rate before the last few decades of the eighteenth. At the same time, it is not actually the first full-dress vision of a secular doomsday. It comes near the end of a considerable series of romantic tales and poems of "the last man" that began in 1805 with the publication in France of *Le dernier homme* by a priest of the *ancien régime* and a critic of *les philosophes*, Jean-Baptiste Cousin de Grainville. In Grainville's novel, the secular end, caused by the exhaustion of the soil and human sterility, gives way in the last pages to the terminal vision of Revelation. God is also very much present throughout the story in the mission of Adam, the first man, whom God has sent back to earth to persuade the last fertile man and woman, Omégare and Syderie, not to reproduce. But nearly all the imaginative force of *Le dernier homme* derives from its secular events, and from its detailed history of the future of the human race. It takes a long stride—although this surely was not Grainville's intention—toward secularism.

Another study of Last Things, which may have been suggested by Grainville's novel, and in turn may have prodded the imagination of Mary Shelley, was her friend Byron's narrative poem "Darkness" (1816). Only 82 lines in length, the poem is nevertheless a complete scenario of a secular world's end, resulting from the sudden extinction of the sun. A longer narrative poem, Thomas Hood's wryly humorous "The Last Man," appeared in the same year as Mary's novel. These and other examples of romantic visions of the endtime are discussed at some length in useful articles by A. J. Sambrook and Henry F. Majewski.[9]

An American postscript to the "last man" theme was supplied several years after its vogue had faded in Europe by three stories of Shelley's contemporary, Edgar Allan Poe. The appeal of eschatology to a morbid imagination such as Poe's must have been irresistible. It is only strange that he did not dwell on it more often or more elaborately. His first world's end scenario was a weak fantasia in the style of Voltaire, "The Conversation of Eiros and Charmion," written in 1839. Here the terminal event is a comet that strikes the earth after scientists assure a respectful public that it has nothing to fear. Better known is Poe's story "The Masque of the Red Death," written three years later. He now chose as his vehicle for destruction a plague that causes profuse bleeding at every pore, a reworking of the ancient idea of a terminal world-fire: blood, like fire, is red. A band of last men is led by a dauntless prince with the ironic name of Prospero. But his courage is useless. He collapses just as he is about to plunge his dagger into the masked figure who symbolizes death. Human effort once more is frustrated by cosmic forces.[10]

Poe drew up his sharpest indictment of human pride in a third tale, "The Colloquy of Monos and Una," a catalogue of romantic protests. The world's end is only vaguely intimated in this story of a conversation between two spirits after death, but its root causes are clearly identified: the folly of the belief in progress, the attempt to control rather than obey natural law, and "the leading evil, Knowledge," which drove men to befoul their natural environment and ignore the gradations in society appointed by God. Taste, beauty, and the social order had all been sacrificed to rude utility. The result was inexorable decay.

Poe's attacks on modern man and his pride, evident in all three tales, provide a link with traditional Biblical eschatology, which blamed the world's end on human moral failure, but whether the romantic eschatologist credited sin or fate, judgment or necessity, the irony remained the same. Modern man was in either case struck down by nature just when he thought himself most invincible. That peculiarly modern heresy, the belief in self-redemption through progress, was in either case overthrown, and man's ultimate weakness before the titanic forces of nature was proved.

This, I think, is the central message of all the "last man" stories of the romantic era. Their connection with private tragedy is clear, and of course they are only a variation on the familiar romantic themes of nostalgia for ruins and times past, the isolation of the self, and longing for a truth above mere utility or pleasure. But all these themes reflect the common experience of the romantic generation. It was a generation of unnerving revolution in politics and society, following hard on a century of steadily deepening skepticism about the underlying structures of Western faith. The Last Man is an anti-Crusoe, conquered rather than conquering, crushed by his solitude, and sure of his defeat.

Picturesque castaway though he may be, the Last Man is also a man of the future, located on the same straight line of historical time—with the probable exception of Poe's fairy-tale Prince Prospero—as George Washington or Napoleon. By and large, the fables, utopias, romances, and fantastic tales of early modern Europe were not set in the future. Their events took place "once upon a time," or in an exotic present. But, as I. F. Clarke and others have noted, all this begins to change toward the close of the eighteenth century.[11] In due course practically every work of utopian, dystopian, or otherwise speculative fiction assigns its characters to a point, often quite specific, in future time. An early illustration, one of the first, is Louis-Sébastien Mercier's L'an 2440, published in 1771, although the wholesale futurizing of speculative fiction did not occur until the next century.

The reason for this remarkable development can be summed up in one rather graceless German word, Historismus, as used and explicated by Friedrich Meinecke in Die Entstehung des Historismus.[12] Or better still, the futurizing of speculative fiction can be attributed to the confluence of Historismus, on the one hand, and the idea of the progress of human knowledge and well-being on the other. Both, in turn, cannot be understood without some grasp of the tradition of historical writing in Greek and Latin antiquity and the uniquely Biblical insistence on a sacred chronology stretching from Creation to Judgment, which invests future time with a transcendent value alien to pagan thought. What happened in the late eighteenth and early nineteenth centuries, put most simply (and ignoring the convolutions of a complex historical process), was the secularization of the Christian hope. The future history of Revelation, thanks to the new rationalism, became the vision of mankind's inexorable worldly betterment through the progress of science and reason. At the same time, thanks to the new romanticism, both the old Platonic and the early modern Newtonian mental habit of viewing the world sub specie aeternitatis, as an order of timeless truth, was exchanged for a historized mind-set that viewed it as forever changing, developing, and evolving, from time past into time future. The Historismus, or historicism, of the romantics amounted to a passion for understanding all things in terms of their temporal unfolding. It is a passion that has stayed with the Western mind despite the dissolution of the romantic movement, and it shows few signs of releasing its grip even today.

Needless to say, the futurizing of speculative fiction by the mutually reinforcing confluence of these new tendencies in Western thought has not always resulted in stories of the world's end. Throughout the nineteenth century, the paradigm of progress produced many tales of future happiness and harmony, fleshed out with details of all the marvels that science, technology, and social engineering could be expected to devise for man's benefit. Discovered in earlier times only on some blessed isle at the other end of the

world, utopia was transferred to our own future, a social order to be constructed and enjoyed by our own grandchildren. In other works, the future
became a place of mystery and adventure. Or progress was imagined, but not
enough to be counted utopian. Dystopias also began to make their appearance, generally as warnings against the consequences of this or that "evil" in
contemporary society, such as the Reform Bill of 1867 in England or the
Prussian defeat of France in 1870.

During the middle decades of the nineteenth century, only a few stories
of the future fall into the category of secular eschatology. A helpful guide is
I. F. Clarke's *Tale of the Future*, which attempts to list in chronological order
every volume of speculative fiction set in the future and published in the
United Kingdom down to 1976.[13] The contributions of British authors obviously receive more than their share of space, but a great part of American
speculative fiction appears as well, along with nearly all foreign-language
works in English translation. For the 1840s, 1850s, and 1860s, Clarke lists a
grand total of only fourteen volumes, most of them not eschatological. A
sharp upturn occurs in the 1870s, with 41 listings; again in the 1880s, with
80 listings; and once again in the 1890s, when 132 volumes of futurist fiction
were published in the United Kingdom. At this point, output levels off, with
no further marked increases until the 1930s.

But what of eschatological futures? For all practical purposes the romance of the world's end, invented quite early in the nineteenth century,
vanished during the heyday of the Industrial Revolution in Europe and North
America. These were the years of the ascendancy of positivism in thought
and of its aesthetic counterpart, realism, in letters and the arts. Belief in
progress, although not unchallenged, was universal. Confidence in the innate
superiority of white Western civilization was well-nigh unshakeable. Even
those mavericks who questioned the fundamental premises of industrial capitalism and the scientific ethos tended to see the future as a time of redemption from present evils, not as a time of ruin and death. W. H. Hudson set
his idyllic vision of *A Crystal Age* (1887) in a remotely future Europe, after
unspecified disasters had put an end to the ugly urban sprawl of the nineteenth century. William Morris's *News from Nowhere* (1891) told of a happy
rustic England purged of capitalism during a great general strike that had
occurred in the middle of the twentieth century.

In the 1890s, however, the tone and texture of thought changed radically, a change foreshadowed by neo-romantics like Hudson and Morris in
England, by the Symbolists in France, by Friedrich Nietzsche in Germany,
and by Fyodor Dostoyevsky in Russia. From the 1890s on to the present day,
Western civilization has been embroiled in troubles of the deepest kind,
troubles not only of substance (which, after all, go back much further!), but

of consciousness and self-esteem. The mental climate has been propitious for thoughts of doomsday.

Between 1890 and 1914 alone, almost every sort of world's end story that one finds in later years was written, published, and accepted by a wide reading public. Great world wars that devastated civilization were fought in the skies and on imaginary battlefields dwarfing those of Verdun and Stalingrad. Fascist dictatorships led to a new Dark Age, class and race struggles plunged civilization into Neolithic savagery, terrorists armed with superweapons menaced global peace. Floods, volcanic eruptions, plagues, epochs of ice, colliding comets, exploding or cooling suns, and alien invaders laid waste to the world. All the grist of the mills of present-day terminal fiction was ready at hand for the writers of the quarter-century that preceded the real-life cataclysm of 1914. They did not miss their chances.

It is customary to describe this period in the history of speculative literature as a fiefdom of the great English novelist H. G. Wells, just as the foregoing quarter-century "belongs" to his eminent French predecessor, Jules Verne. Certainly no one between 1890 and 1914 published as many major novels and stories of the future, or as many classics of eschatological fiction, as Wells. Some of them are still the best of their kind ever written.[14] His first novel, *The Time Machine* (1895), ends the world in three ways: by class conflict, biological degeneration, and the dying of the sun. In *The War of the Worlds* (1898), mankind is nearly obliterated by a technologically superior alien race. Closer to 1914, Wells gave the literature of Last Things two powerful novels of future warfare, *The War in the Air* (1908) and *The World Set Free* (1914). Some of his short stories from this period were also eschatological, including "The Star" (1897), "A Vision of Judgment" (1899), and "The Empire of the Ants" (1905). Nor did he stop writing terminal visions after 1914. They continued to the end of his life, although in his last book, *Mind at the End of Its Tether* (1945), he formally abandoned the hopes for a post-holocaust utopia that had routinely brightened the closing pages of his eschatological fiction.[15]

Extraordinary as Wells's apocalyptic imagination may have been, he was no lonely pathbreaker, and the period from 1890 to 1914 was not really "his." In late Victorian and Edwardian Britain alone, beginning with *After London* (1885) by Richard Jefferies, scores of world's end novels and short stories appeared; some of them bore traces of Wells's influence, but others just as clearly influenced him.

After London is among the most significant of the pre-Wellsian titles for later speculative fiction. Jeffries figures as a mainstream writer of minor rank. He was also a popular naturalist. In *After London* an unknown calamity has wiped out modern civilization, leaving the metropolis a filthy bog exuding poisonous vapors. The new wild England is not a utopia, as in *A Crystal Age* or *News from Nowhere.* Life is harsh, and thoughts of the endtime trouble the narrator, but he wastes no nostalgia on the dead past. All in all, it is manifestly a good thing that London and everything it stood for are gone.

Jefferies died in 1887, still in his thirties, and before his creative powers had fully developed. In the next generation, Wells's generation, the popular appetite for crime, adventure, horror, and science fiction grew immensely, and was satisfied by many skillful specialists in each genre. Terminal visions issued from the facile pens of writers like M. P. Shiel and George Griffith, both, as it happens, the sons of clergymen. Shiel's masterwork is *The Purple Cloud* (1901)—a title that might also be applied, unkindly, to his prose style, which was a bit neo-Gothic in the manner of Poe. The story is an epic of the last man and woman on earth, lone survivors of a volcanic explosion much greater than Krakatoa that filled the earth's atmosphere with deadly hydrocyanic acid. Shiel was the chief practitioner, as well, of the "yellow peril" story of his time, the vision of a future Europe overrun by endless columns of marching Chinese. He wrote three full-scale novels on the theme before 1914, racist Armageddons of truly horrific proportions. The best, and most ferocious, was the first, *The Yellow Danger* (1898). In Shiel's hands, the fear of race-war was also a fear of world war, claiming not millions but hundreds of millions of lives. George Griffith based his career on comparable fears. His apocalyptic formula fused international war, anarchist terror, and innovations in military technology—from aerial bombardment in *The Angel of the Revolution* (1893) to tactical nuclear weapons in *The Lord of Labour* (1911).

The horror story sometimes turned to eschatological scenes, as it does today. William Hope Hodgson's novel of the supernatural, *The House on the Borderland* (1908), includes a mystical journey to the world's end that anticipates in some detail the cosmic eschatology of Olaf Stapledon's *Star Maker.* Hodgson traveled to the endtime again in *The Night Land* (1912), which is the most beloved book in my private Valhalla of imaginative literature. I am so jealous of it (or rather of its heroine!) that at one time I carefully avoided saying anything about it in print. But new editions have made the text more accessible, and I can no longer hope to keep it for myself.[16] *The Night Land* is a formidable romance of terminal things, of the age after the sun has burned black and man stays warm by tapping the energy in the earth's core. It is also a work steeped in the tradition of the tale of supernatural horror, of which Hodgson was a consummate master, although "science-fictional" elements generally predominate. Yet another eschatological romance is Robert Hugh Benson's *Lord of the World* (1908). Benson translates into secular images the Christian doctrine of the world's end, with the forces of righteousness under the command of an underground Pope and the charismatic president of a "progressive" global republic playing the part of Antichrist.

The France of Jules Verne did her best to keep pace with her rival across the channel during *la belle époque*. Verne himself contributed at least one eschatological story, his posthumously published novella *L'éternel Adam* (1910). As his editor notes, it was written in Verne's last years and "uncharacteristically leads to rather pessimistic conclusions, unlike the proud optimism that animates the *Extraordinary Voyages*."[17] Verne's last years (he died in 1905) were not a time of robust self-confidence in the cultural history of France. Social philosophers and novelists dwelled on thoughts of "decadence" and, in particular, on the decline of Latin Europe in the face of vigorous competition from the Teuton and the Anglo-Saxon. Although not eschatological in any strict sense, the works of J.-K. Huysmans, Paul Bourget, Elémir Bourges, and many others conveyed Gallic distress with the ways of the modern world. The cycle of fifteen novels by Joséphin Péladan, *La décadence latine* (1884–1900), expressed the national mood.

Of stories of the world's end, the most widely read was a curious novel that mingled popular science, intellectual history, spiritualism, the belief in progress, and fin-de-siècle gloom, Camille Flammarion's *La fin du monde* (1893). Set in both the near and the far future, borrowing much of its plot from Grainville's *Le dernier homme*, it cannot be called a great work of art, but its science is sound, in terms of then current knowledge. Translations of *La fin du monde* soon appeared in most of the world's languages.[18]

A brisk commerce in popular genre fiction developed in France just as in Britain during this period, which Robert Louit calls "France's pulp era" and "the true golden age of French science fiction."[19] Unfortunately, most of this work did not travel well, and much of it has failed to survive even in the Francophone world. A gifted representative of the French authors of Wells's generation was J.-H. Rosny aîné, who wrote several popular novels about prehistoric life, and one major eschatological romance, *La mort de la terre* (1912).[20] He traces the slow demographic decline of mankind through the millennia, as the planet grows progressively drier and less hospitable to all forms of plant and animal life: in the end, bizarre mineral creatures replace the last men. Also noteworthy from *la belle époque* in France, although far removed from the camp of popular fiction, were the sociologist Gabriel Tarde's post-holocaust utopia, *Fragment d'histoire future* (1904), published in English as *Underground Man* with a preface by H. G. Wells, and Anatole France's gently ironic *L'Île des pingouins* (1908), which sees cyclical returns to barbarism as the dynamic of world history.

In the United States, which had neither a Verne nor a Wells to lead the way, speculative fiction in all its varieties did quite well just the same in the years before the first World War. Fears of national eclipse, although less widespread in the growing and thriving Republic than in Europe, sometimes found a voice, as in John Ames Mitchell's *The Last American* (1889), or in Van Tassel Sutphen's *The Doomsman* (1906), a tale of neo-medieval New York that purloined scenes from *After London*. The most original figure in American speculative fiction, Jack London, filled his dystopia *The Iron Heel* (1907) with apocalyptic imagery, but his only story of a literal world's end was an effective novella, *The Scarlet Plague* (1912). Had he not died so young, London might well have contributed much more to the literature of Last Things. Among his notes for future work is a sketch of a catastrophe that tears the earth away from the sun.[21]

Two of the supreme hack writers of the period in America were Garrett P. Serviss and George Allan England, most of whose stories now rest in well-earned oblivion. They were both enthusiastic producers of disaster fiction in which heroes of science and engineering save the day at the last possible minute, and some of their better work was clearly eschatological. Serviss put his knowledge of astronomy to use—he was a founder of the American Astronomical Society—in a large novel about the flooding of the world by a "watery spiral nebula," *The Second Deluge* (1912). England's principal eschatological romance was *Darkness and Dawn* (1914), a trilogy of novels whose setting is a far-future savage America after a titanic explosion in the earth's crust in 1920 had exterminated nearly all human life.

England may have been thinking, like M. P. Shiel before him, of a great event in natural history when he wrote *Darkness and Dawn:* the blowup of the island of Krakatoa in the East Indies in 1883. But in the year that his work was first published in hard covers, a great event in political history occurred that was to shift radically the content of eschatological fiction: the blowup of the European concert and the first apocalyptic campaigns of the World War of 1914–18. Novelists had foreseen a major European war many times in the decades just before it, but few had anticipated its length, worldwide scale, or costliness in lives and wealth. As Clarke has shown, the majority of future war stories published during the Great Peace of. 1871 to 1914 were tales of warning about the dangers to nations of being overconfident and underprepared. War was seen by the writers of these stories as "normal and romantic."[22] Some also stressed the importance of keeping up to date in military technology, like Stanley Waterloo in his remarkably prescient novel of victory through air power, *Armageddon* (1898). The story of future war that warned against war itself, or gave it eschatological proportions, such as Griffith's *The Angel of the Revolution* or Wells's *The War in the Air,* was exceptional.

After 1914, all this changed. Before 1914, the world most often ended in imagination because of some natural catastrophe; ever since, man himself has become the chief cause of world-ending disasters. In the more than three hundred stories read for this book, the proportion of natural to man-made disasters is roughly two to one in books written before Sarajevo; and thereafter, one to two. Of man-made disasters, it goes without saying, most are world wars fought with the doomsday weapons of modern science.

In other respects, visions of the world's end in fiction produced during what may be called the second Wellsian generation, from 1914 to 1945, resemble their counterparts of the generation of 1890. One constant was Wells himself, who continued writing prolifically throughout these years. Except for a measurable increase in output during the middle and late 1930s, the number of publications per year did not rise appreciably.

Yet there are subtle changes, which become still more pronounced after 1945. A larger number of writers in the literary mainstream turn to speculative fiction and to the sub-genre of secular eschatology. Good examples are Aldous Huxley and J. B. Priestley in Great Britain, Léon Daudet and C.-F. Ramuz in the French-speaking world, Karel Čapek in Czechoslovakia, Hermann Hesse and Franz Werfel in the German-speaking world, and Sinclair Lewis and Stephen Vincent Benét in the United States. Also, the first specialized pulp magazines devoted to science fiction (or "scientifiction" as it was also called) began appearing in the United States in the 1920s and Britain in the 1930s, and science fiction on the Anglo-Saxon model became a popular genre in Germany, Russia, Japan, and other countries previously immune or at least resistant to its charms.

It is the preeminence of the tale of future catastrophic war that most sharply differentiates the eschatological literature of the second Wellsian generation from that of the first. Whatever Wells, Griffith, and a few others had accomplished before 1914, the abundance of fictional warnings of a second world war in the 1920s and 1930s is no less impressive (and futile?) than the abundance of warnings about a third world war after 1945. Wells's *The Shape of Things to Come* (1933) described a world war that started as a border conflict between Germany and Poland in 1940. It degenerated into a chaotic global struggle that no one could stop, wrecking civilization. He had said it all before, with even more pessimistic conclusions, in *The War in the Air*, but *The Shape of Things to Come* is a stronger novel, and it led to an influential film with a screenplay by Wells himself, Alexander Korda's *Things to Come*.

Among the new writers, a good many envisaged long wars producing a gradual spiraling down of civilization to barbarism, in the Wellsian mode. John Collier published a poetic novel along these lines, *Tom's A-Cold*, in the same year that Wells brought out *The Shape of Things to Come*. Edward Shanks's *The People of the Ruins* (1920) is an earlier specimen, although here the cause of downfall is a worldwide series of socialist revolutions, rather than war between nations. Both works are set in Britain long after the débâcle. The war itself, in its final throes, as experienced by the few remaining soldiers, is the center of interest of two exceptional novels published in 1940 by American writers, L. Ron Hubbard's *Final Blackout* and Herbert Best's *The Twenty-Fifth Hour*. The work that had the greatest impact in America, however, was Stephen Vincent Benét's "By the Waters of Babylon" (1937), the story of a young savage who crosses the Hudson to discover the ruins of New York.

Other stories emphasized the horrors of modern weaponry, such as Shaw Desmond's novel of chemical and bacteriological warfare, *Ragnarok* (1926), and Stephen Southwold's *The Gas War of 1940* (1931). *Public Faces* (1933), the work of the celebrated diplomat and historian Harold Nicolson, foresaw the destruction of New York by a single "atomic bomb" delivered by a "rocket aeroplane" capable of crossing the Atlantic in five hours. Nicolson averted war in the nick of time by having his young hero perform a feat of diplomatic legerdemain. But *Public Faces* was pretty fair guesswork for a novel published in 1933.

The fear of the doomsday weapon is really just a special case of a larger fear of speculative fiction since *Frankenstein*, the fear that man will demolish, dehumanize, or enslave himself by his own cleverness, and especially by too much headlong progress in science and technology. Now and then a writer of the interwar years managed to express that fear in a terminal vision without resorting to scenarios of future war. Karel Čapek earned a worldwide reputation for several such visions, from his play *R.U.R.* (1921) to his many-layered fabulation *Valka s Mloky* (*War with the Newts*, 1936). The mad scientist clutching the atomic bomb almost blows up the world in J. B. Priestley's *The Doomsday Men* (1938) and actually does it, by accident, in a brilliant early story of Alfred Bester, "Adam and No Eve" (1941).

Not that nature escapes all blame for the woes of mankind in the fictions of the second Wellsian generation. Wells himself stopped inventing tales of natural catastrophe, but there were plenty of other writers to take his place, such as S. Fowler Wright in his novels of a great world flood, *Deluge* (1928) and *Dawn* (1929); J. J. Connington in a powerful story of mass starvation when a blight kills all plant life, *Nordenholt's Million* (1923); Edwin Balmer and Philip Wylie in their highly successful thriller *When Worlds Collide* (1933); Jacques Spitz in *L'agonie du globe* (1936); and R. C. Sherriff, who arranged to pull down the moon in *The Hopkins Manuscript* (1939). Switzerland's greatest novelist of the period, Charles-Ferdinand Ramuz, turned aside from his usual subjects to produce a richly evocative story of earth's sudden plunge into the sun, *Présence de la mort* (1922), which closes with a scene of spooky rapture of the sort one now expects from Doris Lessing. But no interwar novel can quite match Olaf Stapledon's *Last and First Men* (1930). Stapledon ends the world more than twenty times, in every imaginable way, over a period of two billion years. The ultimate end occurs when mankind, living now on Neptune, is extinguished by the hard radiation from a nearby supernova.

Thanks to the dislocations of war, the 1940s were an era of diminished literary production throughout the Western world. Writers were too busy surviving the horrors of the historical apocalypse to have much time left over for inventing terminal fictions. But what happened in the 1920s, happened in the 1950s, even more strongly. Once peace had returned, memory and fear worked on the imagination to generate a heightened sense of the imminence of Last Things. The 1950s were also a boom decade for speculative fiction generally. The British inventory of I. F. Clarke cited above indicates that the output of stories of the future was about twice as great in the 1950s as it had been in the 1930s. Nor has the boom shown any signs of slackening. The number of titles of speculative fiction doubled again in the 1960s, and doubled once more in the 1970s. Almost as many novels of the future are now published each year as in all the years before 1900 combined.

In the early postwar period American influence prevailed, in science and fantasy fiction as in everything, to the point of inhibiting writers in other countries; translations of American work dominated speculative literature as much as translations of Verne had done nearly a century before. Even the English-language term "science fiction" was adopted everywhere, to characterize the popular ghetto-bound segment of the field.[23] But the Americanizing process had run its course by the late 1960s, and speculative fiction began to flourish in many countries with little need of further stimulus from the United States. Recovery came first in Great Britain. France, Germany, Russia, Poland, Japan, and others quickly followed suit. Today many exceptional works are being written in the languages of all of them, only a small fraction of which make their way into English translations.

The job of keeping up with the world-deluge of speculative literature is of course frightful, and beyond anyone's power to do well. When Brian Aldiss undertook to write his superb history of the field, *Billion Year Spree* (1973), he found himself running out of steam near the end, and could devote only two chapters (of eleven) to the work of the period after 1950. He was harshly criticized. But it is impossible to assign the recent material anything like its proportional share of attention, not only because of its bulk, but also because so much of it relies on the familiar models of earlier speculative fiction.

This is not to say that there has been a deterioration in literary or

imaginative power. Quite the contrary. Much of the new work has lived up
to, and sometimes surpassed, the familiar models. Some of the more innovative writers of science fiction have brought their ghetto into a rapport with
the literary mainstream that has benefited both. More and more, the distinc-
tions between the two tend to fall away, although "tending to fall away"
should not be confused with "vanishing utterly." But even if one ignores for
the moment this commendable détente in literary relations, the weight of
the argument for the self-validating importance of speculative fiction grows
with every passing decade. As J. G. Ballard has well said, "the main 'fact' of
the 20th century is the concept of the unlimited possibility." What separates
our century from all its predecessors except, to some degree, the nineteenth,
is the steadily accelerating force of social change, produced in great measure
by science, technology, and engineering in the fullest meaning of each. The
fiction whose business it is to explore these possibilities, again quoting Ballard,

> far from being an unimportant minor offshoot, in fact represents the main
> literary tradition of the 20th century, and certainly its oldest—a tradition of
> imaginative response to science and technology that runs in an intact line
> through H. G. Wells, Aldous Huxley, the writers of modern American science
> fiction, to such present-day innovators as William Burroughs. . . . No other
> form of fiction has the vocabulary of ideas and images to deal with the present,
> let alone the future.[24]

The abundance of postwar speculative fiction, and especially of that
which identifies itself as science fiction, has brought an abundance of visions
of the world's end. As during the preceding generation, man-made disasters
predominate over the natural variety by a ratio of two to one. As before, the
most popular sort of man-made disaster is the world war fought with the most
advanced military hardware that can be imagined. But there is some increase
in disasters happening by accident, rather than by intention—especially in
the ecological doomsday resulting from waste, pollution, or technologies that
get out of hand. It is also interesting to note that man-made catastrophes
occur relatively much less often in postwar British works of eschatological
fiction than in American works. American feelings of guilt over Hiroshima
and later Vietnam, together with British feelings of impotence over the loss
of empire, may explain the national differences, although this is difficult to
prove. Perhaps a better guess is that Americans, as the suddenly senior part-
ners in the Western alliance, tend to think more often about the responsibilities and perils of military power. In any event, the level of eschatological
anxiety is about the same in the speculative fiction of any Western country
of the postwar era, whatever differences there might be in the imagined
causes of the catastrophe.

The only major change in visions of the world's end written since the second World War, as opposed to those written in the 1920s and 1930s, is the far greater interest of writers in exploiting eschatological themes for psychological and, it may be, ontological studies, in which disaster in the macrocosm is only symbolic of psychic disaster. Or at least so the writers would like to have us think. They may be more concerned with the macrocosm than they know. But certainly the eschatological scenarios of Samuel Beckett, Anna Kavan, J. G. Ballard, Doris Lessing, Samuel Delany, and many others cannot be analyzed in just the same way as one might analyze the work of a Jules Verne or an H. G. Wells.

We have already caught a glimpse of the world's end fiction of the late 1970s, in Chapter One. From the whole libraries of texts published between the mid-1940s and the mid-1970s, there is space here to mention only a few representative titles. Some authors have complicated matters by producing many works, both singly or in series, all of which may be quite good. An example of the quite bad is the shelf of thrillers by the late John Creasey dedicated to the world-saving adventures of one Dr. Palfrey, to say nothing of the frequently apocalyptic formula fiction of John Russell Fearn. Somewhere near the other pole may be found writers like John Wyndham, John Christopher, Edmund Cooper, Brian Aldiss, J. G. Ballard, Michael Moorcock, Edgar Pangborn, Piers Anthony, James Blish, and René Barjavel, each of whom has at least three important novels, and usually a good many short stories, to his credit that qualify as visions of the world's end. Wyndham, the oldest, was already an established producer of routine fantasy and science fiction when the second World War began. After the war he turned to the writing of world's end novels that have a reputation, perhaps not fully deserved, for excellence, and wielded a vast influence throughout the 1950s and 1960s. *The Day of the Triffids* (1951), *The Kraken Wakes* (1953), and *The Chrysalids* (1955) are often compared to the best work of Wells.[25]

Of sterner stuff, but in the same tradition of literary realism, the world's end novels of John Christopher began appearing in 1956, one year after Wyndham's last. *The Death of Grass* recalled J. J. Connington's 1920s novel of worldwide blight, *Nordenholt's Million*. Equally effective are *The World in Winter* (1962) and *A Wrinkle in the Skin* (1965).[26] Christopher's "successor" was J. G. Ballard, who published a great tetralogy of terminal romances in the mid-1960s, *The Wind from Nowhere* (1962), *The Drowned World* (1962), *The Drought* (1965), and *The Crystal World* (1966), dealing in sequence with the assaults on mankind of the four classical elements—air, water, fire, and earth, in that order. In Ballard, however, realism yields to a bleak surrealist irrationalism, an exploration of private hells in the vein of William Burroughs. The theme of the end of the world undergoes a further metamorphosis in the most innovative eschatological series of the 1970s, the "Jherek Car-nelian" stories of Michael Moorcock. Beginning with *An Alien Heat* (1972), Moorcock's comedies of entropy recite the adventures—both moral and amoral—of a jolly band of superhuman revelers "at the end of time."

So far we have cited only British novels, for only one of which—*The Chrysalids*—the end was a war. Even in *The Chrysalids* the war (known as "Tribulation") is a half-legendary past event, directly experienced by none of Wyndham's characters. But in due time, multiple scenarios of terminal wars began making their appearance in British speculative fiction. Some of Brian Aldiss's eschatological works envisage such wars, including *The Canopy of Time* (1959) and *Greybeard* (1964); also Edmund Cooper's, from *Seed of Light* (1959) to *The Last Continent* (1970) and *The Cloud Walker* (1973). Another important series is the collection of short stories by Keith Roberts, *The Chalk Giants* (1974).

In American fiction, too, several authors have made a specialty of ter-minal fictions, written as individual works or in sets, and here the cataclysm is usually a third world war. One thinks, for example, of the stories by Ray Bradbury collected in *The Martian Chronicles* (1950); the stories of David R. Bunch in *Moderan* (1971); and Edgar Pangborn's novels of a post-nuclear America, *Davy* (1964), *The Judgment of Eve* (1966), and *The Company of Glory* (1975). But whether an author contributes many visions of the end, or just one, the fear of a coming terminal war has inspired much of the best speculative fiction published since 1945.

Few stories of World War III compare with Aldous Huxley's only effort, *Ape and Essence* (1948). It would make a powerful film, and with very little trouble, since Huxley wrote it in the form of a film scenario. Two other novels of terminal war did become significant motion pictures, Nevil Shute's *On the Beach* (1957) and Peter George's *Two Hours to Doom* (1958). Shute's novel was filmed by Stanley Kramer under the same title; George's was the basis for Stanley Kubrick's incomparable black comedy, *Dr. Strangelove*. Some of the other novels of future war that demand mention here, but have so far escaped it, are Bernard Wolfe's *Limbo* (1952), Leigh Brackett's *The Long Tomorrow* (1955), Pat Frank's *Alas, Babylon* (1959), Walter M. Miller's *A Canticle for Leibowitz* (1960), Alfred Coppel's *Dark December* (1960), and Robert Merle's *Malevil* (1972). In the last few years, visions of terminal war have become relatively scarce, but Doris Lessing has wrung something new out of the theme in her "space" epic, *Shikasta* (1979).

There is also the tale of the world destroyed by scientific accident or terrorism. A classic case in point is Kurt Vonnegut's fabulation *Cat's Cradle* (1963), and before Vonnegut, Ward Moore's *Greener Than You Think* (1947) and John Bowen's *After the Rain* (1959). Since the late 1960s, novelists have begun to take note of the fashionable prophecies of ecological disaster, usually in a more realistic mode, as in Edmund Cooper's *The Tenth Planet* (1973) and Kate Wilhelm's *Where Late the Sweet Birds Sang* (1976). There is even a brilliant novel of mankind led to suicide by lunatic prophets of ecological purism, *The Bridge* (1973), by D. Keith Mano.

But it is time to stop. All the works studied for this volume are listed in the bibliography at the end. They represent only a selection from a still longer list that a patient student of secular eschatology could compile with just a bit more effort. I have furnished enough signposts to serve the purposes of this chapter. In Parts III, IV, and V it will be our aim to search out the meanings of secular doomsaying: the levels of intention, the underlying world views, and the patterns of expectation for the post-apocalyptic world. Many of the works already encountered will be met again, along with many more still uncited.

In Part II, however, you must let a historian indulge in his favorite failing, the old dodge of *reculer pour mieux sauter.* Historians are chronically reluctant to begin anything, because we know that before our starting point, there was always something else, a prelusive world designated by that indispensable cliché "the historical background." In the case of terminal visions in modern speculative literature, the background takes us very far back indeed, to an *Urwelt* of myth and legend on which the imagination of almost every modern writer has fed voraciously.

PART TWO

◆

Archetypes

3

◆

Circles and Lines

MOST OF THE men and women of letters whose names figured in Chapter Two are atheists, agnostics, or believers so lukewarm as to make no difference. But the old world-pictures of Biblical and pagan faith are by no means forgotten. Even some of the titles chosen for the fictions of secular eschatology betray their power.

From Genesis alone, which deals with primordial endtimes as well as beginnings, there are any number of stories about latter-day inhabitants of latter-day Edens, as well as latter-day Noahs and their Floods. *L'éternel Adam* (1910), "Adam and No Eve" (1941), and *The Last Adam* (1952) all invoke the memory of our fallen parents. *The Second Deluge* (1912), *All Aboard for Ararat* (1941), and "Generation of Noah" (1951) recall the Flood. An ancient metaphor for earthly turpitude is exploited in "By the Waters of Babylon" (1937) and *Alas, Babylon* (1959).

Tribulation, as depicted in the New Testament, finds even more echoes in the secular literature of doomsday. Titles such as "A Dream of Armageddon" (1901), *The Seventh Bowl* (1930), *Day of Wrath* (1936), *Deus Irae* (1976), and *The Final Conflict* (1980) need no explanation. Judgment and the life after death are remembered in "A Vision of Judgment" (1899), "Day of Judgment" (1946), *Limbo* (1952), *The Seventh Day* (1957), *Damnation Alley* (1969), *The Inferno* (1973), and *A Messiah at the End of Time* (1977).

Our debt to paganism also has its place in the literature of Last Things. Greek mythology lives on in *Die Kinder des Saturn* (1959) and *The Furies* (1966), as well as *The Ring of Ritornel* (a scrambling of "eternal return," 1968). *Ragnarok* (1926) and "When the Last Gods Die" (1951) borrow a terminal image from the Nordic Eddas. India is the source of *Kalki* (1978).

But titles furnish only a smattering of clues to the connections beween secular eschatology and traditional visions of the endtime in Western culture. Western man has been at least as unsuccessful, and possibly more so, in expunging the memory of his pre-modern heritage as Muslim, Hindu, Buddhist, or Confucian man. He has tried, but his efforts have met with frequent self-imposed obstacles deeply implanted in the soil of his culture. It is no good denying how deeply. We must chart the depths.

From the beginning, as Frank E. Manuel has pointed out, efforts to determine the structure of world history have yielded only two answers. Either time repeats itself in a cyclical pattern, or it moves forward like an arrow shot from the bow.[1] The archetypal shapes of history, the cyclical and the linear, require two sharply opposed visions of the end: the end as return journey to Paradise, and the end as full stop. Modern Western writers descend from a traditional culture well stocked with both visions. From Greek and Mesopotamian antiquity, the West inherits cyclical images of history, and from Jewish and Christian tradition, it inherits the linear model.

Both models may be traced far back into prehistory. Representing time's course as circular is an extrapolation from the rhythms of everyday life—the revolutions of the heavenly bodies around the earth, the cycle of the seasons, the sequence of animal and human generations. For the early stargazer or farmer, nothing could have been more natural than to assume the periodic decay and destruction of the whole world. Circular motion, like the circle itself, was an indication of health, regularity, obedience to the divine order. If history moved not only in the minor cycles of day and night, full moon and new, summer and winter, but also in a major cycle demanding cosmic death, who could wonder? The thought of such a major cycle, showing that earth and sky were no less mortal than a man or a leaf, was even a consolation, and a confirmation of the oneness and kinship of all being.

But cyclical mythology did not satisfy every need. It did not provide public retribution for oppressed nations; it did not fully console the uprooted and the impoverished, whose numbers grew with the historical advance from tribe and commune to economies based on slavery or serfdom. Even when provision was made for a blissful afterlife as in Egypt or for the dissolution of personhood in transcendental world-negation as in India, cyclical visions ruled out any kind of ultimate earthly triumph. On the contrary, all triumphs on earth were necessarily empty. The greatest empires would fall, the sturdiest races would perish, the greatest wrongs would go unavenged except in a common doom pulling down the just and the unjust together. The moral lesson might seem to be the futility of human effort, a conclusion drawn by many ancient poets and prophets.

To such fatalism the linear model of history replied with the promise of an absolute end of time and a final public judgment vindicating righteousness. The ancient linear view of history, perhaps better represented as a single grand cycle,[2] settled every score. Its end did not simply lead to a new beginning, and a repetition of all the same errors and crimes that had marked history before, but stopped time altogether. In whatever sphere life would resume after the end of history, on earth or in heaven, it would resemble in no way the life of "this" time. If the cyclical vision originated among primitive agriculturists, seeking attunement with nature, the linear vision is perhaps traceable to the nomadic life of warrior-herdsmen, seeking final victory over their enemies.

Yet the difference between cyclical and linear models of history should not obscure the similarities, especially with respect to eschatology. The expectation of a final judgment conveys more hopefulness and greater militance of spirit than the myth of the eternal return, but both eschatologies provide for happy endings, each in its own way. We are indebted to Mircea Eliade for making so emphatic the point that doomsday in the traditional mythic world view is not a nightmare. Let morality collapse, let destruction sweep the earth clean, nevertheless there is a fundamental optimism in all cyclical visions of the end. "In fact," Eliade remarks, "this optimism can be reduced to a consciousness of the normality of the cyclical catastrophe, to the certainty that it has a meaning and, above all, that it is never final."[3]

Consider, for example, the myth of world-destruction by fire, an all but universal expectation in ancient doomsaying. Against this fire mere human beings can do nothing, which breeds a kind of fatalism, to be sure. But the fire is not a meaningless outburst of evil or chaos. Its work of destruction is like the killing frost that comes in winter. It burns away the accumulated debris of the ages. It ends a morally and physically exhausted earth, worn out by time, so that the universe can undergo rebirth.

In short, the end in traditional cultures is the gateway to new life, whether the literal rebirth of cyclicalism or the beginning of eternal joy for God's elect. The end has no "sting." It may be an awesome occurrence, which in itself is surely dreadful, above all in the linear model, since anyone can fear that he is not numbered among the blessed. It may tend to devalue the significance of human effort, above all in the cyclical model. Yet the endtime is ultimately good, and divisible into four parts or phases: a period of growing evil and decay as humankind approaches the final days; an eruption of world calamities, such as conflagrations, floods, plagues, wars, or disturbances in the heavens; the end itself; and the arrival of a restored primal age, or the higher time of eternity. Put in a more general way, we live in bad times, they will get worse, they will end, and all will then be well, meaning "as it should be."

Such a view of the future was universal in pre-modern cultures, which argues that it satisfied perennial needs of the human psyche, including the need for a buffer against the disappointments of life. The price was a retreat from reality, an exaggeration of present discontents coupled with the rainbow promise of retribution or renewal in some golden future. What, in Eliade's terms, glows with psychic health, in Freud's terms bears the unmistakable odor of the narcotic drug.

Since few modern eschatologists have been able to resist the magic of the archetypal symbols, and since mythic visions of the end anticipate in most ways the structure of secular eschatology, it will be useful to look more closely into the substance of ancient prophecy. Our inspection, however brief, will take us into every continent; cultures without terminal visions of some kind have in all probability never existed.

4

•

The Wheel of Time

"A SINGLE DAY WILL bury the human race, and devour whatever fortune has long favored, whatever has been raised high, all fame, all beauty, the great empires of man." The words have the ring of a Biblical prophet, but they appear in the third book of a standard Roman text on the natural sciences by the eminent Stoic philosopher and statesman Seneca.[1] The author does not profess to know how Heaven will choose to blast its creatures, whether by a deluge or by a great fire, or both, but the end is certain, and will arrive in the not too distant future. The very elements of the earth will be dissolved. Heaven will permit nothing to remain untouched by the global catastrophe.

The reason for such a *dies irae*, in Seneca's vision, is the cumulative corruption of the whole earth through vice, a stain that darkens with each passing year until Heaven will be able to bear it no longer. Ludwig Edelstein has elaborately argued the case for Seneca as an early apostle of the idea of progress,[2] but the only progress in which the leathery old Stoic really believed is the advancement of learning, an advancement more than compensated on the balance sheet of history by mankind's moral degeneration. When vice reaches its acme, down will pour Heaven's purifying waters or fires, and the world will begin again.

> The old order will be re-established. Every living thing will be created afresh. The earth will have for inhabitants men ignorant of crime, born under more favorable stars. But their innocence will last only as long as their souls are new. For vice swiftly creeps in.[3]

Seneca's views were not at all strange or crankish in the thought-world

37

of classical antiquity, although it would be too much to claim that every ancient thinker shared them. The great school of philosophers to which he belonged, the Stoics, had been preaching a cyclical view of time since their establishment at the beginning of the third century B.C. by Zeno of Citium. The most celebrated of them all, the emperor Marcus Aurelius, explained his world-weariness as a rational consequence of eschatological wisdom.

At least the Stoics believed in the resolute bearing of the burdens set upon men's shoulders by destiny, no matter how tiresome; their most provocative contemporaries, the Epicureans, taught a doctrine of noninvolvement in life's weary rounds, accompanied by a melancholy view of the human future. The major Epicurean text to survive antiquity, *De Rerum Natura* by the poet Lucretius, expounds a history of the progress of civilization comparable to Seneca's and follows it with a terminal vision drenched in disillusionment. At the end of Book Two, Lucretius assures his readers that the natural world, like a fruit, ripens and then bit by bit decays. In its declining years it will supply too little food to sustain life, so that the ramparts of the world "for all their might, will some day face assault, be stormed, collapse in ruin and in dust." In fact, the downturn has already begun. "Our poor earth, worn out, exhausted, brings to birth no more great eons, Titans, huge majestic beasts, only our own disgusting little days, midges and gnats." The very soil has lost the lush fertility of olden times, and all things "waste away."[4]

Lucretius ignored the question of rebirth to dwell on the course of creation from start to finish during a single cycle, but the Epicurean cosmology is implicitly cyclical. What it took the greatest pains to show, however, was the wholly natural and autonomous character of cosmic change. More than any other ancient cosmology, the Epicurean system was ruthlessly desacralized, almost to the same point as the systems of modern physics. For Lucretius the gods exist, but they do not run the universe. The universe runs itself, and it is mortal, not divine. Lucretius could view its approaching end with satisfaction, since the very mortality of the world helped confirm his ardent naturalism. In this one respect the school he represents diverged from the ancient mainstream, but it preferred its own forms of psychic consolation, and taught, with equanimity, the universal ancient expectation of an endtime. It also endorsed the typical ancient assumption that present-day mankind, thanks to civilization, lives in an age less happy and less virtuous than did the noble barbarian, at least after his invention of the few rude arts that suffice the wise.

Stoicism and Epicureanism date from middle and late classical antiquity. Their eschatologies were adapted, it goes without saying, from traditions centuries older. The idea of cosmic cycles of destruction and rebirth can be found in both Plato and Aristotle, who differed from the Stoics only in foretelling the collapse of civilization, rather than the complete annihilation of the human race, in the endtime. Democritus, one of the first atomists and a contemporary of Socrates, seems to have adhered to a doctrine of cosmic obliteration like that of the Stoics. So, too, did the pre-Socratics Anaxagoras, Heraclitus, and Empedocles. The common sources of all these terminal visions must be sought in two quarters: the wisdom of the ancient Near East, to which Greek philosophy of every school was heavily indebted, and the mythic imagination of the prehistoric Greeks themselves, summed up in the works of Homer and Hesiod.

Time has obscured the tracks of these earliest eschatologies, but they can be followed back at least some of the way. One clue is the many references in Seneca and elsewhere to Berossus of Chaldaea, who made a long-lost Greek translation of ancient Babylonian texts in the third century B.C. that expounded the doctrine of the "Great Year." According to Berossus, the world is periodically destroyed and restored again: by fire when the seven planets are gathered in the sign of Capricorn, by flood when they are gathered in Cancer. The time of fire is the "Great Summer" of the cosmic year, the time of flood its "Great Winter." By one interpretation, the whole cycle requires thirty-six millennia for its completion. Other Babylonian texts foretell the collapse of morals and even the disappearance of sun and moon in the endtime.

More fully documented evidence comes to us from traditional Indian mythology, with its concept of the *Mahāyuga*, Sanskrit for "Great Year," an idea foreshadowed in sacred literature of the earliest (Vedic) period in Indian history. In its final form, the myth of the *Mahāyuga* proposed incredibly long cycles of cosmic rise and fall. Each Great Year lasts 4,320,000 normal years, and ends in the degenerate age known as the *Kali Yuga*, in which mankind now happens to live. One thousand Great Years, in turn, make up a *kalpa*, or day in the life of the divine creator Brahmā, and one hundred years of such "days" constitute the life-span of Brahmā. At the close of this period, writes Heinrich Zimmer, will come "a great, or universal dissolution." All created being, including the heavens, will melt into "the divine, primeval Substance," for a period of rest lasting 311,040 billion years, after which the world will spring into existence again, with a new Brahmā, and continue as before, time without end.[5]

Eliade sees the fantastic arithmetic of the Indian myth in its final form as an embroidery on much earlier and simpler speculation.[6] The heart of it is a four-age doctrine of world history paralleled in the teachings of the other aboriginal Indo-Iranian religions. In the Hindu version, each of the four ages of the Great Year was named after a throw of the dice in a classic Indian game. History began with the *Krita Yuga*, or "foursquare age," when all castes lived holy and obedient lives without effort. The next age, the *Tretā Yuga*, or "age of three," witnessed some deterioration in morality; in the *Dvāpara Yuga*, or "age of two," still more decay occurred, as men adopted the ways of greed and passion. Last of all came the *Kali Yuga*, or "worst age," now in progress, the shortest of the four ages. The whole cycle, or *Mahāyuga*, is said in the *Mahābhārata* to last 12,000 years, followed by a *Pralaya*, or dissolution, de-stroying a world now sunk in total depravity and darkness.

To return to Western mythology, the four-age doctrine of Hinduism appears in almost identical form as the four ages of the earth described by Hesiod in Works and Days, a compilation of the eighth century B.C. The Greek poet traces the decline of the world from ages of gold, silver, and bronze to our modern age of iron; a comparable Mazdean text from Zoroas-trian Iran speaks of ages of gold, silver, steel, and iron. The only difference, and it is not unimportant, lies in the apparent absence of any provision in the Greek or Iranian myths for a return of the golden age. Even this is not certain. Hesiod lets slip at one point his wish that he had lived in an earlier age or had been born later, implying that the golden age will indeed return.[7] At any rate there is firm agreement among all sources that the modern age is the worst, and cannot fail to deteriorate still more in the years remaining. Hesiod warns bitterly of an approaching time when children will be born old, bearing witness to the exhaustion of nature's energy in a wicked world. No Indian prophet of doom could have said it better.

Hindu eschatology and the terminal visions of ancient Greece and Baby-lon clearly belong to a common thought-world. From its probable origin in Mesopotamia or Iran, the myth of recurring dark ages and doomsdays traveled westward through Greece to Rome. From Buddhism, which inherited the cosmology of the Hindus, it even made its way to the Far East, where the neo-Confucian philosopher Shao Yung published a cyclical theory of time in the eleventh century. After a process of unrelenting decay from a golden age long past, Shao expects first the death of all living creatures and later the destruction of the universe. He makes use of traditional Chinese ideas in his cosmology, such as the dialectic of *yin* and *yang*. But his eschatology betrays Buddhist influences.[8]

Not that cyclicalism per se offended Chinese tradition. The Chinese had their own native doctrine of the wheel of time, reminiscent of the teachings of Aristotle and Polybius on the rise and fall of polities. Its focus is the dynastic cycle observable in Chinese history. Dynasties prosper and ulti-mately fail, according to the doctrine, because of the turpitude of emperors, whose bad conduct provokes the certain wrath of Heaven and may cause the ruin of their house. As often in Western mythology, natural disasters such as floods and plagues are blamed on human depravity; the Chinese held that disasters were warnings from Heaven to a corrupt imperial family. Sooner or later, in the nature of things, the fall of every dynasty is inevitable. The crisis of the fall corresponds roughly to an endtime in the Western sense, although it does not involve cosmic doom or the death of mankind.

The Chinese also had their share of primitivist mythology, especially in Taoism, and in parts of the Confucianist canon as well. One much quoted document, a chapter in the *Li Chi*, or Book of Rites, ascribes to Confucius a lecture on the sorry contrast between modern times and pre-Confucian antiquity. One day the Master was walking back and forth on a terrace, "looking sad and sighing." A disciple "was by his side, and said to him, 'Master, what are you sighing about?' " Confucius replied that he grieved for the dear dead days when men had lived according to the *Tao*, the way of Heaven. Kindness was then universal, and selfishness, thievery, and treachery unknown. Rulers had been selected from the ranks of the most able, rather than from a royal family. Today, the *Tao* "has fallen into disuse and obscurity," and men had grown materialistic and proud. They could hope for nothing better than to live by strict rules and regulations in this modern age of "small tranquillity," for spontaneous goodness was now extinct.[9]

There is some dispute among scholars regarding the authenticity of this chapter—perhaps it is more Taoist than Confucianist. But appeals to the wisdom and superior virtue of antiquity were customary among all the chief schools of Chinese philosophy. In Fung Yu-lan's summing-up, "they all agreed that the golden age of man lies in the past rather than the future. The movement of history since then has been one of progressive degeneration."[10] Whatever hope there might be for the future rested in the possibility, voiced many times by reformers and revolutionaries alike in the long history of imperial China, that humanity would return to this or that version of ancient virtue. To students of Western mythopoeic thought, it is all quite familiar. The wondrously socialized Chinese were less preoccupied with eschatological speculation that most other ancient nations, but such ideas as they had, chime with those of the West.

5

•

The Day of the Lord

CHRISTIAN THEOLOGIANS and apologists since Saint Augustine have engaged in a relentless program of invidious comparison between the "timeless nature-wisdom" of the most ancient East and their own supposedly higher God-sent doctrine of the irreversibility of time. Often joined by Jewish scholars, they contend that only in the Biblical tradition, or in its heresies, can the particular and unique acts of God and man achieve real significance. The old wisdom was a wisdom of archetypal gestures by stock figures functioning in the unreal, ahistorical time of myth. The new wisdom of the Bible, so the argument runs, invests concrete human existence with sacred meaning, and validates our earthly struggles. No longer is there "nothing new under the sun." On the contrary, novelty becomes possible at last, from the unique beginning to the terrible, sublime, all-shattering, but surely unique end.[1]

Too much can be made of the difference between the cyclical and the linear models of world history. A curved line, after all, is still a line; and accompanying the straight line of *Heilsgeschichte,* the history of salvation, Christian thinkers allow for repetitive patterns grounded in the nature of both innocent and fallen mankind. More to the point, as noted in Chapter Three, cyclical and linear paradigms of history agree in finding the world meaningful, and the end of the present order of things inevitable. One might even wonder if history does not mean less to Jews and Christians than to Greeks and Chinese. Is not the whole thrust of Judeo-Christian eschatology toward the complete and final annulment of history? Who can assign more than grudging importance to an order of reality scheduled for joyful obliteration, once and for all, perhaps in the quite near future? As Eliade concedes,

42

"in the Messianic conception history must be tolerated because it has an eschatological function, but it can be tolerated only because it is known that, one day or another, it will cease. History is thus abolished . . . in the future." Such an attitude is "antihistorical . . . exactly as are the other traditional conceptions."[2]

It is also possible to argue that theologians, in their zeal, have exaggerated the degree to which the thought of the pagan West was imbued with cyclical notions of time. Arnaldo Momigliano, for one, weighs the evidence for a predominance of cyclicalism among the Greeks and finds it much too skimpy. He is especially persuasive in dealing with the principal surviving texts of Greek historiography.[3] If the cyclical plan of world history had been as fully elaborated and endorsed by pagan thought as the theologians have claimed, why is there so little hard evidence in the writings of pagan historians? It seems at least clear that the curvature of time mattered less in the world views of pagan antiquity, with the exception of India, than the rectilinearity of *Heilsgeschichte* mattered in the world view of the Church.

Yet I cannot deny that the distinction between myths of eternal recurrence and myths of final ending is meaningful in eschatological terms. In the linear model, the end acquires a gravity that it cannot have in the cyclical. The end is once-only, facilitating a once-only judgment of all creaturely being. Justice is done. There are many happenings in both cyclical and linear time, many of them identical or similar to other happenings. But in the linear paradigm the end comes only once. The decision of Heaven is rendered, in this definitive way, without appeal, only once. In secular visions a comparable difference can be seen between the end as prophesied by an Oswald Spengler and the end as prophesied by a Mary Shelley. In Spengler, every end is prefatory to a fresh round of young life. Tragedy is regularly redeemed by comedy. In Shelley's *The Last Man*, history winds down starkly to nothing. Translated from public into personal terms, the cyclical model speaks of recurring crises whereas the linear model speaks of death. In the same way, if the once-only end is followed by salvation, as in Wells's *The Shape of Things to Come*, the saved world-order holds a higher significance than would the rise of a new culture in the Spenglerian schema.

However grave or slight the differences between the two models may be, it is the linear archetypes that modern Western writers more often encounter in the storehouses of their traditional culture, and linear archetypes that they more often assimilate into their own world views. If I am correct in my hypothesis that the linear idea of history culminating in a last judgment first arose among nomadic peoples, it may also be much older than cyclicalism. Eschatologies similar to the Biblical vision of Last Things are reported from many pre-civilized cultures, both modern and ancient. Some have no doubt been influenced by familiarity with Biblical, Koranic, or other written linear sources, but the evidence is too considerable to give all the credit to such sources. Primitive tribes from Australia and the East Indies to pre-Columbian North America predict an eventual end of the world, followed by divine judgment and the entrance of the just, in body or spirit or both, into a life of heavenly reward. Jürgen Moltmann gives the example of the Altaic Tatars of Central Asia. Their myth tells of a great Khan, or emperor, who once lived on earth and who will come again during the endtime to pronounce final judgment, after a powerful intercessor wins a terminal battle in his name against the forces of evil.[4] The nativist Cargo Cults of Melanesia in the 1920s are an almost contemporary instance of the same eschatological hope, inspired by rage against white imperialism.[5]

The best known of pre-civilized eschatological myths of a final judgment, resurrected by Richard Wagner in *Die Götterdämmerung,* is the Norse vision of Ragnarök, the "doom of the Gods." Its first recorded appearance comes in the *Volospá,* "The Sibyl's Prophecy," a poem of Icelandic provenance dating from the tenth century or thereabouts. After recalling events from several periods in world history, including the creation, the poem closes with a striking image of the endtime.

> Brothers shall fight and slay one another, kinsfolk shall break the bonds of kindred. It shall go hard with the world: much of whoredom, an age of axes, an age of swords, shields shall be cloven, an age of storm, an age of wolves, ere the world falls in ruin.

Then giants and demons will arrive from every direction, and the bodies of dead criminals will walk again, sweeping over the earth. At the end of each calamity the poet sings the same refrain: "Fiercely Garm [the hell-hound] bays before the cave of the Rock, the chain shall snap and the Wolf range free!"[6]

Worse is yet to come. The Norse Gods do their best against the monsters, but like the heroes they are, they have to pay for every victory with a death of their own. The last blows fall. "The sun turns to darkness, Earth sinks into the deep, the bright stars vanish from out of the heavens, fume and flame rage together, the lofty blaze plays against the very heavens." The stage is now set for a retribution beyond time, and it arrives in the final section of the poem. "I behold Earth rise again," the Sibyl intones. All sorrows will be healed in the new world. "I see a hall, brighter than the sun, shingled with gold, standing on Gem-lea. The righteous shall dwell therein and live in bliss for ever." Only the wicked remain outside, doomed to eternal torments, wading in poisoned rivers or gnawed by the fiery serpent Nidhogg.[7]

Most Norse scholars agree that the Viking authors of the myth of Ragnarök were influenced by Christian ideas, but it is likely that the story also preserves a nucleus of aboriginal Indo-European folk belief preceding Christianity by many centuries.[8] Still another version of the last judgment occurs in a mythology demonstrably much older than Christianity and the apocalyptic phase of Judaism: the mythology of ancient Iran, given formulation in the sacred texts of Zoroastrianism. The *Gāthās* of Zoroaster, for example, many of which date from the sixth century B.C., teem with eschatological references that may hark back to preliterate sources shared by Germanic mythology.

The first written versions of the Zoroastrian myth view all life as a struggle of cosmic dimensions between the supreme deity, Ahura Mazda, Lord of Light, and Angra Mainyu, the Spirit of Evil. On the Lord's side are ranged all the good impulses of humankind, on the side of Angra Mainyu all evil ones. The contest rages without relief throughout history, as the Lord for his own inscrutable reasons had decreed. On the final day, all men and women are raised from the dead and are subjected to a fiery ordeal. For the pure, the ordeal will prove harmless. But those in whom the shadowy force of the Evil One prevails are horribly burned and thereafter incinerated or hurled into Hell.

Later Zoroastrian accounts of the endtime are still more vivid and detailed, although the materials stem in many instances from pre-Zoroastrian myths found in similar forms in Vedic India, before they were swallowed up in the cyclical doctrine of mature Hinduism. The person of Zoroaster himself is elevated, like Jesus after him, to the status of a world savior. Three direct descendants of the prophet, conceived when virgins bathe in the waters of a lake where his semen is miraculously preserved, will arise at thousand-year intervals to lead humanity in the struggle against evil. The appearance of the last of these, Saoshyans, will inaugurate the last days. In that distant age, men will be born smaller and feebler, and a day will take less time to pass.

The texts also describe a great war at the end, a Zoroastrian Armageddon, featuring a terrible dragon who will devastate the world until a hero slays him with his mace. The soldiers of Ormazd (Ahura Mazda) will fight a pitched battle against the hosts of Ahriman (Angra Mainyu), and will win, signaling the end of time. A river of molten metal will then flood the earth, burning the evil out of every sinner. Ahriman and his attendant demons will perish in the purifying fires, and all humankind, resurrected and redeemed, will live in perfect joy forever with the Lord. Even more completely than in the later Christian myth, Zoroastrianism provides for the triumph of good over evil. In the end, nothing remains of evil but ashes.

The emphasis in all the Iranian eschatological visions, as in the Norse Ragnarök, falls on events that can only be described as cosmic. Although the Iranian prophets enclose history in a mythic beginning and ending, giving it the archetypal shape of a straight line, they took little interest in history as such. It was left to the other great source of linear eschatology in pre-Christian antiquity, the Jews, to elaborate the only historized mythology of their age. The distinctive feature of ancient Judaism is not its monotheism or its ethical doctrine, both found in Iran, but the more or less complete fusion of myth and history achieved in the Bible. For the Jews, reality consisted of a sequence of events strung out along a single time-line: to each a date could be assigned, and through these events God revealed his will and his truth. All later eschatological thought in the West, including the secular literature of Last Things, hinges on this decisive reconception of public time.

The intense historical consciousness of the Jews is bound up with the peculiarities of ancient Hebrew history. A nomadic desert folk in earliest times, they managed to scrape out a precarious existence between the two major centers of agrarian civilization, Egypt and Mesopotamia, without being fully or permanently absorbed by either one. The longer they survived intact, the more their success encouraged them to develop a mythology of ethnic destiny dependent on careful record-keeping and the idea of an almighty God of absolute righteousness who had chosen them for his exclusive service. Experience nourished faith, and faith helped to make possible more faith-confirming experience. The result was a sacred literature in which myth shades imperceptibly into national chronicle.

The myths themselves were mostly borrowed from Mesopotamian and Egyptian sources, including the story of the great Deluge in Genesis 6–8, the myth of a prehistoric end of the world, which has held much fascination for modern writers of doomsday fiction. But even the earliest Jewish prophets showed relatively little interest in eschatology of the standard cosmic variety. In its place they put their own myth of the endtime as the divinely appointed moment for national consummation.

The dream of a utopian future for the hard-pressed children of Israel at first took the form of hopes for a "promised land," a national home assuring to the Jews the place in the sun gained by other races. In the eleventh and tenth centuries B.C., under Saul, David, and Solomon, they realized some of these hopes, but succeeding centuries brought tragedy. Settled in the promised land, they felt drawn to the ways of traditional agrarian culture and stood in peril of losing their distinctive religious faith. Nor was it possible for the Jews to survive as an independent kingdom in their vulnerable position on the rim of Mesopotamia. Local wars for mastery in Palestine proved dangerous enough to Jewish religious and political identity; but in the eighth century B.C. the Assyrians conquered Israel, expelling many of its people, and in the sixth century the southern kingdom, Judah, fell to the Babylonians under Nebuchadnezzar, who promptly transported all but the Judean peasantry to exile in his capital city. Although the Captivity eventually came to an end, periods of Iranian, Greek, and Roman rule followed until the final expulsion of the Jews from Jerusalem by Hadrian in A.D. 135.

The chief concerns of Jewish eschatology, given this background, were twofold: preserving the fierce old nomadic creed against contamination by paganism, and supplying hope of an eventual vindication of God's chosen people, once its infidelities had been sufficiently punished by suffering, and its faith sufficiently tested in the fiery furnaces of history. The second goal was served better than the first, for it proved impossible to insulate Judaism from outside influences. In the sphere of eschatology, the Jews came increasingly under the spell of Zoroastrianism. Their original interest in Last Things had been confined chiefly to questions of national destiny; after prolonged exposure to Iranian beliefs, more compatible with Judaism than other pagan faiths because of Zoroaster's monotheism, the Jews became deeply concerned as well with the fate of the individual and the fate of the earth in the endtime.

But there is little written evidence of the Iranian impact on Jewish eschatology until the second century B.C. The eschatology of the major prophets, from Amos in the eighth century to the "second" Isaiah (Isaiah 40–55) in the sixth, remains centered on national prospects. A day of judgment will come, a day of the Lord, when the Jews and perhaps all nations will receive justice. The prophets expect such a judgment to take the form of a great purge. The wicked will fall, by the sword, by famine and pestilence, in scenes of stupefying carnage and misery. But after judgment comes redemption, for God's favored remnant.

In Isaiah, for example, one reads that the Lord "will empty the earth, split it open and turn it upside down, and scatter its inhabitants." The divine curse will reduce the earth's population until "only a few men are left. . . . So shall it be in all the world, in every nation," the prophet continues, "as when an olive-tree is beaten and stripped, as when the vintage is ended." But after this awful harvest will rise the peaceable kingdom of an anointed hero-king, the Messiah, descended from the house of David. Then wolves and sheep will live together in harmony, lions will eat straw, and little children will choose venomous snakes for playfellows. From a Jerusalem restored to God's love will issue his holy word. Obedient to his commands, "nation shall not lift sword against nation nor ever again be trained for war." (Isaiah 24:1, 6, 13; Isaiah 2:4)

In most of the prophetic texts, the Jews assign to themselves, or rather to those of their number who survive God's terminal wrath, a commanding position in the new earth. Jerusalem is specified as the capital of the coming eternal kingdom, and Israel as the ruler and teacher of all nations, who will be converted to the worship of the one true God. In Ezekiel, even this mercy is not provided. In the endtime the new messianic kingdom in Palestine will be challenged, writes Ezekiel, by a tremendous pagan host under Gog, Prince of Magog. Together with all his forces Gog will be annihilated by the Lord's anger in a series of miraculous interventions so dreadful that it will take the Israelites seven months to bury the dead of their foes. Ezekiel offers nothing further to the Gentile world but God's promise that the messianic theocracy will be "an example of my holiness, for many nations to see." In an earlier passage, he even suggests that the devastated Gentile powers will be like tall trees brought low, like green trees dried up, in order that Israel may be "raised high" and "put forth buds." (Ezekiel 39:27; Ezekiel 17:24)[9]

The return of the Jews to Jerusalem in 538 B.C. opened a new golden age of Judaism, which lasted for more than two hundred years. But Judea throughout this period was only a western province of the Persian empire, and eschatological fervor continued to burn. The post-exilic prophets foresaw that the rebuilding of the Temple and the gathering again of the Jews in their own land would not, alone, suffice to usher in the Lord's kingdom. Haggai, Zechariah, and Joel agree that before the kingdom can come, the Gentile nations will have to fall in battle; Joel seems to require their physical annihilation. In the end, Joel's God warns,

> All the streams of Judah shall be full of water, and a fountain shall spring from the Lord's house and water the gorge of Shittim,. but Egypt shall become a desert and Edom a deserted waste . . . and I will spill their blood, the blood I have not yet spilt. (Joel 3:18–20)

Still later, in the three centuries between the successful revolt of the Maccabees (167–65 B.C.) and the unsuccessful uprising of Simon Bar Cocheba (A.D. 132–35), Jewish eschatological thought underwent drastic changes. The dream of national retribution did not disappear, but in the steadily deteriorating political circumstances of the Jewish people, it became entangled with hopes for individual immortality and a cosmic end beyond historical time that betray the influence of Zoroastrian terminal visions. The primary Biblical source for the new eschatology is Daniel, but there is also an abundance of so-called apocryphal and pseudepigraphic texts, including parts of the Dead Sea Scrolls. Only the fact that Christianity separated itself from Judaism prevents us from adding Revelation and other apocalyptic works of Christian origin to the list of sources of later Jewish eschatology, for they too were written by Jews of the same period, and under the same pressures and influences.

The reputation of Daniel as the supreme eschatological document of the Jewish Bible is perhaps undeserved. There are more tremendous passages in

Isaiah, Ezekiel, and some of the other prophetic books, which tend to be overlooked in synopses of eschatological thought. In any case, Daniel contains only a few foreshadowings of the revolution in future hopes that marks later Judaism. In essence it is another prophecy of Jewish national triumph after God's defeat of the heathen kingdoms. Most of it is keyed specifically to expectation of victory over Judea's then current overlord, the king of Syria, Antiochus IV. More significant for our purposes are such slightly later texts as I Enoch, The Book of Jubilees, and The Testaments of the Twelve Patriarchs; and such writings of the first century A.D. as II Enoch, II Esdras, and The Apocalypse of Baruch. From the Dead Sea Scrolls discovered in the 1940s, the prophecy of Armageddon in The War of the Sons of Light against the Sons of Darkness is especially relevant.

In all this wealth of material, none of it included in the Bible, a variety of new ideas appear. The expectation of a millennial kingdom, a temporary new Jerusalem, which will precede the final judgment, first occurs in II Enoch. Such a kingdom is seen as earthly retribution, but inferior to the heavenly justice scheduled for the end of time. The Messiah, envisioned in the Old Testament as a king whose coming will follow the last judgment, appears now as a lord of hosts, a Zoroastrian hero, who will deliver God's people from bondage, and act as the judge himself on earth's final day.

The judgment in the post-Maccabean texts at last closely resembles the Zoroastrian vision. The dead will be called from their graves and join the living to hear their sentence, which in some accounts will be pronounced for every individual human being, regardless of his nation. The saved—usually only faithful Jews—will be called to their eternal reward, now routinely placed in a heavenly sphere beyond time and history. The damned will be dispatched to Sheol or Gehenna, now conceived as a place of eternal fiery punishment. In short, the end has come to mean cosmic destruction. Either the earth will be purified and transformed, or it will disappear altogether. In either case, this world and time are doomed.

By the first century B.C., with Palestine now part of the Roman Empire, the desperate situation of the Jews had led to the emergence of major eschatological sects, including the militant Zealots and the monastic Essenes, both of whom expected the world's end at any time. The stage was set—from the Christian point of view—for the coming of Jesus of Nazareth.

After the long preparation in Judaism, the arrival of yet one more eschatological prophet seems almost an anticlimax, and doctrinally it was. From a social-historical perspective, however, Christianity did open up new possibilities. Delivered in due course from its Jewish womb, the new religion became the faith not of a provincial priestly elite, nor of a small subject nation with long memories of its nomadic heritage, but the faith of the urban lower classes in an empire that ruled most of the known world. "The history of early Christianity," wrote Engels, "has notable points of resemblance with the modern working-class movement."[10] Both ministered to the poor, both preached salvation, both were persecuted and thrived on the persecution. Through the Christian party in first-century Judaism, the Biblical faith and the Biblical hope were converted from an instrument of national liberation into an instrument of class struggle.

To the converted, the new religion offered three quite different eschatological promises, each with its own distinctive power and appeal. For those among the Roman oppressed classes with the courage to think of winning justice on earth, there was the promise of the Millennium, a temporary messianic kingdom that offered to Jews and Gentiles alike the same satisfactions as the old Judaic vision of a New Jerusalem. For those too world-weary to hope for the success of millennialist politics, there was the promise of an end of time, when the whole world would be destroyed and the unrighteous would reap their grim reward. Both the Millennium and the Last Judgment provided public vindication of the oppressed. Finally, for all righteous men and women regardless of their temporal fortunes, Christianity promised personal resurrection in immortal bodies after earthly death.

But such hopes are obviously not far removed from those furnished in traditional Jewish eschatology, even though they were now extended to a bigger segment of humanity. Nor is Christianity any less future-oriented than Judaism, despite the specious arguments of some Christian theologians that, in their faith, the end has already come because Christ has already come.[11] The much discussed importance of Christ's mission on earth in the first century and his identification as the Messiah did little to slake the thirst of Christian converts for justice and salvation. Like the Jews, they continued to expect the end. Like Judaism, and even more elaborately than Biblical Judaism, Christianity gave its followers reason to await the end with hopeful hearts.

The mythology of the terminal visions in the New Testament closely followed the themes of latter-day Judaism, with its blend of traditional Jewish materials and Zoroastrianism. As Albert Schweitzer long ago made clear, Jesus himself was as much obsessed with thoughts of the endtime as any figure in religious history.[12] The evidence of the Gospels suggests that he expected the end to come very soon. The whole thirteenth chapter of Mark, for example, is heavy-laden with eschatological prophecy ascribed directly to Jesus. According to Mark, Jesus admonished his disciples to be on their guard. In the days to come, they will be persecuted, tempted by false prophets, and hated by all unbelievers. Unparalleled calamities will break over the world. "For nation will make war upon nation, kingdom upon kingdom; there will be earthquakes in many places; there will be famines. With these things the birth-pangs of the new age begin." Jesus expresses sorrow for women who may be pregnant or nursing their young in that coming time. "For those days will bring distress such as never has been until now since the beginning of the world which God created—and will never be again." (Mark 13:8 and 19)

No living thing will be able to survive if God does not "cut short the time," Jesus is reported to have said, but this he will do, signaling the last act of the cosmic drama. The stars will fall, and the sun and moon will be darkened. The Son of Man will descend from heaven with a retinue of angels to gather the elect from all quarters, and immediately thereafter the old heaven and earth will pass away. "I tell you this," Mark quotes Jesus: "the present generation will live to see it all." (Mark 13:30)

Each of the writers of the New Testament added at least something of his own to the eschatological vision of the synoptic Gospels. R. H. Charles traces four stages in the eschatology of Paul, beginning with the horrendous terminal scenes in his two letters to the Thessalonians and ending with the somewhat milder and more spiritualized visions in his letters to the Philippians, the Colossians, and the Ephesians.[13] The second letter of Peter is remarkable for its Stoic (or Zoroastrian) prophecy of the destruction of the world by fire, the only text in the New Testament that envisages such an end for the cosmos as a whole. (II Peter, 3:10)

The eschatological book *par excellence* is of course The Revelation of John, written near the end of the first century A.D. by an unknown author, certainly not the John of the fourth Gospel or the three Epistles. Revelation may be read at one level as a somewhat veiled attack on the Rome of the Caesars, recalling the fulminations of Daniel against Syria. But over the years it has served many other purposes. It is unquestionably the most influential Biblical source for modern doomsayers, and constitutes a grand synthesis of the terminal visions of the ancient West.

The visions of John, as he explained, began on the Greek island of Patmos in the Aegean Sea, where the prophet had been exiled by the authorities for his preaching. The personal note helps to anchor in time and place what is otherwise a cryptic document of mysterious origin. After an encounter with a white-haired Christ who gives him messages for seven Eastern churches, John sees a door opening into heaven. Entering the celestial realm, he witnesses a series of astonishing terminal events in which the future of the world is enacted before his eyes.

The certainty of awesome disasters in the endtime is made explicit from the outset by the breaking of seven seals on a great scroll by a seven-horned lamb representing Christ. Each seal, as it is broken, carries the world closer to its doom. First come the four horsemen of the Apocalypse, empowered to bring war, famine, and death. When the lamb breaks the fifth seal, the Christian martyrs call upon God to avenge their blood. When he breaks the sixth, a violent earthquake occurs. "Every mountain and island was moved from its place" and the stars fall out of the sky "like figs shaken down by a gale." (Revelation 6:13–14)

The opening of the seventh seal leads to an ominous silence, thirty minutes in duration, and then seven angels appear, blowing seven trumpets in succession, to announce a holocaust of fire, the death of ocean life, the poisoning of the rivers, the dimming of the heavenly bodies, a plague of giant locusts with human faces, and a murderous assault by squadrons of fire-breathing warhorses. All the same, as John reports with the acerbity of an Old Testament prophet, the mortals who survived these calamities "still did not abjure the gods their hands had fashioned, nor cease their worship of devils and of idols. . . . Nor did they repent of their murders, their sorcery, their fornication, their robberies." (9:20–21) The wickedness of the last men, as in so many other ancient eschatological visions, is almost incalculable.

A second septet of angels come forward next, bearing seven bowls of wrath to continue the chastisement of sinful humanity. The disasters of this third round are much the same, with the addition of disease, drought, and a titanic hailstorm. Babylon, the world capital of evil, and a code word for Rome, is struck down with plagues and fire. Returning to earth on a white horse, Christ slays the kings of the earth and their armies at Armageddon, chains up Satan, and rules in glory with his resurrected martyrs for a thousand years.

In the final episodes of Revelation, which immediately follow the Millennium, Satan is released from bondage. He drums up a mighty host to oppose the army of God, "but fire came down on them from heaven and consumed them; and the Devil, their seducer, was flung into the lake of fire and sulphur . . . there to be tormented day and night for ever." (20:10) The dead are resurrected, final judgment is pronounced, and the world comes to an end. Sky and earth and sea all vanish, to be replaced by a golden new Jerusalem 12,000 furlongs square, where the saved will live happily ever after. But the damned will die eternally in the infernal lake "that burns with sulphurous flames." (21:8)

So goes the vision traditionally attributed to John the Evangelist. Although there is no total destruction of the world by fire, as in II Peter, the Lord punishes his creatures with fire at least six times, from the disaster summoned by the first trumpet to the final disposition of the damned in the burning lake of Hell. The two world wars of the endtime, recalling the last battle between the armies of Ormazd and Ahriman in Zoroastrian myth, and the divine counterattack on the legions of Gog in Ezekiel, provide an alternative terminal vision. But there are also natural disasters, such as earth-quakes, storms, and droughts. Pestilence does its worst, along with monsters. Revelation is a warehouse catalogue of calamities. When the end finally arrives after the sparely described interlude of the Millennium, it is an abso-lute end, so far as earth and its history are concerned. The battered universe vanishes, and time is rolled up. Revelation is exhilarating, no doubt, and especially for underdogs sure of their faith. It is also terrifying. With its last words, a prayer to Christ to return soon, the Christian Bible comes to an awesome close.

6

◆

From Sacred to Secular

SUCH ARE THE GREAT mythic archetypes of the endtime handed down to modern man from antiquity. The cyclical eschatologies—Taoist and Confucian, Hindu and Buddhist, Babylonian and Greek, Platonic and Stoic—envisioned an end programmed into history by the very rhythm of the cosmos. In the main, cyclical views thrived best among the peasantries and ruling classes of settled agrarian civilizations, mingling hope and fatalism, comfort and resignation, mitigating the harshness of life without ignoring the evils of the day. Each individual could interpret his culture's terminal vision to mean whatever best suited his needs and circumstances. The powerful found a way to express feelings of guilt and uneasiness, and yet justify their continuation in power; the weak could take refuge in the knowledge that even the powerful would some day go under. For everyone, discontent was absorbed into reassurance that public time followed the circular course of personal and natural time.

The linear eschatologies, for their part—precivilized and pastoralist, Germanic and Iranian, Jewish and Christian, and, a little later, Islamic—supplied many of the same consolations, with the steadying power of the cyclical vision replaced by a view of time that encouraged political militance. The example of utopian primitivism in the revolutionary Taoism of the Han Dynasty in China shows that cyclical views could also be adapted to radical politics, but the linear model was on the whole more adaptable. As in Judaism, it could promote the cause of a weak nation striving for its place in the ancient sun; or as in early Christianity, it could appeal to oppressed masses thirsting for justice in a world of intolerable extremes of wealth and dissolving social morale.

54

In due course, however, Christianity underwent a transformation that would have appalled its founder. During the fourth century, the old faith of the estranged urban masses became the faith of imperial Rome. Present-day critics who lament the instant co-optation of avant-garde movements by the media, or Marxists who have suffered through the un-Marxing of both social-ism and communism in twentieth-century Europe, can well understand the ironies of a Romanized Christianity. John of Patmos had reserved the first resurrection, the partial resurrection of the Millennium, for Christian mar-tyrs. But martyrdom swiftly receded into the legendary past after the Chris-tian church supplanted the cults of Jupiter and Caesar.

High on the agenda of the imperial church was the defusing of eschatol-ogy. In the second and third centuries, eschatological fervor had continued to warm the imaginations of the devout. The Montanist sect of the second century, which eventually captured the most acute theological mind of his generation, Tertullian of Carthage, had proclaimed that the end of the world was imminent. The writings of such early Fathers as Irenaeus, Cyprian, and Lactantius bristled with terminal forebodings. But in the fourth century the church started to pipe a somewhat different tune. It might have done so anyway, since Christ's Second Coming was by now embarrassingly late, and many theologians had begun to look inward, like Origen, for a consolation more quiet and intimate than the high drama of the endtime could supply. All the same, one suspects that the real embarrassment of Biblical eschatol-ogy to the churchmen of the fourth century was its potential for making trouble. As a newly installed pillar of imperial civilization, the church had the task of teaching respect for law and order. The time had come for Chris-tians to "settle down."

One strategy was to transfer some of the hopes of millennialism to the Roman empire itself, in its new guise as a Christian polity. A progressivist faction surfaced in the fourth century, represented by Eusebius of Caesarea and Saint Ambrose, Bishop of Milan, which saw hope for the betterment of mankind in a Christ-centered public order.[1] This ancient liberalism soon sputtered and died in the unpropitious climate of the fifth century, when the Western empire fell to barbarian conquerors, but the Roman church survived the Roman state and, indeed, helped to inspire and educate its successors. The church finally found a comfortable compromise between the fiery escha-tology of the Bible and the needs of a largely conservative, agrarian society in the theology of Saint Augustine, Bishop of Hippo.

Augustine did not deny that the world would some day literally end, as prophesied in scripture. Yet he scolded Christians who imagined that a replica of heaven could be raised up in this world of sorrows. Dreams of a terrestrial millennium were foolish, since, as he argued ingeniously from a free interpretation of holy writ, the thousand-year reign mentioned in the Bible had already begun, with Christ's first coming. It was simply the Christian era itself, the era in which Christ's healing grace was already available, and Christ's church already ruled men's hearts. As for the end of time, no one could say just when it would happen. The expression "one thousand years" did not mean one hundred decades. One thousand was the cube of the number ten, suggesting length, breadth, and height, and therefore only a symbol of the "fullness of time," an ample age without any fixed term knowable to mankind. In reality the end might be several thousand years distant.

In the last chapter of *The City of God*, Augustine summed up his schema of world history as an experience lasting six cosmic days, corresponding to the six days of creation. The first five had already passed, from Adam to the birth of Christ. The sixth, the so-called millennium, "is now passing, and cannot be measured by any number of generations, as it has been said, 'It is not for you to know the times, which the Father hath put in His own power.' (Acts 1:7)"[2] When it did finally end, in however many earthly years, the Jews would be converted and Antichrist would arise to persecute the faithful. Then Christ would come again in glory. "Christ shall judge; the dead shall rise; the good and the wicked shall be separated; the world shall be burned and renewed."[3]

The Bishop was thus able to have his cake and eat it too. Without demythologizing the expectation of an endtime, as some Christian Platonists of the early church had sought to do, he could render such an expectation relatively harmless by denying any knowledge that the end was near at hand. The coming of Antichrist was put off to a remote future epoch. The millennium was for all practical purposes eliminated altogether. The present age, with all its woes, could now be seen as fundamentally good, since God had built his church on its Roman rock, and to all men the risen Christ offered his love. At the same time, Augustine did not endorse the hopes for progress of his more politically minded predecessors of the fourth century. The church, not the empire, was the voice of God here below; states existed only because men were too sinful to live without them.

Augustine's eschatology became the official teaching of the church throughout the Middle Ages, and served its mistress well. It consoled, without inflaming. Disaffected Christians seeking stronger visions had to look elsewhere, often returning to the Bible for their authority. An eschatological underground flourished for many centuries after Augustine, breaking out into the open from time to time, and then disappearing from view again, as the church mobilized its forces on behalf of social stability and established power.

Much of the story is well told in Norman Cohn's *The Pursuit of the Millennium*. Cohn finds that major outbreaks of millennialist activism often occurred among the uprooted poor in areas of overpopulation, or in the wake of great disasters, or both. Even settled and prospering populations could be jolted into eschatological concern by extraordinary happenings. The irruption into Europe of fresh barbarian hordes such as the Magyars, the Vikings, and the Mongols was interpreted as the arrival of "the hosts of Gog and Magog" of Revelation 20:8. Muhammad, who himself had filled the Koran with eschatological visions much like those of the New Testament, was easily identified as Antichrist. The Black Death of the fourteenth century was correlated with Biblical warnings of plagues in the endtime. But for the alienated poor, the established order itself seemed to be doing the work of Satan best: the church with all its wealth, the great landowners, even the mysterious Jew, whose rabbis still stubbornly denied Christ but whose affairs seemed to prosper in spite of everything.

In any event, the history of Europe from the early Middle Ages through the Reformation abounds with prophets and movements professing revealed knowledge of the endtime. The supreme example is the twelfth-century Italian monk Joachim of Floris, who announced that Antichrist was already alive and would soon seize power. Immediately thereafter, perhaps in the year 1260, the last age of world history would begin, a reign of monks supplanting the authority of the secular clergy, and bringing history to a radiant finale. Joachim was often quoted, and misquoted, by the many apocalyptic preachers who followed him. Radical prophecies of the endtime were proclaimed in the later Middle Ages by Fra Dolcino and his Apostolic Brethren, by the Franciscan Jean de Roquetaillade, by the Taborites of Bohemia, and others.[4]

Despite the weight of the Augustinian tradition, partisans of various kings, emperors, and popes also resorted now and again to apocalyptic prophecy. From the textual evidence gathered by Bernard McGinn, one may even surmise that such partisans were more common than defenders of the oppressed. Medieval apocalypticism, he writes, was "not primarily a movement from below, a manifestation of popular religion," as Cohn maintains, but rather "for the most part, an attempt by a group of educated religious *literati* to interpret the times, to support their patrons, to console their supporters, and to move men to pursue specified aims at once political and religious in nature."[5] Nothing was easier than to identify a given pope or ruler with Antichrist, or, alternatively, with the reign of the returning Christ; if radicals could play the game, so could the advocates of the mighty, and often did. Joachim himself, regardless of the uses to which Joachite prophecy were later put, was hardly a revolutionary. McGinn supplies illustrations of his thesis from many sources, including Pope Gregory I in the sixth century, Saint Bonaventure in the thirteenth, and Telesphorus of Cosenza, a tractarian of the fourteenth century whose vision of the endtime brands a coming German emperor as Antichrist and gives the role of defender of the true faith to a king of France.

Apocalypticism found a place as well in the Reformation of the sixteenth century. A variety of dissident elements in the disintegrating feudal order with a variety of motives struck out against kings, emperors, magnates, and popes alike, and encountered fierce resistance. Kings, emperors, magnates, and popes—as in the Middle Ages—also fought among themselves. Endtime prophecy became a familiar weapon in the wars of words and faiths that ensued.

Many Protestants echoed Augustine in proclaiming that the millennium had been inaugurated by the risen Christ. But now, they said, it was a thousand years and more after Augustine's death, and the millennium had ended. Satan had been loosed once more and Antichrist ruled in the persons of the latter-day popes of Rome, faithful vicars of Christ no longer but masters of deceit and iniquity. In 1540 Luther noted that exactly 5,500 years had transpired since the Creation; mankind was therefore in the middle of the sixth millennium, or day, of earthly history, and the end drew near. "For the sixth millennium will not be finished, just as the three days of Christ's death were not completed."[6] Luther's disciple Melanchthon suggested that the year of Christ's Second Coming might be 1680. The Zwinglian Henry Bullinger, in one hundred sermons preached on the Apocalypse in 1573, agreed that the end would come late in the seventeenth century, just 666 years (the code number of the apocalyptic beast in Revelation 13:18) after Antichrist's arrival.

The Protestant mainstream did not favor revolutionary action to establish any sort of temporal divine kingdom. The chief objective of Luther and many of his contemporaries was to overthrow the power of Antichrist, meaning the power of Rome, and then to prepare for the Parousia, the return of Christ. The millennium of the early church had come and gone; in these final days, Christ's flock was obliged to center its hopes on the approaching bliss of Heaven. Protestant eschatology thus dovetailed well with the worldly needs of the princes and advancing bourgeoisie of sixteenth-century Europe. It helped justify the assertion of independence from Roman authority, without demanding a social revolution on behalf of the popular masses.

But there is no reason to suppose that the Reformers were insincere in their expectation of an imminent end. Unlike the majority of Roman churchmen, many of them did indeed see little time left before Christ's return in glory. Swelling the power of local aristocrats and urban ruling classes was not, certainly not in any conscious way, the goal of their theology. Their state of mind was radically eschatological, and only in later times did Protestants often abandon their universalist vision of Last Things to preach a doctrine of merely individual judgment and resurrection or, still later, merely earthly reform and progress.[7]

Meanwhile, another tendency emerged in Protestant thought as early as the 1520s, a tendency organically linked to the millennialism of the Middle Ages, but anathema to Luther and even Calvin. The Protestant "left wing," whose spokesmen included the redoubtable Thomas Münzer and the half-mad Anabaptist tyrants of the Westphalian town of Münster, revived the Montanism of the second century and announced that the millennium, far from being over, had not yet even begun.

Spiritual leader of the German peasants in their uprising of 1524–26, Münzer preached explicitly to the poor. He insisted that the rich and the powerful, whether Roman or Lutheran, could not be God's elect. Fidelity to Christ's gospel compelled him to assert that from the downtrodden poor men of the land God would call an army of his faithful to battle. The high and mighty would be exterminated, and the millennium of the chosen would ensue. As for Antichrist, he was obviously none other than that celebrated whore of the German princes, Martin Luther! Many Catholics had reached the same conclusion.

Millennialism erupted many times throughout the sixteenth and seventeenth centuries, often among oppressed or dissident strata of society with revolutionary goals. The coming millennial reign of Christ's saints was a common theme of Puritan divines, especially popular during the tumultuous years of the English Civil War and the Cromwellian Commonwealth. The Puritans brought eschatology to the New World, where Michael Wigglesworth's poem *The Day of Doom* (1662), says Perry Miller, became "the first best seller in the annals of the American book trade."[8] The German Pietists also subscribed to millennialism, as did such eminent English theologians of the seventeenth century as Joseph Mede and Thomas Burnet, studied at length in Ernest Lee Tuveson's *Millennium and Utopia*. Tuveson's main object is to show how millennialism eventually faded into the modern belief in progress, but during the seventeenth century the expectation was of a literal end. As late as the 1680s Burnet predicted in his *Theory of the Earth* that the globe would be engulfed in a great fire starting at Rome, and then, purified, would rise again under conditions much like those of Eden to serve as the home of a perfect race of wise and happy Methuselahs.[9]

Much more evidence is available, but the point is easily made that for the first seventeen hundred years of Christian belief, visions of the end burned in the minds of the faithful with a heat as hot as the final fires themselves. Such visions were not always meant to be taken word for word, but they were visions of a real end. The power of the eschatological imagination, with its sharp contrasts between good and evil, light and darkness, with its dreams of absolute salvation and absolute degradation, and its furious denial of the durability of the established world-order, is felt repeatedly in all the vicissitudes of the history of the Christian era.

The passage from that era to our own post-Christian culture occurred between the middle of the seventeenth century and the middle of the nineteenth. There is not space to do it justice here.[10] But it is a unique and perilous spiritual journey. At one time, not so very long ago, the only significant body of unbelievers in any Western country was the Jewish community, which had its own ancient and well-developed eschatological faith. Today, and for several generations past, believing Jews and Christians are a curious remnant, functioning as last-ditch defenders of a dying feudalism and a decadent capitalism, often in spite of themselves. The suddenness of the change, measured in historian's time, strains credulity.

What we call the "secularization" of Jewish and Christian belief, including the secularization of eschatology, was not one process but three, each cutting a different way. It was the metamorphosis of the forms and creeds of traditional religious faith into new ones that preserve unmistakable traces and even essences of the old. It was also the replacement of Jewish and Christian values by analogous modern values that satisfy the same needs without appreciable residues of Judaism or Christianity. Finally, it was the expropriation, for secular purposes, of the symbolic language of traditional belief.

All three processes have occurred in the history of eschatology as in most other fields of traditional thought. For example, some post-Christian thinkers and writers have reconceived traditional eschatological doctrine so as to eliminate a literal public end, together with all mythology, but they keep what Frank Kermode identifies as "the sense of an ending." Romantic tragedy, in Goethe's *Young Werther* or Byron's *Manfred*, illustrates such a reconception. Not a little of the moral and psychological force of Christian eschatology survives. In the second instance, other post-Christian thinkers and writers have imagined ends comparable in awesomeness to any foreseen by religion, ends with natural or historical causes that sometimes supply opportunities for salvations comparable in grandeur. How much the secular vision may owe to sacred archetypes is often difficult to measure. In the third case, traditional belief furnishes symbolic materials that are taken over and put to new uses, as when a modern dictator proclaims a thousand-year Reich or when his critics dub him the Antichrist or liken the world war he unleashed to the Biblical Armageddon.

The present work attends primarily to the second of these three modes of secularization, studying modern terminal visions that are neither outgrowths nor echoes of the traditional myths, but distinctively modern analogues. Yet in saying this, I am well aware that no modern analogue of the sacred archetypes can ever be wholly independent of its predecessors in traditional culture. Whether the analogous visions would have arisen without that traditional culture is impossible to know. What we do know is that the culture once flourished, and had chance to touch everything that followed it. The existence of traditional terminal visions has beyond all doubt helped to plant in various modern minds the thought of an endtime, along with ideas of what forms the end might take. The substance of the old eschatologies has also invaded modern visions of the end; likewise their symbolic paraphernalia. In the real world we cannot hope to find a pure example of any of the three modes of secularization. In any given situation, all three will be involved to some degree.

Just when the transition in eschatology from sacred to secular took place in modern history is debatable. But it is safe to guess that the various secular alternatives to Biblical futurism had all matured by the early nineteenth century. The ideas of "progress" and "utopia" had emerged to supplant the sacred myths of heaven and the millennium; it remains a lively issue among scholars whether these ideas were the "bastard offspring" of the Biblical hope, as Emil Brunner contends, or simply modern analogues constructed from modern materials.[11] Visions of the end were also beginning to make their appearance, either as overtures to social philosophies of utopian transformation, or as expressions of cultural despair and fatigue.

Yet such visions were relatively late in coming, by contrast with ideas of progress or utopism in its chiefly didactic early phase. The advanced thought of the eighteenth century had been conspicuously free of apocalyptic thunder: it stressed reform and progress, in a spirit of sweet reasonableness. But after the crash of the *ancien régime*, after the romantic rebellion against the Enlightenment, the uproar of Napoleon, and the harsh beginnings of the new industrialism, modern culture lost some of the innocence of its founding fathers. It had acquired scars and wrinkles of its own, and only then, in the first decades of the nineteenth century, did thoughts of the end once more become fully relevant to the cultural situation of Western man.

Against this background romantic belletrists like Mary Shelley and Edgar Allan Poe entertained visions of the world's end through plague or cosmic disasters. Arthur Schopenhauer and a morbidly admiring younger generation of self-conscious pessimists questioned the value of all worldly striving. Scientists began to speculate about the mortality of the universe. Conservatives compared modern Europe in all her smoky glory with the once powerful but finally fallen Rome. Socialists and anarchists inveighed with the passion of Amos or Jeremiah against the iniquities of capitalism and prophesied its end in scenes of apocalyptic grandeur. Anyone alive in the 1980s can feel almost at home in the world of the early nineteenth century. We have reached our starting point—once again. We are ready to begin exploring in greater depth the terminal visions of the two centuries of the Secular Age.

PART THREE

◆

The Etiology of Doomsaying

7

◆

Fears

THE SCENE IS EARTH, after the end. A young inventor and scientist, Steven Krane, crawls across the burned land toward the sea. He has a crushed leg, injured in his drop by parachute from his spacecraft. No one but Krane lives, from all the millions of his fellow human beings. Nothing lives. The planet is a cinder, consumed in the terminal fire of a nuclear chain reaction. Some time before, Krane had stumbled on "a catalyst that would induce atomic disintegration of iron and give 10×10^{10} foot-pounds of energy for every gram of fuel."[1] An older scientist had warned him that if even a drop of the catalyst escaped through the rocket tubes of his spaceship, it would trigger a global cataclysm, but the young man had refused to pay heed. He had launched. He had destroyed the world.

Krane continues his painful passage across the ashes of the dead planet. His only companion, a dog named Umber, came down with him but cannot be found. Obeying a compulsion he does not understand, Krane drags himself toward the sea. The old scientist Hallmyer appears to him in a hallucination, taunting and scorning him. Hallmyer pours a goblet of cold water into the dust, just out of his reach. Krane is consoled and urged on by another hallucination, the vision of his fiancée Evelyn, who reminds him of his cottage on the shore where they will live together as Adam and Eve. Her warnings help save him from the terrifying attack of the only other living creature on earth, the once faithful Umber, now a wild animal maddened with hunger. Krane kills Umber with his revolver.

When he finally reaches the sea, Evelyn's ghost vanishes. The waters of the ocean cradle him, like a loving mother. "Then he knew. This was not the end of life. There could never be an end to life. Within his body, within the rotting tissues rocking gently in the sea was the source of ten million lives." From his cells and from the micro-organisms infesting them, life will regenerate. "It would begin again the same old repeated cycle that had begun perhaps with the rotting corpse of some last survivor of interstellar travel." No Evelyn, no Eve, is required in Krane's silent Eden. "Only the sea, the great mother of life was needed. The sea had called him back to her depths that presently life might emerge once more, and he was content."[2]

"Adam and No Eve" by Alfred Bester, the source of this terminal vision, is by no means an imperishable classic of world literature. But in just thirteen pages it manages to touch nearly all the levels of meaning and motive in the secular literature of Last Things. The archetypes are there, too. The last man is a new Adam, guilty like the original Adam of the sin of pride and the crime of defiance. His Eve is "no Eve," but rather the eternal feminine, a Holy Mother calling him to her watery bosom so that he can regenerate the world with the seed of his flesh. The terminal catastrophe, both Biblical and Greek, is a literal *ekpyrosis*, and life is represented as a cycle of eternal return. The story can be read in Freudian-Jungian terms as the conquest of Thanatos by Eros, and of father-hatred by mother-love, with Krane finding peace by descent into the deepest caverns of the collective unconscious. At the same time, "Adam and No Eve" is a typical expression of modern man's fear of the Frankensteinian powers of his own science and technology. He knows only too well that such powers can always get out of hand, with disastrous consequences. Nor does the story ignore his dread of nature, which science has reinforced in a thousand ways since the days of Rudolf Clausius and Charles Darwin. In "Adam and No Eve," Krane's fatal catalyst ignites the world-fire, but could not have done so if the elements themselves, in this case iron, were not inherently unstable. A final touch is supplied by Umber, loyal comrade under civilized conditions, but awful beast of the apocalypse and exemplar of nature red in tooth and claw after the catastrophe has incinerated the last can of dog food.

To study the etiology of doomsaying, to understand why stories of the endtime are still told in an age that has largely abandoned its Biblical faith in tribulation and judgment, we must sort out the symptoms and sources of modern anxiety, both in history proper and in the history of ideas. Or to try yet another metaphor, we must undertake a stratigraphy of fear.

The fears of secular eschatologists, and of modern man generally, can be separated into three layers. The lowest layer, and the first to be deposited, is the private fear that starts in earliest childhood, the fear of separation, of powerlessness, of sexual rivals, of loneliness, of failing, of dying. Such fear is universal; it also takes on a somewhat different intensity with a somewhat different combination of psychic ingredients in each individual writer of eschatological fiction. Whether the writer knows it or not, every story of the world's end draws power from, and illuminates in one way or another, the ends and beginnings of the self.

The second layer in the stratigraphy of fear is what we have just called the dread of nature: the sense already well developed in primitive man and in the child's world that external reality is full of dangers. Wolves lurk in the shadows, and the sky can fall. Fears of nature are often projections of internal conflicts, but just as often they are quite rational, based on perceptions of real menaces to health and life. All the natural sciences have their eschatologies, from the big bangs and heat-deaths of cosmic physics to the minuscule but deadly jungles of microbiology. Much of the old fear of the supernatural, and especially of God's wrath, has been translated into fear of nature, adding further to its psychic energies.

At the highest level of consciousness and concern, at least in the terminal visions of twentieth-century writers, is a third assortment of fears centered on what can be done to man by man himself. Stories of the mad or reckless scientist, the lethal effects of technology and industry on the environment, and apocalyptic wars of class and race and nation, like fears of nature, may sometimes give expression to more deeply buried and more private anxieties. But they are also, like fears of nature, grounded in authentic modern experience and knowledge.

In the chapters that follow, fictions will be explored as studies in this or that mode of terminal fear. But as with the sample cores of geologists, many of our literary cores will contain deposits from every layer, together with psychic fossils from pre-modern myth and faith.

8

◆

The Excluded Self

ONE CONVENIENT STARTING point for the investigation of the psychology of terminal visions is the research done since the second World War into the effects of disaster, impending or actual, on individuals and groups. The war itself supplied a harrowing assortment of disasters: bombing raids on densely populated cities, the attempted race-murder of the world's Jews, millions of deaths on the battlefield, the sinking of whole fleets, and much more. It came after years of steadily mounting terrified expectation, and it climaxed with the debut of weapons so apocalyptic that any future war in which they are used unrestrictedly will result in the physical destruction of the warring peoples, and any others caught in their crossfire.

On the one hand, the mass panic predicted before the war by novelists and social psychologists alike did not materialize. Populations and armies in disaster behaved responsibly, cooperatively, and sometimes even cheerfully, resulting in what Martha Wolfenstein has called the "post-disaster utopia," a period of exceptional social harmony immediately subsequent to any kind of catastrophic happening, remembered with nostalgia by the participants in later years.[1] "We have seen," writes Allen H. Barton at the close of a detailed study of communities in disaster, "that there is little truth to the assumption that disaster instantly strips the mask of civilization from people and reveals all their darker impulses; neither does it turn people into catatonics or render them hysterical and irrational."[2]

On the other hand, expectations of disaster (and expectations of panic!) may betray neuroses on the part of the prophets, a point well treated by Wolfenstein. Mentally stable individuals, even when they realize that disasters may actually befall their world in the future, do not often allow themselves to become emotionally disturbed by the prospect. They assume or hope that the world will muddle through, take what precautions seem practicable, and go about their daily business. The less stable or neurotic personality, by contrast, finds reality difficult to accept. He lacks the full powers of self-control in facing reality available to "normal" people. "The individual," notes Wolfenstein, "who fears that he may not be able to control his own destructive impulses anticipates on the basis of projection that explosive forces in the external world may break through restraining bonds."[3] In other words, his subconscious suggests to him that the world will blow up at any time because he knows that he himself is likely to blow up at any time. The more stable person, by the same token, projects his stability on to the world.

Worse yet, in imagining universal death and destruction, the neurotic may also be venting repressed hostility. Sadistic desires that cannot be fulfilled in overt behavior find play in relishing the doom scheduled to befall others. As Susan Sontag has observed, in an essay on disaster films, such spectacles release the viewer from all normal obligations. He can identify with the survivors and take pleasure in the fall of the rich and the mighty. He can "give outlet to cruel or at least amoral feelings."[4] He becomes, for an hour or two, the high court of the world.

There is the further possibility that visions of the end express neurotic feelings of guilt. Since in childhood we are repeatedly warned of the calamities that will smite us if we fail to obey authority, we grow up with irrational beliefs that everything that happens is "a reward or a punishment meted out by higher powers."[5] Hence, we may produce or obsessively consume scenarios of the endtime because we feel guilty about our misconduct, which includes our sadism, whether acted out or not. In Wolfenstein's conjecture, "Fear of death may express an unconscious expectation of talion punishment for death wishes towards others. Where an external danger situation exists it may readily be incorporated into a pre-existing fantasy of anticipated retaliation."[6]

Wolfenstein is not thinking of the authors or readers of eschatological fictions in particular, but clearly the individual who is morbidly preoccupied with visions of Last Things may be an individual who needs the services of a psychiatrist, or at any rate has emotional problems which he should try to understand and solve. For other individuals, the great majority of writers and readers of terminal fictions, interest in doomsday no doubt fails to reach the intensity of a neurotic fixation. Doomsday fictions may even be mildly therapeutic. Bruno Bettelheim suggests that facing up to well-entrenched fears, as the child does when he bravely weathers the telling of a horrific fairy tale by the Brothers Grimm, has the effect—if properly managed—of dispelling the fears and building self-confidence.[7] Stories of the world's end are something like Grimms' Tales for grown-ups.

But setting aside for the moment the question of whether eschatological fictions are in any sense neurotic, we can hardly deny that they traffic in situations of the most fundamental relevance to the health and well-being of the self. They cut to the bone. In almost every instance they confront in a uniquely dramatic form the fact of death. They enable us to imagine ourselves heroically evading death, as we identify with the survivors of the world-disaster. They also quite often give us the chance to re-live anxieties of separation from loved ones, and the healing that occurs when new ties are formed, or old ones restored. All the central impulses of Eros, the wish for life and love, come into play in the typical eschatological tale, and propel its characters through their endtime struggles. If sometimes Thanatos, with its lust for destruction and self-destruction, gets the upper hand, the author generally takes pains to show that his own sympathies, nevertheless, lie with Eros.

To begin: the fear of dying. Obviously nothing is more universal in terminal fictions than death. Since the certainty of an ultimate personal endtime is also the most overwhelming datum of the human condition, it is safe to guess that every public endtime in fiction serves its readers to some degree as metaphor and reminder of their own mortality. Not all terminal stories make death their central concern. But they all find a place for it, and some of them are veritable *danses macabres*.

Byron's poem "Darkness" and Poe's story "The Masque of the Red Death" offer the romantic image of death at its grisliest. The narrator of Thomas Hood's poem "The Last Man" is a hangman by profession, who so resents the appearance of a fellow survivor that he plies his trade one last time: again, death is the main player on the stage. In more recent terminal visions, death and dying often dominate stories of the last survivors of a final war. Some are little more than countdowns to extinction, but the device of the countdown, however simple, can prove remarkably effective. Such is the case with Mordecai Roshwald's *Level 7*, where communications with the subterranean shelters of the postwar society break off level by level, as each succumbs to radiation sickness, until life remains only in the smallest and deepest. Eventually the denizens of Level 7 start dying, too, one by one, as the diarist waits for the inevitable signs of his own annihilation. Nevil Shute adopts the same narrative strategy in his *On the Beach*, except that death approaches by degrees of latitude, rather than depth. Edward Bryant in "Among the Dead" carries the strategy to its ultimate grotesquerie: three survivors in a world stripped clean of all living things measure the time left by eating their way through the fresh-frozen bodies in a cryogenics vault in alphabetical order, from "A" to "Z."

The movement in twentieth-century philosophy that makes a specialty of reminding man of his mortality, existentialism, has nothing to say about public endtimes, by the very nature of its forming premises. But the theater and fiction of "the absurd," whose history is interlaced with that of existentialism, has now and then allowed itself to deal in eschatological metaphors. Once again, the gaze of the reader (or theatergoer) is fixed on the face of death. Samuel Beckett's *Endgame*, although patently a parable about the burdens of existence, borrows many of the conventions of the doomsday tale. The protagonists Clov and Hamm live in a "shelter." The time is "zero." Outside, everything is dead, nature no longer exists, seeds will never sprout, the sky is gray, the universe stinks of corpses, the sea is still and tideless. Repeatedly, the players announce that the earth will not replenish itself, that it is dead, extinguished, "corpsed." Beckett "forbears to enlighten us," writes Maurice Valency, "as to whether he is describing the end of a man or the end of the world. . . . It hardly matters. Dramatically the result is the same, and the figure is sufficiently capacious to receive either interpretation or both."[8] A still more explicitly eschatological scene from the absurdist canon is Béranger's vision of the universe in flames in Eugène Ionesco's *Le piéton de l'air*, where doomsday appears as a future event seen only by the clairvoyant hero, as in Revelation. The implication is that some day all men will see what he sees: that life ends irrevocably in death, and that beyond the fiery curtain, which consumes saints as well as sinners, there is no heaven, no survival, only absolute emptiness.

But such intensity of concentration on mortality is comparatively rare in terminal fictions. More to the point is their grasp, desperate or exultant, of the possibilities for life that remain. Even a story of almost certain total oblivion like Shelley's *The Last Man* dwells less on death and dying than on the cruelty of death, and the horrors of loneliness. As we noted earlier, Shelley was moved to write it by her loss of Byron and her husband. All companions dead at last, her hero dedicates himself at the end of the novel to sailing the coastlines of the world in a search for other survivors, although he has little hope of success.

In many later stories of doomsday, the pathetically dwindling band of fugitives portrayed in *The Last Man* develops into a post-disaster utopia, a family or community or brotherhood in which the protagonist can put down new roots. He may do a lot better for himself than in the old days. Terminal fictions are full of scenes of food-gathering and feasting, erotic gratification, the formation of warm and loving relationships among survivors, new simplicities and rough comforts that compare favorably indeed with the humdrum, or the decadence, of pre-disaster society. From the point of view of the individual life-cycle, the post-disaster utopia is analogous to a fondly remembered childhood, or to the ideal home and family that adults—beyond the identity crisis—dream of creating in order to fit the freshly identified self into a larger structure of relationships. The love and security sacrificed during the "catastrophe" of growing up are recaptured. The more acute the sufferings of the time of separation, the more keen the joys of coming home again.

Home, for example, is the last redoubt of William Hope Hodgson's *The Night Land*, the immense metal Pyramid where most of earth's endtime generations live and die after the burning out of the sun, surrounded by enemies both natural and unnatural. The young hero leaves its security to rescue his beloved, whose own refuge has depleted its power-source and has been overrun by monsters. He risks everything for her, almost loses her several times, and finally brings her back to the Pyramid, where they will live happily ever after. He has proved his manhood, she her womanhood. The redoubt holds them safe in its warm uterine depths. Outside, in the Night Land, death waits patiently. Even the Pyramid will some day run out of energy, like the heroine's home. But until the very end, the fierce love of man and woman and the joyful fellowship of the Pyramid will keep the human flame alive. The whole story, whatever else it signifies, is a celebration of Eros.

Hodgson's novel belongs to a special category of fictions set millions of years in the future, in which the real catastrophe is the exhaustion of nature herself. Brian Aldiss tells much the same story in *Hothouse*. His plot, too, is circular: the hero is first seen as a child living with his tribe in a tropical rain forest; the hero's *Wanderzeit* of high adventure follows; then as a grown man he returns to the forest with his wife and baby, where they and their descendants will live out the time that remains before the rapidly expanding sun goes nova. Aldiss has updated Hodgson's astrophysics, but not his narrative strategy or his stress on love and community as defenses against death's sting.

Fictions that deal with catastrophes of the near future give ampler opportunity for developing contrasts between the present day and the glamors of the endtime. R. C. Sherriff, in the opening pages of *The Hopkins Manuscript*, depicts in some detail the prosaic existence of a middle-aged poultry breeder and astronomy buff in the months before the catastrophe. The end comes, as the moon smashes into the earth, but contrary to the expectations of the scientific community, millions survive—including Hopkins and his prize hen. Hopkins is now a figure of some importance in what remains of his little world in Hampshire. The few local survivors come to his bachelor home for shelter. Everyone works contentedly, and there is a worldwide epoch of recovery, "a wonderful period which lasted for wellnigh two years," recalled later by Hopkins as the happiest years of his life.[9]

The post-disaster utopia becomes almost a cliché in the world's end stories of the 1950s and thereafter. It is the besieged farmhouse and later the

Isle of Wight in John Wyndham's *The Day of the Triffids*, the strange new London of ice and snow and Anglo-Saxon Eskimos in John Christopher's *The World in Winter*, the Fort Repose of Pat Frank's *Alas, Babylon*, the Saxham of J. T. McIntosh's *The Fittest*, the Mars of Ray Bradbury's "The Million-Year Picnic," the Winnebago camper with its six oddly assorted survivors in Piers Anthony's *Rings of Ice*. Robert Merle in *Malevil* lovingly recreates the early Middle Ages as a handful of lusty survivors living in a stone castle in rural France recover from the horrors of World War III. Walter M. Miller, Jr., furnishes a similar setting, with a monastery instead of a castle, in the first part of *A Canticle for Leibowitz*. Edgar Pangborn evokes a simpler and often more caring America, reminiscent of colonial times, in *The Company of Glory* and *Davy*.

The stages in recovery from disaster, and its joys as well as dangers, are carefully delineated in an otherwise routine novel by Edmund Cooper, *All Fools' Day*. The hero, Matthew Greville, is a poet manqué and a London advertising executive whose outward success in the business world brings him no contentment. His wife has pushed him to the top, by sleeping with the people who can help him get there. He despises his work, his wife, and himself, in equal measure. The catastrophe, a new kind of radiation emitted by the sun, which drives all the sane people of the world to madness and suicide, spares Matthew Greville and other creative and unstable folk like him. The world has been inherited by its "fools." It is full of terrors, described by Cooper with his usual husky realism, but the real point of the story is Greville's gathering self-respect, as he peels off the layers of his soiled past and finds more honest love and companionship than he has ever known.

The first stage in his redemption comes when he makes his way to safety with Liz, a young woman whom he has rescued from a pack of wild dogs. He knows of a haven, a secluded cottage built on a little island in a Norfolk lake; together, they get away from London, survive ambush by adolescent hoodlums, and live for some time in peace and pleasure on their island, described as a kind of "shabby Eden." They share their Paradise briefly with a loveable old scholar, late of the University of East Anglia. After his death they leave to look for Liz's sister, and wind up in a larger Eden, joining forces with a community of eccentric but warm-hearted anarchists, who call themselves the Band of Hope. Like Pangborn's Company of Glory, the Band of Hope proves to be the nucleus of a regenerated civilization. Under Greville's inspired leadership, the anarchists trek to Cornwall. Eden is again enlarged. A whole new society evolves on the peninsula, while the rest of England struggles on in chaos and madness. In an epilogue, the reader is transported into the early twenty-first century to witness Greville's death during an expedition to the ruins of London. Now a venerable patriarch, he dies happily, thinking of his beloved Liz. "It was a fine summer morning, promising a long warm day."[10]

Even in stories where the endtime is short and survival impossible, the terminal utopia of love and tenderness often makes its appearance in some form or other. All of Melbourne, and Dwight Towers, Moira Davidson, and the Holmes family in particular, become a post-disaster utopian community in Shute's *On the Beach*. The confrontation with death generates an intimacy of spirit among the last men and women that would otherwise never have emerged, an intimacy of wholeness and goodness unattainable in the everyday present. In the same way, Alfred Coppel lets the endtime work a small miracle for a man and his ex-wife, who spend earth's last hours together in "Last Night of Summer." Richard Matheson carries his hero still further back in the life-cycle of love, to his mother's lap, at the end of "The Last Day." He had planned to stay away, thinking they would quarrel about religion, but he soon realizes that he has no one else to turn to. "In a wide world, about to be burned," he asks himself, "was there any other person who loved him above all others?"[11]

Eschatological fictions not only help us cope with fears of death and separation. They grant the individual a unique opportunity to face and perhaps conquer the fears of powerlessness that begin for all of us in earliest childhood. The last man, or one of a handful of last men, is a figure of immeasurable power and importance. Whoever he was before the end, he is now someone to reckon with. Survivorship, as the hangman discovers to his chagrin in the poem by Thomas Hood, can crown even a beggar.

So it happens that many survivors of the endtime, especially those who were already adults when the end came, find post-disaster life exhilarating. In addition to the new love and fellowship, there is the chance to be Adam and Eve, king of the world, savior of mankind. As in the Rubáiyát, "the sorry scheme of things" has been shattered to bits, by the author at least, and his hero can now "remould it nearer to the heart's desire." Or try. All adventure fiction, of course, appeals to similar impulses in its writers and readers, but few imaginary situations offer so much challenge and responsibility as those of the endtime.

One of the great prototypical heroes of the endtime is Allan Stern, consulting engineer in Manhattan before the end, and father of a whole new world after it, in *Darkness and Dawn* by George Allan England. Stern and his loyal secretary Beatrice fall asleep in their office on the top floor of New York's tallest skyscraper in the year 1920 and wake up many centuries later. Poisonous gases had escaped from an explosion in the earth's crust, killing nearly everyone. Their lives were saved, and in fact suspended, by the flukish effects of a less than fatal concentration of the toxin at the great height of Stern's office, and now they appear to be the last true human beings on earth. As the engineer comes to realize his situation, his dismay is overpowered by a strange sense of excitement. "Stern, deep down in his heart, caught some glimmering insight of the future and was glad." Everything in the world belongs to the two of them, and together they will restore civilization. With the help of a barbarian tribe whose ancestors had survived the world cataclysm high in the Rocky Mountains, they do just that, in three large volumes. Throughout, nothing daunts the intrepid lovers. They approach every new challenge "with a buoyant sense of conquest."[12]

Some of the enthusiasm of England's characters may be due to the author's time and place: England was an American living in the age of Teddy Roosevelt. He wrote primarily for the pulp magazines, which demanded manly heroes and faithful heroines. But there are too many other heroic or at least happy characters throughout the long history of eschatological fiction to rely entirely on explanations of time, place, or market.

Consider *Greybeard,* a comparatively recent novel by Brian Aldiss, who is a good deal more than a writer for the pulps, and an Englishman living in the considerably more chastened age of Harold Macmillan and Harold Wilson. His hero is no young engineer. Known as "Greybeard," he is a man in his mid-50s when the novel begins, and the world has come to an end, thanks to disastrous nuclear bomb tests in outer space and an ensuing world war. Nearly all human beings and many other mammals were sterilized when the bomb tests temporarily ripped open the Van Allen belts, exposing the planet to hard radiation. But Greybeard and his good wife Martha are not brooding dotards. Despite everything, Greybeard has to admit to himself that he feels "a terrible pleasure." He will not confess it to outsiders, "but somewhere it is there, a little stoaty thing that makes of a global disaster a personal triumph." He has been "lucky, wonderfully lucky."[13] He does not save the world, but he lives a decent life, and he will do what he can for the shy new race growing up almost invisibly in the woods, a race of fertile young savages who will some day inherit the earth.

Within the range suggested by the contrasting yet somehow kindred figures of Allan Stern and Greybeard, is a vast population of heroes of the endtime, who find fulfillment in their survivorship. Often the hero is hard and tough, a flinty man of destiny like the artilleryman, "grim set on living," in Wells's *The War of the Worlds,* or the airman John Cabal in the same author's screenplay, *Things to Come.* He is the tycoon and dictator Nordenholt in *Nordenholt's Million* by J. J. Connington, the valiant squire John Blundell in the Earl of Halsbury's *1944,* the mysterious lieutenant of L. Ron Hubbard's *Final Blackout,* and the resourceful Hugh Fitzharding of Herbert

Best's *The Twenty-Fifth Hour.* More recently, he is John Custance, London engineer, and his unloveable sidekick Mr. Pirrie, who lead a party of armed and desperate survivors to the safety of a rural redoubt in *The Death of Grass* by John Christopher. He is space captain Idris Hamilton in Edmund Cooper's *The Tenth Planet* and Hell's Angel Hell Tanner in Roger Zelazny's *Damnation Alley* and Vic the scavenger in Harlan Ellison's "A Boy and His Dog." He may be a woman, like Mil Lambert, matriarch of Nether Saxham in J. T. McIntosh's *The Fittest*, or—going all the way back to a novel first published in 1893—the glamorous but unflinching anarchist Natasha in George Griffith's *The Angel of the Revolution.*

Other heroes and heroines could be named who are appreciably less rugged than these, from the hapless Brother Francis of *A Canticle for Leibowitz* to the genial storyteller Demetrios of *The Company of Glory*, but the special interest of the tough ones is the short distance that separates them from the anti-heroes and villains of eschatological fiction, characters who share the unique power of the hero-figures, but who use it wickedly or fail to use it at all. In an endtime situation, where does survival end and crime begin? Although few authors have much difficulty deciding, the reader may not find it so easy. Depending on one's ethical and political convictions, a given character may be seen as good or evil. Even if writer and reader can agree on the moral issue, there is the further problem of the extent to which literature (eschatological or otherwise) is designed to satisfy the hunger of its readers (and sometimes of its writers) for violence and death.

Psychoanalytic theory suggests that such a hunger is no less part of the human condition than the desire for life, love, and fulfillment through useful work. Destructive impulses are related organically to the same fears of powerlessness that nourish fantasies about heroically saving the world or surviving its end. A sense of powerlessness can invoke all the devils of Thanatos: uncontrollable rage, bitter hatred, insatiable gluttony and lust, the desire to destroy supposed enemies and oppressors, self-loathing, and cravings for humiliation and death. All sorts of scenes in terminal literature serve these devils well, especially the visions of mass destruction during the catastrophe itself, whatever it may be, and the reigns of lawlessness and terror that so often follow. As for the heroes, and in particular the "tough" heroes, nothing is simpler for readers and writers alike than to admire them for the wrong reasons. Just as one may admire James Bond because he kills people and seduces innumerable gorgeous women, so one may admire the heroes of the endtime because in the name of survival or the rebuilding of civilization they are "driven" to behavior that would be unacceptable in "normal" times.

It is also possible to admire (or detest) the anti-heroes and villains for the right reasons. Certainly there are enough of them. The thanatotic temptations of the endtime are endless, a point lost on few writers of eschatological fiction. In this instance, the model is perhaps Thomas Hood's "The Last Man." Hood chose the same premise for doomsday as Mary Shelley: a universal pestilence, worse than the Black Death of the fourteenth century. As we have already seen, his last man is a professional executioner. When the curtain rises in the year 2001, the hangman—who is also the narrator of the poem—is singing "a merry lay," thankful to be alive when all others are dead. His happiness is shattered by the discovery that he is not the last man after all. Up the heath comes "a jolly knave," innocently delighted to see another survivor. Under his breath, the hangman curses the beggar. "If it were not for that beggar man," he reflects, "I'd be the King of the earth." Darkly, he promises himself that "an hour should come / To make him rue his birth."[14] They roam together briefly.

As the story continues, Hood re-creates the class struggle in this smallest of human microcosms. The hangman holds the beggar in contempt as his social inferior, and is enraged when he surprises the poor fellow dressed for fun in the robe and crown of a king. It irks him to see a man "lording so braggart-like / That was born to his beggar's fare, / And how he had stolen the royal crown / His betters were meant to wear." A mock trial follows, capped by a real execution. The hangman knows his business, and now he is indeed the last man. Wild dogs seize the dangling corpse, leaving only "ribbons of rags." At last the poem's anti-hero experiences loneliness, and the pangs of conscience. In the final stanza, he yearns for someone to render him the same service that he provided for the beggar. "For hanging looks sweet."[15]

Hood's work can be read on a number of levels. It expresses fear of nature, which can let pestilence loose and send dogs to devour the cadavers. It is a parable of post-revolutionary Europe, a world of common folk aspiring to great things in a society beginning to unravel. Its last men, a lackey of the old legal order and a simple beggar, reproduce under changed conditions the ancient struggle between exploiters and exploited. Hood was a poet of humanitarian protest, a forerunner of the social realism of later generations. But his gallows humor, another hallmark of his art, gives him a superb instrument for psychological, as well as social, analysis. The hangman is a madman. His joy at being the only survivor, his resentment of the harmless and happy-go-lucky beggar, his murder of the man, and his final wish for death for himself add up to a fairly convincing portrait of psychosis, which the catastrophe of the endtime did not create, but only unleashed.

In 1901, three-quarters of a century after Hood published "The Last Man," the son of a Methodist minister brought out one of the closest analyses of good and evil in eschatological fiction. The book is *The Purple Cloud* by M. P. Shiel. We discussed it briefly in Chapter Two. As the story begins, a

Chicago multimillionaire has left an enormous fortune in his will to the first man who sets foot on the North Pole. Whoever does it will be rich and famous. The protagonist—hero, anti-hero, and villain all in one—is Dr. Adam Jeffson, whose ambitious fiancée poisons the doctor selected for the latest polar expedition, so that Jeffson can take his place. But a dour Scotsman prophesies that doom will befall the world if any human being reaches a spot so plainly proscribed by the Almighty. The failure of dozens of previous expeditions proves that it is forbidden ground, as forbidden as the fruit of the tree of knowledge in Genesis.

Adam Jeffson, like his Biblical namesake, is a man with few defenses against temptation. He deliberately chooses to ignore the clues that point to his fiancée's responsibility for the murder of the other physician. As the expedition closes in on the Pole, the terrible desire to win the prize infects Jeffson more and more. He kills a colleague in a duel, after killing another by accident. Nine miles from the Pole, tormented by evil thoughts, Jeffson abandons the two remaining members of the expedition to dash on ahead. He finds a mysterious lake on the site of the Pole, and in fear and horror returns to his comrades, but they have died in a storm, and he is alone. Making his way back to civilization, he discovers that the Scotsman's apocalyptic warning was accurate. On the same day that he visited the Pole, the world did come to an end. Every human being on the planet had been killed by a vast purple cloud of vaporized hydrocyanic acid released from a volcanic eruption in the South Sea. The cloud did not quite reach either pole, or Jeffson would have died as well.

Tainted by his black thoughts and actions before the end, Jeffson is now free to commit whatever crimes he likes with impunity. He dreams of searching for another human being—in order to kill him. But he can find no one. He has fantasies of playing the Oriental despot, and carries them out, dressing up like a sultan. In a fit of hellish inspiration, he burns London to the ground, then sails to France and burns city after city. At times he repents of what he has done, but returns to his career of pyromania again and again, putting the torch to Paris, Calcutta, Peking, San Francisco, Constantinople. He dreams that one Chinaman still lives and resolves to kill him. There is no Chinaman, but when he finally does encounter a fellow-survivor, a beautiful young Turkish woman, he draws his dagger. "The crookedest and the slyest of the guiles of the Pit was whispering to me, tongue in cheek, 'Kill, kill—and wallow.' "[16]

A lightning bolt prevents the murder of Adam Jeffson's Eve. From this point forward the forces of life gain strength steadily over those of death. Jeffson treats his companion badly, refusing to mate with her, but he cannot bring himself to kill her. When she attempts suicide rather than leave him, he uses his medical skills to save her life. Eventually, he capitulates to her stronger will, and agrees to settle down with her and replenish the race.

Told so baldly, Shiel's tale sounds like just another example of what Michael Moorcock calls "Shaggy God stories."[17] But thanks to Shiel's odd mastery of the style of Gothic horror, and a paradoxical gift for touches of convincing realism, *The Purple Cloud* somehow works. It works above all as a study of the morbid fascination of death and destruction. The outrageousness of Jeffson, his uncontrollable pyromania, his frantic egoism, his blood-lust, are entirely credible, however much Shiel labors to spoil their credibility with supernaturalist blather about the struggle between cosmic forces of "White" and "Black" or with incidents that can be interpreted only as divine interference, such as the striking of Jeffson's dagger by lightning. One wonders how many readers of *The Purple Cloud* over the years—it has been reprinted more than once—found themselves darkly identifying with Jeffson the world-destroying Nero, rather than with Jeffson the reluctant hubby and dad.

Villains (as opposed to evil anti-heroes) appear with tedious predictability in the literature of the endtime, and like villains in fiction generally, they are treated as mere objects, foils for the hero's heroism. Only very occasionally does a villain receive enough of the writer's attention to repay psychopathological study or quench a reader's thirst for thanatotic thrills. Among the exceptions are the figures of Renshaw in John Bowen's *After the Rain*, Jack in William Golding's *Lord of the Flies*, and Collingwood in Alfred Coppel's *Dark December*. A particularly memorable villain, because of his puritanism, emotional flatness, and rigidity—rather like Heinrich Himmler as psychoanalyzed by Peter Loewenberg[18]—is Commander James William Geraghty of the U.S. Navy, the highest-ranking officer to survive World War III in *Commander-1* by Peter George. The story ends with Geraghty's cold-hearted killing of his enemies and the beginnings of the fascistic world order that he plans for earth's few remaining inhabitants.

But when a writer succeeds in emulating Hood and Shiel, and making the protagonist of his story the principal evildoer, he can delve more deeply into the mechanics of Thanatos. James Gould Cozzens gives himself this opportunity in his only work of speculative fiction, the short novel *Castaway*, first published in 1934. Very much like J. G. Ballard's considerably later *Concrete Island*, the Cozzens story is an inversion of Defoe's *Robinson Crusoe*, but without Ballard's customary moral ambiguity. The anti-hero, Mr. Lecky, is a figure of hopeless mediocrity, a bungler, an ignoramus, an unimaginative specimen of human garbage, "cast ashore" in a well-stocked modern department store after an undisclosed catastrophe has apparently emptied the city of New York. Whereas Crusoe rebuilt civilization from little, Mr. Lecky can only waste and wreck and go mad, although he has all the treasures of civilization ready at hand. He kills the one other person he finds in the store, a shadowy ape-thing who is very likely a phantom of himself, and feels "no more remorse than Cain, his prototype." The story ends where it begins, with Mr. Lecky still alone, but finally stripped of the delusion that he can ever "have for his own the stock of this great store."[19] Cozzens's moral is obvious: man, simply as man, without benefit of learning or skill or laws, is a clumsy shambling killer. The endtime is Cozzens's laboratory for examining humanity under controlled conditions. As in a remarkably similar novel of the same period by Horace Horsnell, *Man Alone*, Cozzens isolates the natural man, and what he finds is a flabby parody of *Homo sapiens*.

In *The Black Corridor*, Michael Moorcock also isolates the natural man, but one capable of endless feats of rationalization about his own irrationality, in the character of Captain Ryan, commander of a spaceship whose passengers, in suspended animation, are the survivors of a worldwide holocaust. Or are the passengers in fact all dead, victims one by one of Ryan's homicidal paranoia? After a series of sinister hallucinatory experiences on shipboard, and a series of flashbacks to Ryan's equally sinister adventures before take-off, the reader is left to draw his own conclusions. At the end Ryan is once again quite calm. He writes in his personal diary:

> All the horror and humiliation and wretchedness of Earth is far behind us. We shall be starting a new race, soon. And the world we'll build will be a cleaner world. A sane world. A world built according to knowledge and sanity—not fear and guilt.[20]

It sounds very rational indeed. But what if the good ship *Hope Dempsey* (named after Ryan's mother) actually contains only a glib lunatic and a dozen corpses?

In the immunity uniquely available to criminals in the endtime lurks the further possibility of crime against oneself. Vice and suicide are easier to get away with than murder in normal times, but they take on a special perverse allure in terminal situations. A distinguished group of authors of eschatological fiction have used the end of the world as a background for exploring the psychology of self-destruction. One of the first, the poet James Elroy Flecker, imagines in "The Last Generation," a short story dating from 1908, that the world will come to an end after the insane leader of a successful proletarian revolution requires the sterilization of all women and the execution of all newborn infants and their parents. The aging survivors of this endtime society amuse themselves by joining mutual extermination clubs and indulging in tremendous feats of gluttony, arson, and carousing. Here suicide—in the form of refusal to procreate—is the cause, and not just a grim adornment, of the endtime.

Since Flecker, a number of writers have played creatively with the idea of mankind's possible self-destruction through mass suicide. D. Keith Mano's *The Bridge* duplicates Flecker's scenario, except that the villains are guilt-maddened ecologists rather than terminally embittered radicals. Gore Vidal's two sardonic novels about the religious worship of death, *Messiah* and *Kalki*, have some of the same things to say, as does C. M. Kornbluth in the closing scene of "Shark Ship." Bernard Wolfe addresses the relationship between masochism and aggression in his brilliantly and explicitly Freudian novel, *Limbo*, in which a fourth world war is caused rather than prevented by a worldwide frenzy of self-mutilation by would-be pacifists. A roughly comparable holocaust follows roughly comparable madness in David R. Bunch's *Moderan*.

The master of the narrative of self-destruction is the contemporary English writer J. G. Ballard. In Ballard's case there need be no guesswork about the author's intentions in choosing the world's end as the setting of so many of his fictions. In an interview given in 1975, he explains that none of his novels of world disaster (except *The Wind from Nowhere*) concerns disaster. He uses the classic formula of the English disaster novel—referring to Wells, Wyndham, and others—in order to turn it upside down. The transformation that occurs in the terminal landscape is exploited "to reflect and marry with the internal transformation, the psychological transformation, of the characters." His three novels of the mid-1970s, *Crash*, *Concrete Island*, and *High-Rise*, stories of surrealist violence in present-day London that require no endtime, do not represent a departure from his earlier work, he argues, since once again the disasters in the outer world serve only to mirror the happenings in inner space.[21] Of course what an author intends to achieve, and what he says he intends to achieve, and what he does achieve, are often three different kettles of fish.

I would argue, and shall argue in Chapter Sixteen, that Ballard's fiction deals in a literal way with Last Things, no matter what Ballard himself says. But he is not wrong in characterizing the novels of worldwide disaster that he wrote in the 1960s as studies in psychological transformation. Among other things, they are just that. Many of his short stories work the same vein. The question remains, who is being transformed, and into what?

The essential Ballardian protagonist, whom we meet in stories of all sorts, is a quiet, withdrawn, introverted professional man in the grip of a morbid and ultimately self-destructive obsession, which he may share with some of the other characters in the narrative. The transformation, often well under way when the story begins, consists of the protagonist's inexorable engulfment in his mania. But Ballard never views the mania clinically. Under the cover of a style that is superficially objective and realistic—somewhat in the manner of Kafka—he watches his hero's annihilation from the inside, and with enough empathy to persuade the unwary reader that annihilation is well worth the trouble. Or is it annihilation? Perhaps not. Perhaps even the internal disaster is only an illusion, a trick with mirrors, concealing a still deeper experience, an experience of self-discovery for which the destruction of the self, like the destruction of the world, is only a metaphor of catharsis, a symbolic cleansing and clearing. Either way, Ballard plays a dangerous game, the sort of game his literary idol William Burroughs plays in *Naked Lunch*. [22]

The obsessions themselves fall easily into three categories: those drawn from nature (darkness, prehistoric life, *femmes fatales*, the sea, the desert), whose sexual undercurrent is unmistakably Oedipal; those drawn from technology (clocks, automobiles, apartment buildings, highways, airplanes), which have phallic or homoerotic associations; and ontological obsessions with time and timelessness, being and non-being, whose sexuality, if any, is polymorphous. An example of the first is "The Delta at Sunset," in which a misanthropic archeologist with a badly infected foot suffers from hallucinations and refuses to leave the site of his expedition in a remote corner of Mexico to get medical help. The prospect is that he will die, but his phantasmal vision of the snake-infested beaches of Paleocene lagoons has pushed him over the brink into a state of archaic consciousness where ordinary life and work no longer matter. In *Crash*, a television writer becomes obsessed with car accidents. After the death of a similarly obsessed friend in a spectacular crash, he plans to have a crash of his own. The ontological stories are illustrated by "The Overloaded Man," the tale of a lecturer at a business school who resigns his post and stays home every day, systematically learning how to perceive the contents of ordinary objects only as forms. When he has fully mastered his new skill, so that all things now have only a geometrical reality for him, like a Mondrian painting, he kills his shrewish wife and drowns himself in a pond, feeling completely free at last.

You will notice that none of these three stories involves a world's end. Clearly, Ballard does not need and has never needed eschatological images to fulfill his declared purpose of studying psychological transformation. But images of the endtime appear with some frequency in his work nonetheless, and they give it a roundness and a resonance that much enhances its credibility at a number of levels. In the quartet of novels cited in Chapter Two (*The Wind from Nowhere, The Drowned World, The Drought*, and *The Crystal World*), the world comes to an end as the result of a steadily accelerating global windstorm, an increase in temperature, the cessation of rainfall, and, finally, a cosmic catastrophe that progressively changes all matter into crystals of timeless space. In each instance, with the partial exception of the first, heroes and other characters act out their own self-annihilating destinies against a background of world annihilation. Several of Ballard's shorter pieces also require a literal world's end, such as "Deep End," "The Reptile Enclosure," and "The Voices of Time." His recent novel, *The Unlimited Dream Company*, is a powerful solipsistic fantasy that imagines the end of the world through its absorption into the flesh and mind of the protagonist, who dies early in the narrative, but somehow—like Christ?—manages to return to life.

The Drowned World, first published in 1962, is as good an example as any of Ballard's use of terminal situations. The protagonist is Robert Kerans, a lean, introspective biologist of forty with a *"fin de siècle* temperament." His obsessions are chiefly of the uterine variety, and the landscape that Ballard creates with such suffocating skill is one of his favorites, a world that has regressed in climate, topography, and biology to prehistoric times—in *The Drowned World*, to conditions approximating those of the Permian or Triassic periods. He explains the cause of the catastrophe in a deliberately perfunctory way, in a kind of ironic bow to Wellsian conventions. Solar storms have stripped away the outer layers of the ionosphere, we are told, raising the earth's temperature and admitting all sorts of hard radiation. The ice caps have melted, flooding coastal areas. Tropical plants thrive. The fertility of mammals including *Homo sapiens* has dropped off sharply, while reptiles and amphibians multiply. Fewer than five million human beings survive, clustered in the polar latitudes, which are now subtropical. Since children are rarely born nowadays, "a point might ultimately be reached where a second Adam and Eve found themselves alone in a new Eden."[23]

Kerans belongs to a government expedition charged with studying conditions in the swamps and lagoons of what used to be Europe. His commanding officer, Col. Riggs, is the kind of man that Wells or Wyndham might have admired: buoyant, rational, energetic, intelligent, good-humored, a worthy representative of modern man. Unfortunately, modern man happens to be obsolete. The different between Kerans and Riggs is summed up in a single exchange between them early in the novel. The Colonel wonders if Kerans ever bothers to listen to his radio. " 'Never,' Kerans said. 'Is there any point? We know all the news for the next three million years.' "[24]

But there is news, within Riggs's frame of reference. Headquarters has just radioed orders to pack up and return to base. Riggs's second in command, Lt. Hardman, who had grown increasingly withdrawn in recent months, promptly deserts. The others assume that he has headed north, but Kerans knows instinctively the direction that Hardman took: it had to be south, into the rising heat, into the Triassic landscape of his dreams, which an associate of Kerans describes as biological memories. The same dreams haunt Kerans, and some of his colleagues as well. Just as the earth is returning physically to the Triassic period, so men's brains are undergoing an evolutionary, or devolutionary, transformation. They feel the southward pull, the drag of "archaeopsychic time," the hunger for "the lost but forever beckoning and unattainable shores of the amnionic paradise."[25]

Hardman is later found, moving south, but he eludes his rescuers and continues on his journey. Riggs and the expedition return home, leaving Kerans behind by his own choice. An outlaw ship turns up, commanded by an insane albino pirate who symbolizes all the rapacity and manipulative impulses of modern Western civilization. Kerans barely misses being killed, but the experience does not bring him to his "senses." On the contrary, he now knows that he must follow Hardman. Hotly pursued by an uncomprehending Riggs, who had rescued him from the pirate, he flees southward. In a great Triassic jungle he finds Hardman, blind and starving, and gives him some food. Hardman plunges on alone. Kerans does likewise, completely lost, attacked by alligators and giant bats, "a second Adam searching for the forgotten paradises of the reborn Sun."[26]

Measured by the standards of everyday consciousness, Hardman and Kerans are suicidal madmen, running from life, reverting to the unconscious floating existence of the fetus. Heat, hunger, and hostile fauna will soon kill them both. A tragedy? Not necessarily. Ballard tells us that his American publisher had wanted him to change the ending, to make it a happy ending. "I said: 'no, God, this *is* a happy story.' " *The Drowned World*, for Ballard, is a story of "psychic fulfillment," of changes that "lead us to our real psychological goals."[27]

To take Ballard's argument one step further, the deaths of Hardman and Kerans, although real enough in the waking logic of the story, are something quite different in the logic of the unconscious. They can be compared to the uncovering of the mouth of a hidden cave, allowing access into the psychic underworld. Doris Lessing follows an almost identical strategy in *Briefing for a Descent into Hell*. Both she and Ballard argue that by re-establishing contact with the life-renewing dialectics of the archaic we can break out of the cul-de-sac of modernity, with its false view of man as the clean, antiseptic, white-coated expert in full rational control of his world and himself.

Curiously enough, Lessing has now turned to eschatological fiction herself, in works such as *The Memoirs of a Survivor*, which will be studied in Chapter Fourteen. But she by and large avoids the sadomasochistic imagery of Ballard. Another kindred spirit who does use it, but with more delicacy than Ballard, is Anna Kavan in her eschatological novel *Ice*. The narrator's morbid fascination with the heroine, a thin silver-haired young woman, and the strange fatalism and timidity of the woman herself, with her "victim's look," match the suicidal impulses of mankind in the vaguely sketched end-time. Wars rage. Mercenaries roam the landscape. An ice age has also descended, and it is unclear whether the world will end by the ice of glaciers or the fire of guns. No one really cares. People feel no horror when they see others die, a trait of Ballard's characters, too, The only warmth in the book comes at the very end, when the narrator and the object of his obsession finally resolve their differences and drive off into a blizzard. The heated car is a room, a home, a refuge, a temporary utopia. "I knew," says the narrator,

> there was no escape from the ice, from the ever-diminishing remnant of time that encapsuled us. I made the most of the minutes. The miles and the minutes flew past. The weight of the gun in my pocket was reassuring.[28]

Our theme has been the self, and its fears, as they are caught and magnified in eschatological fiction. The self comes into the world kicking and screaming. Powerless, frightened, needing love and nourishment, it struggles toward maturity for most of its existence, and never quite arrives. It seeks to overcome alienation and exclusion, and almost always, except in dreaming, fails. Writers like Ballard and Kavan bring us face to face with extraordinarily dangerous truths that we dare not dodge.

9

◆

The Universe as the Jaws of Hell

"NATURE STANDS IN not the slightest need of propagation," Mme. Delbène advises her favorite pupil in *L'histoire de Juliette*, "and the total disappearance of mankind . . . would grieve her very little; she would no more pause in her career than if the whole species of rabbits or chickens were suddenly to be wiped off the face of the earth."[1] A libertine philosopher-nun possible only in the novels of the Marquis de Sade, Delbène expresses a type of anxiety that became more or less inevitable with the emergence of the modern secular consciousness: the fear that nature—uprooted from her divine ground—could no longer welcome, succor, or perhaps even tolerate human life.

Blind trust in nature seldom characterized pre-modern thought. From the earliest Mesopotamian myths, nature regularly devastated the human world, either as the agency of divine wrath or as an ordained concomitant of disorder in state and society. But nature was not truly autonomous. Through her, man only caught glimpses of divine power at work. She spoke neither the first nor the last word.

In a godless universe, three views of nature suggest themselves. Nature can be worshipped as a surrogate deity, an all-encompassing reality in which man regains his lost home and recaptures feelings of transcendental worth and purpose. Such was the use put to the idea of nature by the first systematic atheist thinker of modern times, the Baron d'Holbach. The romantic poets of Wordsworth's generation followed his example, in the style of thought appropriate to their quite different world view. A second approach, descended from Bacon on one side and Biblical tradition on the other, sees nature as man's to exploit freely in the service of human needs. This view was adopted with enthusiasm by many scientists, entrepreneurs, and statesmen during the Industrial Revolution of the nineteenth century. In either case, the relationship between man and nature gives cause for hope, and nature enhances human well-being.

But the third view of nature possible in a universe without God is the crushing thought of Sade, that nature is indifferent to human aspiration, and wholly absorbed in her own mindless processes, which now and then casually lay waste to all that reason or goodness can fashion. If man himself is no more than a product of such processes, and subject to their laws, how can he presume to dictate to nature? How can he expect always to hold her vast energies in check and harness them for human pleasure? His own crimes and vices, Sade recognized, are tools for destruction appointed by nature to help preserve a "wise economy" in the order of things. So also are famine and pestilence and natural disasters. To follow nature, each of us must give free rein to his deepest impulses, no matter how selfish and cruel. "The luckless ones chance puts in our clutches, or who excite our passions, have their place in Nature's scheme as do the stars in the firmament and the sun that gives us light."[2] Mme. Delbène concludes that interference in natural wolfishness would be as great a crime against nature as disturbing the heavens.

Yet can there be a crime against nature? Logically, no. Sade elsewhere concedes that anything within our power to do is also by definition natural and therefore good. Another of his heroes, the judge Curval in *Les 120 journées de Sodome*, confesses to his colleagues his fierce desire to perform the very deed that Mme. Delbène had proscribed. "Ah, how many times, by God, have I not longed to be able to assail the sun, snatch it out of the universe, make a general darkness, or use that star to burn the world!"[3] Only man's inability to commit cosmic mayhem makes it wrong for him to do so; not the act in itself.

Behind all this swaggering villainy lies a veritable horror of nature, and of man's subjection to her, that Sade only rarely uncovers to his readers. Curval wishes to extinguish the sun because he loathes nature, and himself as her child. Like all of Sade's protagonists, he is the helpless captive of a lust that cannot be slaked, inhabiting a world full of injustice and misery where destruction is both necessary and inevitable. In the words of a character from *La nouvelle Justine*, "This most sublime life of men is to nature of no greater importance than that of an oyster, and she has abandoned us all equally."[4] Sade took no joy in the flowers of his evil and no joy in the natural freedom that allowed everything only for the sake of destroying everything.

Sade's private hell as a sexual psychopath gave his work a twist that separates it from most other serious modern thought. But the heart of his message is universal: nature has abandoned man (since there is no God), and nature may at any time wipe him out, or prune his numbers, if the remorseless laws of cause and effect happen to require it. One of the founders of modern political economy, the Reverend Thomas Malthus, offered views not far removed from Sade's in his tough-minded *Essay on the Principle of Population.* The first edition of the *Essay* appeared in 1798, only one year after the publication of *La nouvelle Justine* and *L'histoire de Juliette.* Malthus maintained that poverty was the perennial lot of man because population always tends to run ahead of the supply of food. When there are too many people, their numbers are cut down by war, famine, and disease. When there are too few, population swiftly surges up to the limit again. The result is poverty for the great mass of people, which, said Malthus, can be mitigated only by sexual restraint or by "vice," for example, sodomy and the use of contraceptives.

As a Christian, Malthus recommended restraint. But his concept of the balance of nature is virtually identical to Sade's. Disaster is nature's way of keeping a species under control. That Malthus was able to square his unsentimental understanding of nature with Christian belief is hardly unusual for someone of his time; pure secularism was a rarity in the England of his generation. But his failure to draw the same radical theological and moral conclusions that Sade drew takes away nothing from the radicalism of his idea of nature. It was later to help Charles Darwin arrive at his theory of evolution by natural selection, and it signals, just like the novels of Sade, the beginnings of a major shift in modern consciousness.

Another harbinger of the shift, as we have seen, is the spate of "last man" stories published during the first quarter of the nineteenth century. In all of them, forces of nature were the cause of man's extinction. Nature continued to take the blame in the majority of terminal visions in literature published down to 1914. Even since then, she has been held responsible for innumerable world's ends, by flood, earthquake, comet, plague, uprising of insects, or whatever. Of late, she has also put in appearances as the raped and bleeding mother who gains her revenge, in various tales of ecological doom.

To be sure, a work of fiction is not always what it seems. When a writer like Anna Kavan cannot decide, in her novel *Ice,* whether the world will end by warfare or by advancing glaciers, it is tempting to assume that she may be using the end of the world as a metaphor for something else, for personal or social disintegration, or both. Yet even for Kavan, the metaphor of advancing glaciers—Brian Aldiss thinks it may refer obliquely to the "snow" or heroin to which she has was long addicted[5]—has a chance of working because it connects with real fears of modern man concerning the processes of nature. Kavan did not write about advancing moonbeams or clams or tea trolleys. Her choice of glaciers takes advantage of the disturbing discoveries of nineteenth-century geology. Ice, not very long ago, did cover much of the heartland of the civilization of modern man. It could do so again, and in any case it symbolizes the instability and danger of the natural order, on which man depends for his well-being.

Disclosing the instability and danger of the natural order has been a major part of the work of scientists in all fields in the past two centuries, and the abundance of natural disasters in the literature of Last Things owes much to their achievements. Earlier, the scientific world-picture had stressed the underlying harmony of man and nature. Both had been created by a reasonable Supreme Being, and functioned according to the same mathematically precise laws, which reason—a faculty natural in mankind—fully revealed without supernatural aid. Only ignorant or willful disobedience of these laws could bring man into fundamental conflict with the machinery of the cosmos. But by the late eighteenth century, the sciences had begun to investigate problems and collect evidence that challenged the steady-state model of the universe favored by the philosophers of the Enlightenment.

As efforts were made, for example, to reconstruct the natural history of the earth and its life forms, it became necessary to account for the accumulating evidence of geology and paleontology that the earth was not always as it appeared today. How could one explain fossils of marine creatures found on high ground, creatures that in some instances had no living descendants? Such evidence pointed to great disasters in the earth's history, disasters that had caused the extinction of species and the creation of new ones. Even the planets themselves might, in the speculations of the Comte de Buffon, have resulted from a tremendous catastrophe, the near collision of the sun with a comet, forcing the ejection of solar material that had in turn condensed into planetary bodies. Buffon's ideas became unfashionable for a time, but were revived in the late nineteenth century by A. W. Bickerton and others, and dominated astronomical thought for generations.

Meanwhile, catastrophism grew rapidly into a new orthodoxy in geology, with the chief controversies centering only on whether the great world-cataclysms that had produced the geological eras of the past were floods, earthquakes, volcanic eruptions, or some combination of these. Georges Cuvier, the major geologist of the first third of the nineteenth century, effected a synthesis of catastrophist thinking that collapsed after his death but left an indelible impression on the public and scientific mind. Even when geologists no longer accepted catastrophism as a universal causal explanation, the fact of relatively sudden changes in the climate, topography, and flora and fauna of the earth at various points in natural history remained well established. Other formidable discoveries, such as those of Cuvier's pupil Louis Agassiz, led to the idea of successive eras of glaciation, or "ice ages."

The second half of the nineteenth century brought to light fresh horrors: Rudolf Clausius's second law of thermodynamics, the "heat-death" of the universe, along with a prediction by Hermann von Helmholtz of the inevitable cooling of the sun in a matter of hundreds of thousands, or, in later revised estimates, ten million years; Charles Darwin's picture of the origin of species through the ruthless natural selection of random variations; and the discovery by Louis Pasteur and others of the microbiological jungle that spawns disease and pestilence. Fuller knowledge of comets, meteors, stellar novae, and other deadly wonders of outer space fed the imagination of disaster as well. Any writer of fiction could draw the obvious moral: nature was not the anthropomorphic mother of romantic myth or the mighty whirling mechanism of Newtonian physics, but a stage of endless slaughter and catastrophe. Anything that had happened before could happen again, here and now; and at best the whole universe was sinking by degrees into the cool calamity of heat-death.

Yet it is arguable that none of the theories and discoveries of science between, say, 1750 and 1900, would have caused more than brief alarm if not for one other event: the event that Friedrich Nietzsche billed in *The Joyful Wisdom* as the death of God. The steady decay of Jewish and Christian faith after the middle of the eighteenth century deprived nature of her divine origins and purposes. Natural disasters could no longer be viewed in any literal sense as "acts of God," as punishments or tests of man imposed by an ultimately loving Father for his own ultimately good ends. Except for those whose faith remained intact or who subscribed to any of the various idealist or vitalist cosmologies that in effect turned nature herself into a god, the disasters of the natural order were simply disasters, the blind and brutal doings of an intrinsically pointless universe.

Thomas Henry Huxley—agnostic, humanist, man of science—crystallized the thoughts of thousands of his contemporaries in 1894 when he declared war on the "cosmic process." Nature's ways, he wrote, should never be man's. What lay before the human race was "a constant struggle to maintain and improve, in opposition to the State of Nature, the State of Art of an organized polity." The natural instinct of "unlimited self-assertion" disclosed by Darwin, the biological equivalent of original sin, had to be replaced by morality, the love of the common good, "until the evolution of our globe shall have entered so far upon its downward course that the cosmic process resumes its sway; and once more, the State of Nature prevails over the surface of our planet."[6] In that same year, 1894, Huxley's onetime biology student H. G. Wells was preaching a similar sermon in his own way, in a magazine serial story that he entitled *The Time Machine*. Their views on the relationship between man and nature in a godless cosmos were nearly identical.

The twentieth century, for all its incredible proliferation of science and scientists, has not yielded any fundamental reconstruction of the world-picture assembled by Darwin and Clausius and all the other luminaries of science from the period just discussed. Or rather, it has yielded no fundamental reconstruction of the empirical basis for T. H. Huxley's concept of man's distance from nature. Nor has what Basil Willey once described as "the secular drift" slowed appreciably, in spite of all sorts of ingenious theological contortions and seasons of revived religiosity. The majority of thinking men and women in the Western world throughout this century, as in the latter part of the preceding century, have been agnostics, atheists, or believers so passive and confused in their belief that it counts for little.

In biology the Darwinian synthesis has held firm in its essentials, notwithstanding great progress in genetics, and a considerable broadening and deepening of the fossil record. Such apocalyptic events as the sudden disappearance of the dinosaurs at the end of the Cretaceous period or the glaciation of the Pleistocene epoch are better known in this century, but still not definitively explained. Astronomers have extended the life of the sun by several billion years, showing that earth will become much hotter (in the sun's "red giant" phase before its collapse to a "white dwarf"). But our star remains mortal all the same, along with its brood of planets. New cosmic catastrophes such as supernovae, black holes, and the "Big Bang" that is plausibly theorized to have created our universe some fifteen billion years ago and may launch the next universe after entropy has done its inevitable worst, supply the eschatological imagination with all sorts of nourishment, beyond what the astronomers of the nineteenth century had to offer.

Yet the new theories and data have not appreciably altered the values of the man-nature equation. The tension between the two remains as before. If anything, it has been increased, especially by the psychology of Sigmund Freud and some of his followers, with its disturbing analysis of the unconscious as a treacherous swamp of raw natural energies that poisons our dreams and demands relentless monitoring and control by society, or by the reasoning ego, or both.

The problem of man *versus* nature is seldom a central theme of twentieth-century philosophy, but only because most modern philosophers have learned to despair of finding useable truth in the natural order. Twentieth-century positivism has expressly proscribed the grounding of ethical, ontological, or aesthetic values in scientific knowledge, although most positivists would agree with Bertrand Russell in his essay "A Free Man's Worship" that in a universe with no knowable purpose or meaning, man must take responsibility for himself. Certain of no help from gods, as Russell intoned, man must resolve to play the "weary but unyielding Atlas," sustaining "the world that his own ideals have fashioned despite the trampling march of unconscious power."[7]

The existentialist movement of the middle decades of the century, at least in the version promulgated by Jean-Paul Sartre, turned away from nature in almost the same measure as the positivists. For Sartre nature belongs to the realm of *l'en-soi*, being in itself, being that exists without will or freedom, being that is opaque and silent. The art and literature produced under the influence of existentialism adds its own voice. *The Plague*, Albert Camus's masterpiece, uses an outbreak of bubonic plague as a symbol of all the evil and adversity in the world of experience, natural and man-made alike, which must be fought tirelessly in battles that are always followed by yet more battles. The same treatment of nature as emblematic of the massive dehumanizing stupidity of *l'en-soi* appears in Eugène Ionesco's absurdist play *Rhinoceros*. As Percy Shelley's skylark, in the familiar ode, supplies an example of man's efforts to bring the human and the natural together, so Ionesco's pachyderm is a grotesquely apt symbol of man's estrangement.

Terminal fictions imagining disasters visited on man by nature can be sorted into three broad categories. One of these is the entropic romance, the vision of man at the end of the natural history of the solar system, or the universe. Here the term "disaster" must be used rather loosely, since there is no implication of suddenness. Great as the disaster may be, it occurs in infinitely slow motion, over millennia or thousands of millennia. The second category consists of fictions of the ruin of the earth or its biosphere by disasters in the more ordinary sense, such as falling comets or geological catastrophes. Into the third group fall stories of man's overthrow by rival life-forms, ranging from bacteria to alien invaders. Each category has its own special terrors, although authors sometimes emulate John the Evangelist by introducing more than one kind of disaster into the same work.

The entropic romance, strictly speaking, did not become possible until the second half of the nineteenth century, after Clausius and others had firmly established the second law of thermodynamics in the canon of modern physics, and after astronomers had turned their attention in a systematic way to measurements of the sun's energy and theories of solar mechanics. But even before these events, writers had at their disposal the Epicurean paradigm of a gradual wearing-out of the natural order. This venerable view had been challenged, and, it seemed, overthrown by Newtonian physics, with its insistence on the uniformity and stability of natural processes. But belief in the decay of nature continued to find its adherents throughout the eighteenth century and on into the nineteenth, especially among those who had theological or metaphysical quarrels with the Enlightenment.

We have seen traces of such a belief in the two principal "last man"

novels of the romantic period, by Mary Shelley and J.-B. Cousin de Grainville. The traces are negligible in Shelley, but quite significant in Grainville's
Le dernier homme, where the world's end results directly from the exhaustion
of natural forces. The moon burns up, consumed by a great volcano. The sun
does not die altogether, but it grows pale and weak. Crops no longer flourish,
as the soil loses its fertility. Men themselves become barren, until at last there
is only one couple able to have children. Personified as a genie with supernatural powers, nature fights back, using trickery to encourage the last couple
to reproduce, but its stratagems fail and God lets the world come to a merciful
end.

In the terminal fictions of the later part of the nineteenth century, the
remnants of the Epicurean paradigm blended with the physics of Clausius
and Helmholtz, and a number of funereal visions of the far future began to
make their appearance. The one passage that sticks in everyone's memory
comes near the end of Wells's *The Time Machine*, where the Time Traveller
leaves the degenerate future society of Eloi and Morlocks to visit the last days
of earth. The planet no longer rotates. The sun is red and cool, motionless
on the western horizon. In this eternal twilight, man no longer exists. The
Time Traveller watches giant crabs crawling across the lurid beach, beside a
still sea, until—thousands of years later—even the crabs have disappeared,
the thin air is bitter cold, and the only motion he detects is that of a black
thing with tentacles, "hopping fitfully about." All the images are of death
and dying: the blood-red color of the sun, its position low in the western sky,
the terminal symbolism of the beach, the chilling silence, the "evil" eyes and
hungry mouth of the crab-monster as it moves to attack our hero, the black-
ness of a total solar eclipse that takes place during the last moments of his
journey. Wells also discussed the demise of the solar system in a sketch
entitled "The Man of the Year Million," published in 1893. Here, a global
brotherhood of enlightened supermen with enormous brains puts up a brave
fight against the encroaching cold from its strongholds deep in the earth.
The surface of the planet is thickly mantled with ice and all life there is
extinct. As the hero of another story by Wells solemnly proclaims:

> These Earthlings do not yet dare to see what our Mother Nature is. . . . They
> do not see that except for our eyes and wills, she is purposeless and blind. She
> is not awful, she is horrible. . . . She made us by accident; all her children
> are bastards—undesired; she will cherish or expose them, pet or starve or
> torment without rhyme or reason. She does not heed, she does not care.[8]

The device of the terminal redoubt, the last home of man in a dying
universe, with its inevitable suggestion of heroic humanity pitted against
hideous nature, turns up in several fin-de-siècle romances in addition to

Wells's "The Man of the Year Million." The French sociologist Gabriel Tarde left behind after his death the manuscript of a fascinating short novel, *Fragment d'histoire future*, in which a prosperous and united mankind is struck down at the peak of its glory by a kind of solar anemia. Little heat reaches earth from the sun, and a remnant of the human race flees underground to take advantage of the warmth near the planetary core. The remnant builds a scientific utopia that relies for its well-being on strict birth control.

The masterpiece of "last redoubt" stories is Hodgson's *The Night Land*, which we explored in the preceding chapter as a tale of love and heroism. It deserves a second look here, as a tale of mankind's struggle against a bleak and hostile nature in the endtime. The setting is several million years from now, when the sun no longer shines at all. The earth's surface has grown too cold to support life, but one hundred miles below the frozen surface in a "valley" created by the cracking of the planet in an earlier disaster, the last human beings live in their pyramid, a metal marvel of science eight miles high powered by a force known as the "Earth-Current." The land around the Pyramid, the Night Land, is warmed by volcanic fire-holes. The monsters who live there are mostly the devolved descendants of *Homo sapiens*, "mixt and made monstrous or diverse by foul or foolish breeding."[9] In this entropic hell, man is safe for the time being, but he can take little comfort in his future prospects. Eventually the Earth-Current will fail, and the Pyramid will fall.

Several years before publishing *The Night Land*, Hodgson reached the endtime in another major novel, *The House on the Borderland*, in which the protagonist has a vision of the death of the sun. As the earth whitens with eternal snow, the sun turns darker and darker shades of red, growing colder all the while. The other stars die too, until nothing remains but two enormous central suns symbolizing the good and evil in the cosmos. Despite Wellsian touches purloined from *The Time Machine*, this earlier novel stands closer in technique and world view to Olaf Stapledon's *Star Maker* than to any work of Wells.

For historians of science, and its popularization, a fin-de-siècle literary relic of special interest is *La fin du monde* by Camille Flammarion. The author was a professional astronomer and science writer, whose *Astronomie populaire*, first published in 1880, soon became one of the best-known books of its kind in the Western world. In *La fin du monde* he presents a story of the solar system ten million years from now that draws liberally on his knowledge of the astronomy of his time. Mankind is toppled just as it has gained complete mastery of itself and of nature. Cold and drought drive it back to savagery except for two equatorial cities of iron and glass, the last heroic citadels of a doomed race, situated in the dry beds of the former Pacific and Indian oceans. Eventually all life on earth comes to an end.

As astrophysicists shifted in the twentieth century to a quite different theory of the sun's source of energy from that proposed by Helmholtz, and as the new 100-inch telescope at Mount Wilson disclosed the existence of other galaxies than our own, the probable amount of space and time in the universe was enlarged beyond anything imagined in Flammarion's day. Not only did the remaining life predicted for the sun increase by a factor of one thousand, but it became possible for the first time to construct theoretical models of the history and future of the entire universe on the basis of detailed knowledge of stellar and galactic evolution through billions of years. Oddly, or perhaps not so oddly, eschatological fiction continued to present visions of the end of all things, undaunted by the hugely expanded time-scale of the new astronomy.

To stories of the death of the sun were soon added stories of the death of the galaxy or the whole universe of galaxies. Many of these offer cyclical concepts of universal collapse and resurrection, a theme we shall save for Chapter Fifteen. They include Olaf Stapledon's *Star Maker*, James Blish's *The Triumph of Time*, Brian Aldiss's *The Canopy of Time*, Michael Moorcock's *The End of All Songs*, and George Zebrowski's *Macrolife*. Many are fundamentally hopeful fictions, of the heroic survival of man through the eons and the continuation or rebirth of life in the next cycle and even beyond. In Poul Anderson's *Tau Zero*, the death and rebirth of the universe shrinks to the dimension of a mere episode in the flight to safety of a man and his spaceship, a flight that Joe De Bolt and John R. Pfeiffer call "a direct metaphor for the myth of progress—advance or die."[10] The entropic disintegration of the cosmos becomes just one more hurdle that the natural order places in the way of negentropic man.

Entropy is a concept of many uses, a point further illustrated by Pamela Zoline's story "The Heat Death of the Universe," which mingles notes on entropy with glimpses of the nervous breakdown of an embattled housewife. But in the realm of purely apocalyptic fiction, the failure of earth's own sun remains a popular agency of disaster, as it was in the nineteenth century. One of the supremely imaginative works in this category, whose hero we met earlier, is Brian Aldiss's *Hothouse*. The time is one billion years from now, when the sun has expanded, turning earth into a tropical nightmare. As in James Blish's "The Thing in the Attic" (from *The Seedling Stars*), the men of the future are a vastly altered race of agile creatures no bigger than monkeys, who live in trees. Blish's tree folk are "Adapted Men," deliberately engineered by human scientists as part of a program to enable mankind to colonize alien worlds. But in *Hothouse* they are the product of devolution. Earth's changing climate and the rise of many deadly new varieties of plant and insect life have destroyed civilization. The devolved green-skinned descendants of man shelter in the branches of a banyan tree that covers a whole continent on the daylight side of the no longer rotating planet. Their simple matriarchal life calls to mind the Indians of the Amazon or the Papuans of New Guinea.

But existence is far more hazardous in Aldiss's future world than anywhere on earth today. Death is a daily event, inflicted chiefly by a fantastic array of carnivorous and poisonous jungle plants—the wiltmilts, the killer-willows, the bellyelms, the trappersnappers, and many others. The overheated earth "was no longer a place for mind. It was a place for growth, for vegetables . . . green in tooth and claw," full of "idiot hatred of all life but [their] own." Human life has become as cheap as that of flies or ants today, and the other mammals have long since met with extinction. "Over everything, indifferent begetter of all this carnage, shone the sun."[11]

Worse is in store. The hero learns, near the end of the novel, that in a matter of generations the sun will become a nova and incinerate all life on the planet. After many adventures, however, he has made his peace with the forest. Things are what they are. Everything happens as it must. No matter how murderous nature's world may be, it is our world, we have our place in it, and sooner or later everything will end, in accordance with the inexorable laws of astrophysics.

Another category of terminal fictions imagines ends of the world caused in the relatively near future by great cosmic accidents and disorders of earth's climate and crust. Again, science is called in to provide rational explanations of the endtime. In a way, stories of this sort reflect a deeper pessimism about Mother Nature than those dealing with the longer term. Just as death in old age seems far less a tragedy than in youth, so the near-future world cataclysm gives nature a more ruthless face than the endtimes of entropy. The point is well made in H. G. Wells's "The Star," which draws a striking contrast between the everyday world of humanity, going about its essentially innocent business, and the random destructiveness of a rogue planet that invades the solar system. The intruder blunders into Neptune, burns white-hot from the force of the collision, and nearly wrecks the earth with heat, floods, storms, and other calamities as it hurtles by. The first scientist to foresee the catastrophe looks up at the star, then still far away,

> as one might look into the eyes of a brave enemy. "You may kill me," he said after a silence. "But I can hold you—and all the universe for that matter—in the grip of this little brain. I would not change. Even now."[12]

Man's mind is defiant, but his body is helpless against the immense brute force of the cosmos.

Not always. The sudden celestial calamity often gives scope for heroism, too. A representative American story from the same period as "The Star" is *The Second Deluge* by Garrett P. Serviss. One of the founders of the American Astronomical Society and the author of popular books and articles on astronomy, Serviss approached life in the "can-do" spirit of the Progressive Era, joining enthusiasm for science and technology with an elitist philosophy of social reform similar to Wells's. His sequel to *The War of the Worlds*, a pot-boiler in which no less a personage than Thomas Alva Edison helps mankind carry the war to the enemy's home planet, was published in 1898 as *Edison's Conquest of Mars*.

The Second Deluge, another novel of technological derring-do, was inspired by the visit of Halley's Comet in 1910. Here, the menace comes not from Martians but from a "spiral nebula" full of water that dumps six miles of rain on the planet, drowning even Mt. Everest. The scientific Noah who rescues a handpicked remnant of mankind in his metal ark is Cosmo Versál, an independently wealthy genius and an irascible realist. He alone correctly foresees the coming doom, and he alone takes rational steps to survive it. An upthrust of dry land in Colorado becomes the base of a manly new America, supplied with atomic energy by the invention of one of Cosmo's protégés and purified by a program of systematic eugenics taught by Cosmo himself. Despite the worst that nature could do, the new race of mankind will be "far superior, in every respect, to the old world that was drowned."[13]

Heroics, American-style, are the order of the day in many later narratives of cosmic disaster, from those two-fisted novels of the 1930s, *When Worlds Collide* and *After Worlds Collide*, by Edwin Balmer and Philip Wylie, to the most persuasive of "comet" novels, *Lucifer's Hammer*, by Larry Niven and Jerry Pournelle. Balmer and Wylie add to the celestial excitement a war between parties of Asian communist and American survivors. In *Lucifer's Hammer* the forces of science and reason win their armageddon against cannibalistic Luddite fanatics in what remains of California. Heroics, Scottish-style, are provided by Fred and Geoffrey Hoyle in *The Inferno*. The disaster in this instance is a tremendous explosion at the center of the galaxy. Only the Highlands and a few other far northern areas weather the cooking of the planet. The Hoyles's protagonist, a Gaelic-speaking Scottish physicist, undergoes a kind of racial reversion to clan chieftain when civilization disintegrates, but he retains many of its values as well, in confrontations with less humane rivals.

Similar opportunities for heroism arise in tales of geological disaster, ends of the world brought about by convulsions of the earth itself. Such ends are the oldest of all, going back to the myth of the Flood preserved in The Epic of Gilgamesh and in Genesis. Worldwide floods are relatively common in speculative fiction, with earthquakes, vulcanism, droughts, and ice ages rounding out the list. Again, nature acts as the bludgeoning destroyer, vast and implacable, and man has his chance to stand up to her, for whatever his efforts may be worth.

In romances of geological disaster, no writer has done a better job of capturing the contrast between the awfulness of nature and the fragile strength of her human opponents than John Christopher. His faith in the ability of decent men, specifically decent Englishmen, to withstand the worst she can do while making as little fuss about it as possible, occupies a special niche in eschatological fiction. In *A Wrinkle in the Skin*, published in America as *The Ragged Edge*, nature's hammer falls in the form of a chain of worldwide earthquakes. Living alone on the island of Guernsey, our hero is Matthew Cotter, a tomato grower and ex-journalist, whose daughter Jane has gone to England for her university years. He misses her keenly, but otherwise his existence is a happy one. By a miracle he happens to be outdoors in the middle of the night when the island is rocked by the terminal quakes, which heave and roar for hours, and pulverize civilization.

The next morning, Cotter tours the island, searching for survivors. He rescues a boy of ten from the rubble, and together they locate a treasure trove of canned food. The rest of the story takes the familiar form of a heroic quest. Accompanied by the boy, Cotter goes in search of his daughter. They get to the mainland easily enough, since the quakes have drained the Channel, but when they finally reach Jane's part of England, they find only a new sea. The two comrades return to the Channel and settle down on Alderney with a small community of mainland refugees met earlier in the story.

Throughout, Christopher stresses the enormous power of nature, which in one pointless night of violence has shaken civilization to bits and turned the majority of the survivors into animals or lunatics. It takes only a few days without law and order to make wolves of ordinary Englishmen, wolves who rape and pillage at will. Others merely panic and become their victims, or go mad, like the manic-depressive ship captain who entertains Cotter, pretending that nothing has happened. At one point a doctor reflects that the behavior of the survivors is as erratic and destructive as that of ants streaming from a crushed anthill. But by the end of the novel, we see that some few men and women, the real survivors, the real human beings, have the strength of purpose and character to cut their way through the jungles of the endtime, and eventually to rebuild civilization. The fittest—in every sense—will prevail.

In another of Christopher's novels of geological disaster, *The World in Winter* (*The Long Winter* in the U.S.), the central figure is a London television news editor, Andrew Leedon. This time, doomsday is a new ice age, coming on suddenly. The story is complicated by the survival of a belt of nations in tropical latitudes. Leedon flees to Nigeria and painfully works his way up in what is now very much a black man's world. But on a Nigerian expedition to icebound Britain, he betrays the Africans and joins forces with David Cartwell, a tough civil servant under his veneer of charm and sophistication, who stayed behind to form a guerrilla army in London. The army will probably become the next government of Britain. Cartwell has learned the fundamental lessons of survival in disaster: discipline, organization, putting first things first. He has come as far as he has by securing ample food supplies for his men and letting other survivors starve, or killing them, "when they wouldn't starve quietly."[14] Since the alternative is anarchy and extinction, there is no alternative. Thanks to men such as Cartwell and Leedon, Britain will some day live again, the same minimally happy ending supplied in yet another recent novel of a new ice age, *The Sixth Winter*, by Douglas Orgill and John Gribbin.

But as in stories of cosmic disaster, so in geological doomsdays. When nature strikes with overwhelming force, protagonists must settle for less, or may fail entirely. In *Ice!* by Arnold Federbush, the only formula for survival that works is wholesale adoption of the Eskimo way of life. The efforts of the meteorologist-hero Mark Haney to rally worldwide cooperation by shortwave radio during a terminal snow blitz prove useless. His former mistress, who had once lived among the Eskimos of Greenland, becomes the leader of a survival group trekking southward with a dog pack as the novel ends. Her way, not Mark's, is the only appropriate adaptive response for a human race re-entering the Pleistocene epoch by courtesy of Mother Nature.

Mark Haney's failure recalls the struggles of a much earlier hero of the literature of Last Things, the valiant Targ of J.-H. Rosny's *La mort de la terre*. Targ has waged a relentless war against the great drought that dooms humanity after millennia of progress. One by one, earth's settlements have accepted the "irresistible will" of the planet and have submitted without complaint to euthanasia. When the last community agrees on a plan for voluntary phased euthanasia, Targ and his wife and sister alone refuse to cooperate. They flee to a small oasis, where Targ has located enough water to keep them alive for two years. It is too late. Targ's wife and children are killed in an earthquake that engulfs their oasis, his sister takes poison, and Targ is left alone, the last man.

But the story does not stop with Targ's useless defiance of the elements. Rosny supplies one more event, which verges on our third major category of ends inflicted on mankind by nature, catastrophes resulting from challenges by other terrestrial species, or by invaders from outer space. Although Targ continues to spurn euthanasia, he finally gives up the struggle to live. He allows himself to be devoured by ferromagnets, members of a strange new mineral race which is destined to replace mankind as the next lords of creation. As man's power has dwindled through the centuries, that of the ferromagnets has grown, since they need no water to sustain life.

Acting more as scavengers than as hostile forces, the ferromagnets are not directly responsible for the end of mankind. But they do fulfill nature's plan for replacing *Homo sapiens* with a species better adapted to radically altered circumstances. In other stories, the attack on mankind by other forms of life is far more direct. In all but a few, inspiration flows from the view of life expounded by Charles Darwin and his various successors and popularizers. The literature of the biological doomsday brims with references to extinct species, contests for food and living space, mutations that upset the ecological balance, and mindless struggle in the rain forest, the anthill, the ocean deeps, the microscopic world, wherever life is found and its suffering is disclosed to the patient biologist. Instead of the juggernaut, nature appears in tales of biological disaster as the mother of sharks and tigers and tentacled horrors from Mars. She is no longer quite so vast or indifferent, but she is much more obviously hostile, and much less obviously maternal.

One classic situation in eschatological fiction, with many Biblical resonances, is the pestilence that runs wild and wipes out all or most of the human race. Plague is the killer in Shelley's *The Last Man,* in Hood's poem of the same title, and in Poe's "The Masque of the Red Death." But these early narratives of worldwide pestilence lack the clear focus of later stories, if only because the natural causes of disease were not yet known in the first half of the nineteenth century. The microbiological discoveries of Pasteur and Koch occurred in the second half. Joined to the theory of evolution by natural selection, a product of the same era, they enabled writers to interpret disease as just another instance of nature's feral offspring hard at work attacking and devouring their appointed victims, not unlike the consumption of lambs by wolves. By the turn of the century, world-destroying plagues were an established part of the repertoire of the scientific romancer. Jack London's *The Scarlet Plague* strikes down all but a few hundred members of the human race, through the action of a germ so virulent that no bacteriologist lives long enough to prepare a serum against it. Van Tassel Sutphen's *The Doomsman* is set in the twenty-first century after a plague known as "The Terror" needed only a few days to decimate mankind in 1925.

Of more recent stories, the best known is George R. Stewart's *Earth Abides,* a reworking of *The Scarlet Plague.* Again, the pestilence spreads too swiftly to contain. "No one was sure in what part of the world it had originated; aided by airplane travel, it had sprung up almost simultaneously in every center of civilization, outrunning all attempts at quarantine."[15] There is even a chance that the virus had escaped from "some laboratory of bacteriological warfare." No one knows. In any event, most of humanity dies. A few individuals survive because of natural immunity, but as in the Jack London story, they quickly revert to savagery. Stewart takes an austerely ecological view of the tragedy, prefacing his narrative with a meditation on nature's penchant for writing off whole species:

As for man, there is little reason to think that he can in the long run escape the fate of other creatures, and if there is a biological law of flux and reflux, his situation is now a highly perilous one. During ten thousand years his numbers have been on the upgrade in spite of wars, pestilences, and famines. This increase in population has become more and more rapid. Biologically, man has for too long a time been rolling an uninterrupted run of sevens.[16]

In *Earth Abides*, the next roll is snake eyes. By the end, its protagonist—a former graduate student of ecology—has given up all hope of reviving civilization among his Neolithic descendants. Known as the "Last American," he discontinues the school lessons he has given for many years and starts teaching the youngsters of the tribe a more valuable skill: how to make bows and arrows.

Micro-organic disaster may also occur in the form of blights that ignore man and the other animals but deprive them of the plant life on which they all depend for sustenance. J. J. Connington (nom-de-plume of the Belfast chemist Alfred Walter Stewart) produced such a scenario in *Nordenholt's Million*. The evildoer is a mutated denitrifying bacterium, which originates— by a nice, if improbable, twist of literary irony—when a fireball of lightning strikes a specimen dish in the study of a London science writer named Wotherspoon, who is surely an irreverent caricature of H. G. Wells. The new bacterial strain takes root in Regent's Park, then quickly annexes the rest of London, spreads throughout England, and eventually conquers the planet. By breaking down all nitrogenous material in the soil, the mutant converts it into loose sterile sand in which plants cannot grow. The prognosis for mankind is death by starvation within the year.

From this point on, *Nordenholt's Million* becomes the story of the titanic efforts of one man, the platinum tycoon Nordenholt, to beat nature at her own game by ruthlessly seizing power and mobilizing the best talents of the British nation in the Clyde Valley for a crash program of bacteriological research and mass production of nitrogenous material. All remaining food supplies are rounded up to keep the Clyde Valley workers alive. On Nordenholt's orders the rest of the country, after sabotage of its communications and transport facilities, is abandoned to starvation. Forty-five million men, women, and children die. But it is far better to let them die, Nordenholt argues, than to prolong their lives for a short while and in the process lose mankind's last chance for racial survival. Men similar to the tycoon pursue similar policies in Japan and the United States. Elsewhere in the world death and chaos are the only rulers. "All that had once been arable land became a desert strewn with the bones of men."[17]

Connington gives his hero ample opportunity to lecture on his philosophy of life, a philosophy of the purest Darwinism, supplemented by technocratic fascism. To compete and succeed in the real world, and above all in the world of the new bacterium, men must stop their "gabble about Democracy" and submit their affairs to scientific management. Life is struggle. Just as in lower nature, victory goes to the strong and the organized. "Of course," Nordenholt tells his chief lieutenant, "the brute is the basis. A wolf-pack will give you a microcosm of a nation: family life, struggles between wolf and wolf for a living, co-operation against an external enemy or prey."[18] Civilization softens the struggle up to a point, but it does not abrogate the responsibility to take whatever measures are needed to ensure survival in an unsentimental cosmos.

The same "lifeboat ethics," in Garrett Hardin's phrase,[19] permeate *The Death of Grass* (published in the U.S. as *No Blade of Grass*), an effective story of blight, famine, and the survival of the strong by John Christopher. *The Death of Grass* avoids the technocracy of Connington's novel, but its view of nature, and of nature's laws as they apply to man, does not differ all that much. A virus that unselectively kills all grasses, including wheat and rice, causes worldwide hunger and the breakdown of public order. Christopher's protagonist, a London engineer, leads a band of armed survivors through a lawless England to his brother's farm in the hills of Westmorland. They kill remorselessly in self-defense as they go, and in the dénouement the engineer is forced to shoot his own brother to save his group. There is no place for squeamishness or charity in the new order. "Nature was wiping a cloth across the slate of human history, leaving it empty for the pathetic scrawls of those few who, here and there over the face of the globe, would survive."[20]

Tales of assault by the creatures of the macro-organic world, such as J. T. McIntosh's Darwinian fable, *The Fittest*, add little to the picture of life presented by Stewart, Connington, and Christopher, except perhaps the enhancement of the horror of it all, since the attackers are now creatures that man can see, creatures with eyes and limbs and brains of their own. In the McIntosh story, common household pets join rats and mice as man's relentless enemies, revealing in Mother Nature the traitor as well as the savage. Other examples are H. G. Wells's "The Empire of the Ants," Jacques Spitz's *La guerre des mouches*, and Arthur Herzog's *The Swarm*. In *The Day of the Triffids* by John Wyndham, a giant mobile plant is the implacable enemy. Olaf Stapledon's *Darkness and the Light* shows mankind falling before armies of overgrown rats, and in a singular episode of the same author's *Last Men in London*, earth's first high civilization is ruthlessly exterminated by hordes of shaggy beasts: with the ingenious twist that the fallen civilization had been built by lemurs, and the shaggy beasts are our own ancestors.

The worst nightmares of all involve murderous attacks on *Homo sapiens* by intelligent beings from other planets. Dumb brutes or barely animate viruses have only instinct, and the laws of biochemistry, to direct them. Aliens, whose level of development is usually "higher" than man's, can be held to stricter account. When even they prove ferocious, treating mankind as a dangerous rival, an irritating pest, or a source of slave labor or food, they show Mother Nature at her most purposefully malign.

Such is manifestly the view of nature in Wells's *The War of the Worlds*, perhaps his best novel, and one in which his biological *Weltanschauung* figures prominently. Despite superior technology and obvious sophistication as social animals, Wells's Martians are not humanitarians. They believe that "life is an incessant struggle for existence." Because their own world has grown too harsh to support life, these beings, with "intellects vast and cool and unsympathetic," have determined to make earth their home. Just as mankind itself has wrought "ruthless and utter destruction . . . not only upon animals, such as the vanished bison and the dodo, but upon its own inferior races"—a reference to the Tasmanians, who died out in the 1870s—so the Martians propose to clear their new planet of the vermin that infest its surface.[21] The war of the worlds is, unexpectedly, won by earth. But the victory is entirely a matter of jungle economics. The Martians are attacked and destroyed by earth's microbes, an order of life unknown and apparently unsuspected on Mars, and one against which they have no line of defense.

The theme of alien invasion pioneered by Wells has attracted hundreds of writers and film-makers since *The War of the Worlds*. Some of the worthier successors to Wells's story are John Wyndham's *The Kraken Wakes*, Keith Roberts's *The Furies*, and Thomas M. Disch's *The Genocides*. Wyndham and Roberts allow man to win, after much loss of life, but Disch requires his obliteration. In *The Genocides* the unseen aliens whose machines convert earth into a farm for the raising of skyscraper-tall food plants deal with man as man himself would deal with garden pests. The helpless hero is dismayed at the ease of the aliens' victory.

> What was worse, what he could not endure was the suspicion that it all meant nothing, that the process of their annihilation was something quite mechanical: that mankind's destroyers were not, in other words, fighting a war but merely spraying the garden.[22]

His suspicion turns out to be correct. The reader's only indication of what the aliens think of mankind is contained in a report to their headquarters, describing the "incineration of the artifact" known as Duluth-Superior, and the unfortunate escape from its flaming ruins of some 200 to 340 of the "large mammals" who had constructed it. Duluth is the last such "artifact" on earth. Now that it has been properly leveled and sown, most of the aliens' work is done. The insignificant remnant of mammalian fugitives will be tracked down and torched by robot exterminators.[23]

The one danger in seeing aliens as forces of nature is that sometimes extra-terrestrial enemies (or even non-human terrestrial ones) turn out to be metaphors for more familiar human adversaries. This is especially true of space opera, which teems with Nazis, Communists, sinister Orientals, and Western imperialists hiding under horns and scales. Nor does anyone who reads Karel Čapek's *War with the Newts* come away with the impression that the great Czech writer wanted to warn mankind about the amphibian menace. But since man, too, belongs to nature in the view of modern science, the whole problem of nature's hellishness has still deeper implications that carry us out of this chapter and into the next.

10

◆

Report from Cainsmarsh

IN OLD AGE, weary of storytelling, H. G. Wells wrote a series of secular sermons crudely masked as fictions; often the characters impatiently lift the mask themselves, somewhere near the end of the tale. But when he got his teeth into a good anti-hero, preferably a caricature of someone he knew and detested, the literary results were not wholly disastrous. *The Croquet Player* is one of these sermons, a short novel redeemed in part by the light it throws on Wells's state of mind at age seventy, and in part by its delightfully malicious portrait of Georgie and his dragon of an aunt, who travel the world together, do-gooding and playing croquet.

On the terrace of a French resort hotel, Georgie listens, with mounting distress in spite of himself, to the ravings of an English country doctor recently settled in Cainsmarsh in the Fens. The doctor is convinced that Cainsmarsh is haunted. Suicides and murders run higher than normal. The dour inhabitants are subject to inexplicable fits of rage and fears of who knows what. A Paleolithic skull recovered near the marshes, on display in a Cambridgeshire museum, has given the doctor nightmares. But Georgie soon discovers that all the talk of hauntings is nonsense. The doctor is a mental patient at a local sanitarium; "Cainsmarsh" does not exist, and there is nothing unusual about the district where he actually practices. His psychiatrist, a formidable figure rather more like T. H. Huxley than Sigmund Freud, explains everything.

Having taken care of the literary formalities, Wells now tucks into his sermon, delivered by the psychiatrist. Cainsmarsh cannot be found on any map, he says, because, in case one or two readers may have dozed off, Cainsmarsh is really the world. The whole human world is haunted, not by

105

the sin of Cain or by the ghosts of cave men, but by mankind's genetic inheritance of brutishness, malice, and greed from its animal past. "Man, Sir, unmasked and disillusioned, is the same fearing, snarling, fighting beast he was a hundred thousand years ago. These are no metaphors, Sir. What I tell you is the monstrous reality." The psychiatrist continues for another few pages, calling for unspecified transformations of human consciousness. Georgie politely retreats to play croquet with his aunt, and the story is over. "I suppose the outlook *is* pretty black," the croquet player admits. "I suppose there may be frightful wars, air-raids, and pogroms ahead of us. But what am *I* to do about it? What was the good of bow-wow-wowing at me?"[1]

The Croquet Player was published in 1937, and the wars, air-raids, and pogroms followed it right on schedule. No one was less surprised than H. G. Wells. He had been regularly predicting such calamities for close on half a century. When all the terminal fictions are added up, the greater number, as we mentioned earlier, consist of stories about ends contrived by man himself, by the descendants of the brute who left his ugly skull in the low hills above Cainsmarsh and whose sort "had slouched and snarled over the marshes for a hundred times the length of all recorded history."[2] Notice, however, that Wells really seeks to exonerate man, even as he condemns him. Who can feel personally responsible for his animal inheritance? Does not the ultimate blame still fall on nature, the author of all life?

The answer to this question depends on the world view of the person responding, a topic due for consideration in later chapters. For many respondents, the answer will surely be yes. The villain is not man as such, but his genes and chromosomes, his glands, his racial memories, the energies churning in the id, a chain of circumstance traceable all the way back to the first blobs of protoplasm that quivered in the rich organic soup of earth's primeval oceans. For other respondents, the answer will be no, with or without qualifications. The villain is not nature, but the cultures of man, or modern Western culture in particular, or some aspects and tendencies of that culture. For still others, the Biblical faith remains essentially correct, in fixing blame on the corruption of man's will through sheer impiety.

Yet there is a sense in which all three lines of argument run parallel, and even amount to the same thing. In each case, the eschatologist affirms that the responsibility—if not the blame—rests with man, as he is. Whether he is what he is because of nature, culture, or original sin, the difference may not matter fundamentally. Whether it does matter fundamentally depends, once again, on world views.

It may also depend to some degree on what part of the world one happens to be viewing. Natural scientists, who spend most of their lives studying nature, find it difficult to connect the activities of man with the question of the world's end. A survey of scientists conducted by Malcolm W. Browne for the *New York Times* in 1978, in a piece entitled "Doomsday Debate," found that no one regarded war as likely to end the human race. All the scientists interviewed limited themselves to natural causes. Popularizations of the thinking of the scientific community such as Isaac Asimov's *A Choice of Catastrophes* and Kenneth Heuer's much earlier volume, *The End of the World,* devote only a few chapters (three of fifteen in Asimov, one of eight in Heuer) to the prospects for a man-made world's end.[3]

But men and women of letters, scientifically trained or not, seldom let humanity off so easily, not even Isaac Asimov himself wearing his other hat as a writer of fiction. During the last hundred years, they have produced a considerable array of visions of terminal wars among the races and nations of mankind. Less abundant, but only by contrast, are stories of an end of the world that results from the accidents or miscalculations of scientists. In other narratives, in smaller but roughly equal numbers, the eschatological event is a revolution, an act of terrorism, or a breakdown of the machinery of society for economic or ecological reasons.

Man may also share responsibility with nature in stories of Last Things in which nature is entirely to blame for the original catastrophe, but in which man bungles clear opportunities to survive the challenge. A pair of novels that appeared within months of one another in the late 1930s illustrates my point: *La guerre des mouches* by the French novelist Jacques Spitz and *The Hopkins Manuscript* by his English contemporary R. C. Sherriff. In both books mankind is faced with disaster at the hands of nature, a plague of intelligent flies in the case of *La guerre des mouches,* the fall of the moon into the earth in the case of *The Hopkins Manuscript.* But as the stories unfold, the attention of the reader comes to center on the criminal absurdity of the human response. In the novel by Spitz, published in 1938 near the end of the Spanish Civil War, the Spanish fascists rejoice at the death of every loyalist as the Iberian peninsula is invaded by swarms of killer flies, and the loyalists rejoice at the death of every fascist, until no more Spaniards are left. As in the real world of 1938, the French offer their Latin brothers no aid. England imagines herself immune from attack because of the Channel. Hitler's Germany, accusing the Jews of attracting the flies by their abominable odor, exterminates every Jew in the Reich before turning to its defense. *La guerre des mouches* is not a bad novel of natural horror, but its real interest, by the end, has shifted from the unfeeling filthiness of our common mother to the lunatic disarray of the family of man. In Sherriff's story, mankind survives the fall of the moon into the Atlantic basin with incredibly little damage, but then muffs everything by engaging in a terminal war over the rich mineral spoils.

What are the sources of the bad conscience of modern man, which lies behind all these scenarios of man-made disaster? Intellectual history may help us rather less than it did in studying the background of narratives of the world's end from natural causes. But it can still help. Theories and prophecies of the general collapse of civilization have been circulating in Western social thought and social science for several generations, and they have exerted an undeniable influence on the imaginations of all of us.

One point to make clear at the outset is the relatively recent arrival of eschatological fictions in which man literally destroys his own civilization, species, or planet. The first serious examples come along only in the 1890s, and there are not many of those. In the fictions of the period from 1890 down to 1914, massive devastation of man by man occurs in just a few sensational novels of war, revolution, and terrorism. Even these are usually fitted out with "happy" endings. But after 1914 man-made dooms are the rule, not the exception.

The place of theory and ideology in all this is uncertain. The apocalyptic implications of Marxism and some of the other leading schools of socialist and anarchist thought in the second half of the nineteenth century surely have their echoes in much of the speculative fiction of the generation active just before 1914. The writers were often involved in politics themselves, as well as letters: Bernard Shaw, H. G. Wells, William Morris, and Ignatius Donnelly, to name a few. But what matters here is the powerfully eschatological thrust of nineteenth-century socialism and anarchism. The pallid social democrats and apparatchiki of the late twentieth century may make it difficult for us to remember how passionate these men and women really were, and how convinced that world-historical changes loomed in the near future. The very warmth of their visions alerted literary folk to the possibility of dramatic defeats as well as victories.

Another stimulus to the speculative imagination came from what may be called the romance of applied science. All through the second half of the nineteenth century geniuses of engineering, with the help of physics and chemistry, transformed the face of Western industrial life. By the 1890s, as telephones and dynamite and electric power came into general use, as iron-clad warships steamed through the Suez Canal and tourists climbed the Eiffel Tower, all things seemed possible. So much was expected, thanks to the rapid rate of scientific and technical progress in the final decades of the century, that anyone with a touch of imagination could foresee man's acquisition of powers great enough to destroy civilization, if ever they fell into the "wrong" hands. Even Jules Verne let his mind play with such possibilities, as early as 1879, in *Les cinq cent millions de la Bégum*. A diabolical German professor from Jena builds a dystopia called Stahlstadt (Steel City), armed with an immense cannon whose shells freeze and suffocate everyone within range of their mysterious power. The professor's schemes are foiled, but Verne's novel is one of the first of many anticipations of scientific and technical villainy in speculative fiction, and sometimes the villains prevail.

From science, too, sprang the versatile idea of evolution by natural selection or, in Herbert Spencer's misleading phrase, "the survival of the fittest." The notion of a struggle to the death among individuals and groups was taken up by all kinds of thinkers and writers and put to various uses in the half-century before the first World War. We mentioned it in the preceding chapter as a source of ideas about catastrophic conflict between species, such as men and Martians. But it could just as well be invoked to rationalize warfare between the races of mankind, or the extermination of inferior races. Thinkers such as the Austrian sociologist Ludwig Gumplowicz in *Der Rassen-kampf* and the British eugenicist and statistician Karl Pearson in *National Life from the Standpoint of Science* stamped visions of racial struggle with the authority of science. Justifying warfare among nations on Darwinian grounds posed no greater problems. Once the idea was abroad that great life-and-death conflicts are inevitable and, for that matter, enjoined by laws of nature, imagining racial, class, or national wars of eschatological proportions was an easy next step.

Darwinism fell out of favor among social scientists after its gruesome exploitation in Nazi Germany, but the continuing influence of biology on social thought has been seen more recently in two contrasting movements: sociobiology, with its stress on the aggressiveness and tribalism of the "natural" man; and the environmental sciences, with their many prophecies of the exhaustion of resources and the lethal pollution by man of the planet's ecosystems. Sociobiology and ecology alike have spawned a whole new catastrophism in the social sciences in the 1970s and 1980s, which already rivals anything accomplished by the Darwinists of a century ago.

To all this should be added a number of tendencies in social scientific thought with mostly internal origins, such as theories of the business cycle in economics, which anyone can force to eschatological conclusions, although few professional economists have done so, and the many organicist theories of the rise and fall of civilization associated with Oswald Spengler, Arnold J. Toynbee, Pitirim A. Sorokin, and others. An early and deeply impressive example of doomsaying that blended both political economy and historical organicism was *The Law of Civilization and Decay*, published in 1895 by Henry Adam's younger brother, Brooks Adams. The event that inspired him to write, significantly, was the business panic of 1893.

Disasters, sometimes much weightier than the panic of 1893 in the scales of world history, may have as much to do with the writing and reading of stories of man-made doomsdays as all the theories and doctrines put together—not to mention their impact on the theories and doctrines themselves. We have already taken note in Chapter Six of Norman Cohn's observation that the most fervent visions of the end in medieval Western Christendom and again during the Reformation flourished among the most disoriented and atomized segments of the poor. Michael Barkun, using Cohn's work as one of his points of departure in *Disaster and the Millennium*, develops a general theory of the positive correlation between disastrous changes in the status of social groups and their receptivity to doomsaying and millennialist cults throughout history. He adds that although rural enclaves were once the most vulnerable to millennialism, whole nations and the world community at large can now easily fall prey to apocalyptic hysteria, transmitted through the media and sometimes stage-managed by governments in the interest of ruling elites.

What is true of communities may also apply to modern writers of terminal visions and to their readers. General strikes, racial violence, world and civil wars, acts of genocide, business depressions, bloody revolutions, weapons races, and diplomatic crises turning on feats of hair-raising brinksmanship are all familiar man-made disasters or near-disasters of modern history that could well suggest narratives of doomsday to literary folk. In many cases, as during the Cold War of the late 1940s and 1950s, anxiety is deliberately multiplied by the propaganda of states in the pursuit of alleged national interests.

Changes in the themes chosen by writers over the past hundred years help us sort out the relative influence of theory and doctrine, on the one hand, and events and material circumstances, on the other. From the 1880s to 1914, in the scenarios of man-made ends of the world studied for this book, nearly all envisaged disaster as the result either of social revolutions or wars, in roughly equal numbers. During the war and interwar years, 1914 to 1945, the accidents and miscalculations of scientists overtook revolution as a cause of world's ends. But by a margin of something like three to one most of the doomsdays attributable to human action were world wars fought with weapons of mass destruction. From 1945 to 1965, world wars continued to dominate the field in roughly the same proportions. Blunders of science remained a fairly popular alternative to war. After 1965, however, a significant shift in scenarios took place, with just over half still forecasting terminal wars, and the rest evenly divided between the accidents and miscalculations of scientists and catastrophic events in the environment.

The most salient observation prompted by this evidence is the profound effect of the first and second World Wars and the U.S.-Soviet Cold War on the apocalyptic imagination. When war is fresh in memory, stories of the world's end as a result of armageddons are plentiful. By the same token, the

East-West détente of recent years and the rise of a new generation of writers who have little or no first-hand knowledge of the second World War may help explain the modest decline in the production of stories of terminal wars since the late 1960s. But one must not forget the contribution of state propaganda, crisis diplomacy, popular journalism, and growing stockpiles of doomsday weapons in keeping fears alive. The decline in terminal war stories is relative, not absolute.

In other respects, our inventory of trends confirms the important role of doctrine and theory in stimulating the writing of eschatological fiction. Although the high drama of the revolutions of 1789 and 1848, as well as the Paris Commune of 1871, had not entirely faded from memory, the decades just before the first World War were far more noteworthy for talk about revolution than for revolution itself. Forecasts abounded of the imminent breakdown of industrial capitalism in the Western world through a war of the classes or the activities of terrorists. Politicians, ideologists, journalists, sociologists, utopographers, and many others debated the "social problem" interminably. The visions of the endtime in literature from this period reflect the debate with some accuracy. Yet from the early 1920s onward, despite a great revolution having just occurred in Russia, followed by a ruinous civil war, despite serious revolutionary outbreaks in Germany and Hungary, despite the chaos in China, writers lost almost all interest in revolution as a setting for doomsday. It is probably no coincidence that since the early 1920s there has also been a fall in the intellectual level if not in the quantity of theoretical debate about revolution as a lever for social transformation.

Another index to the power of ideas is the upsurge of novels during the past ten or fifteen years centered on the possibility of man's destruction of the biosphere by waste, overuse, and pollution. Here again, the gravity of the destruction so far recorded does not begin to equal the warnings of future events disseminated by natural and social scientists, politicians, environmental action groups, and the like. The fears may be grounded in empirical fact, but they are, up to now, just fears. Yet they have set off shock waves of concern that are responsible for a wide range of stories of environmental doom. By contrast the quite real, quite sudden, and mostly unforeseen worldwide economic depression that began in 1929 and lasted until the late 1930s appears to have inspired few works of eschatological fiction. Nothing is easier than to imagine a collapse of civilization by extrapolating from the worst years of the Great Depression. But the doctrines of orthodox and even Marxist political economy do not call for such a collapse. Orthodox political economy requires a cyclical return of prosperity, and Marxism affirms that when the capitalist economy is fully mature, the final business depression of the series will bring on a worker's revolution that prevents the collapse of civilization and raises it to unimaginably higher levels of achievement. Writers of speculative fiction may not be especially proficient in economic theory, but they know enough, one assumes, to feel uneasy with forecasts of the catastrophic unraveling of society through economic failure.

In looking more closely at the fictions themselves, the best place to begin is with the literature of revolution and terrorism that occupied such a relatively large place in eschatological visions before 1914—or, perhaps more accurately, before the mid-1920s. As is well known, a spate of utopian and dystopian novels were written in the late 1880s and early 1890s throughout the Western world. In one way or another virtually all this work addressed the "social problem," the closely intertwined phenomena of industrial and urban growth, poverty, and class struggle in an emergent global economic system that was also currently in the throes of a protracted business depression. Between 1885 and 1891 alone, there appeared *After London* by Richard Jefferies, *A Crystal Age* by W. H. Hudson, *Looking Backward* by Edward Bellamy, *Freiland* by Theodor Hertzka, *News from Nowhere* by William Morris, *Caesar's Column* by Ignatius Donnelly, and *Sozialdemokratische Zukunftsbilder* by Eugen Richter, all in all a substantial marshaling of visions of the best and worst that might be expected in the social future of mankind. These are also the years of such masterpieces of the romance of labor in revolt as Emile Zola's *Germinal* and Gerhard Hauptmann's *Die Weber.*

Most of the prophets expected the best, but even for some of them the cost was high. It is sometimes overlooked that William Morris included in his otherwise Edenic *News from Nowhere* a lengthy and generally quite tough-minded chapter on the history of the transition from capitalism to the garden world of the future. The transition fell just short of eschatology. It includes scenes of massacre, para-military fascism, a great general strike, and the temporary breakdown of civilization. The price of the collapse of urbanism and plutocracy in *After London* is a return to the Middle Ages, with few of the Edenic qualities of Morris's vision. Donnelly ascribes iron ruthlessness to his revolutionaries, the Brotherhood of Destruction, in *Caesar's Column*, while making clear his own preference for the peaceful removal of capitalism by a tender-hearted democratic populism. But in the late twentieth century of his imagination, it is too late for democracy. The Brotherhood defeats the plutocrats in a worldwide bloodbath that takes the lives of three-quarters of civilized mankind. Most of the rest, except for a saved remnant in a remote corner of Africa, revert to barbarism. Civilization will be restored, but not for centuries.

In the year before Donnelly brought out his vision of a proletarian Day of Wrath, which became a best-seller almost as famous in its time as *Looking Backward*, his countryman John Ames Mitchell published *The Last American,* a wistfully satirical novella that anticipated nothing less than the suicide of modern man. An expedition of neo-medieval Persians sails into the harbor of New York in the year 2951 and finds the metropolis empty. As the Persians tour the city and later Washington, they collect evidence of the tragedy for their history books. Bizarre fluctuations of climate are held partly responsible, but it soon becomes obvious that the meteorological ploy is one of Mitchell's jokes. The real cause of the catastrophe was social disintegration. Extremes of wealth and poverty, greed and commercialism, the loss of moral fiber of the original European stock, the rebellion of the poor led by Irish immigrants, a short-lived "Hy-Burnyan" dictatorship, and finally collapse; such was the sad history of the "Mehrikan" people. Europe has apparently vanished as well. When the Last American is found alive in the ruins of the nation's capital, and then killed in a scuffle, the Persian admiral takes his skull home to present to the museum in Teheran. But Mitchell leaves no doubt about his message even before the story begins. He dedicates his volume "to those thoughtful Persians who can read a warning in the sudden rise and swift extinction of a foolish people."[4]

The degeneration through luxury and idleness of the rich and the bestialization of the poor sketched by Mitchell in *The Last American* is, of course, precisely the theme of Wells's *The Time Machine*. In addition to furnishing an unforgettable picture of the end of the natural world, *The Time Machine* directly addresses the class struggle of late nineteenth-century Europe, extrapolating it into a far future in which bloody revolution has not occurred, but something much worse: the biological degeneration of both rich and poor, and their separation into two subhuman new species. The once oppressed workers have become cannibals with the inhuman cunning of sewer rats, and their former masters are now mindless creatures kept alive to supply the devolved workers with fresh meat. What Wells is saying, very simply, is that failure to solve the social problem will dehumanize rich and poor alike, and finally destroy civilization itself.

In the year before the publication of *The Time Machine* in serial form, George Griffith brought out his first novel, *The Angel of the Revolution*, and a few months later his second, a sequel, *Olga Romanoff*. Both books are popular thrillers innocent of literary ambition, but seething with all the ideas in the air of Europe in the 1890s about class struggle, anarchist terror, secret weapons, and the chances of war among the Great Powers. What sets Griffith apart from most of his fellow writers of potboilers is a gift for inspired exaggeration, an apocalyptic imagination that may fail utterly at the level of psychological insight but succeeds, where the George Merediths and Henry Jameses failed just as utterly, in grasping the readiness of the collective mind of modern man for mass destruction. For a sample of his rhetoric, consider the opening scene of *The Angel of the Revolution*. Our hero Richard Arnold, a poor and unknown genius starving in a South London tenement house, has just invented a workable flying machine. He quickly perceives that it could be used by evil rulers to tighten the grip of their oppression over the downtrodden of the world. He takes a lonely evening walk on the Embankment along the Thames, thinking out loud.

> The next war will be the most frightful carnival of destruction that the world has ever seen; but what would it be like if I were to give one of the nations of Europe the power of raining death and desolation on its enemies from the skies! No, no! Such a power, if used at all, should only be used against and not for the despotisms that afflict the earth with the curse of war![5]

As it happens, young Arnold's soliloquy is overheard by a member of the Inner Circle of the Brotherhood, also known as the Terror, a worldwide confederacy of nihilists, anarchists, and socialists who have infiltrated all the world's armies and governments with the express aim of helping modern capitalist civilization destroy itself. Arnold turns over the plans for his airship to the Brotherhood, together with another of his inventions, a high explosive that makes a stick of dynamite seem like a firecracker. When a world war breaks out in 1904 involving all the Powers, East and West, the Brotherhood bides its time, waiting for the right moment to intervene with Arnold's irresistible airships. The carnage is beyond all human experience. Some eight million troops and five million civilians perish in less than a year, but the Brotherhood knows when to strike. Revolution cripples every national army, the rich are eliminated by taxation, and from the ruins a new world order emerges, dominated by a federation of the Anglo-Saxon peoples under the political tutelage of the Brotherhood.

Olga Romanoff, Griffith's next romance, follows the story into the twenty-first century. A counter-revolution is launched by the ruthless but beautiful descendant of the last Russian tsar. The Brotherhood, which has now become the remote mountain nation of Aeria, can prevent the triumph of Olga's forces, but has to withdraw at the critical moment and let her win in another tremendous armageddon of the air because its scientists learn that a comet will soon destroy all life on the surface of the earth. In the end, only two hundred and fifty carefully selected Aerians survive in deep underground shelters. A new world will arise out of the ashes of the old, peopled entirely by the grandchildren of the heroic anarchists of 1904.

Griffith's novels are melodramas filled with one-dimensional characters in the lowest traditions of pulp romance. They got worse, as his popularity grew. But how many writers foresaw, as early as 1893, the all-importance of air power, or world wars killing tens of millions of people, or leagues of militant revolutionaries who could infiltrate armies and take over great modern states? Not even H. G. Wells came so close to anticipating the shape of the twentieth century, or at least not so soon. Griffith's wars are constructed on the scale of the real armageddons of our time. His Brotherhood achieves in imagination what Lenin, Trotsky, and Mao Tse-tung much later achieved in the real world.

Of course both Griffith and Wells had plenty of competition. Tales of anarchists plotting to destroy the world were legion in the 1890s, further illustrated by the still dustier volumes of Edward Douglas Fawcett (*Hartmann, the Anarchist; or, the Doom of the Great City*) and T. Mullet Ellis (*Zalma*). Just a bit later on, the James Elroy Flecker story we have already examined for its scenario of race suicide, "The Last Generation," opens with the mad leader of an army of proletarians ranting against progress and civilization in Birmingham Town Hall. When his revolution triumphs and he has conquered the world, the revolutionary chieftain resolves to end human misery and suffering forever by banning reproduction.

For a few years after World War One, the Bolshevik revolution in Russia inspired a number of awful-warning stories somewhat predictive of George Orwell's *1984*, but more apocalyptic in tone, of which the most persuasive is no doubt *The People of the Ruins: A Story of the English Revolution and After,* by Edward Shanks. Socialist revolutions reduce mankind to the Dark Ages, and a hero from the twentieth century, preserved by suspended animation, fails in his mission to rescue the barbarous English from the more barbarous Welsh. Before putting a bullet through his head, he has

> a vision of the world sinking further below the point from which in his youth he had seen it. . . . Cities would be burnt, bridges broken down, tall towers destroyed and all the wealth and learning of humanity would shiver to a few shards and a little dust.[6]

But tales of the world's end through revolution become increasingly rarer as the twentieth century wears on. Karel Čapek's *War with the Newts*, at one level, is a metaphor for catastrophic class struggle, but his story has other values. After 1945, revolution and the war of the classes have been exploited in Western speculative fiction for their dystopian, rather than for their eschatological, interest. Thanks to Comrade Stalin, and his counterparts in the so-called Free World, revolution has lost much of its old apocalyptic glamor, becoming a synonym for the quite different terror of the all-engulfing superstate.

It would be more useful at this point for us to take up another theme from the novels of George Griffith, the theme of the scientist or inventor and his weapon of total destruction. In some narratives of the endtime, he appears as a one-man engine of doom, able to do the work of a whole party of anarchists—for "good" or "evil," as the case may be. Such prototypes as Dr. Frankenstein, Dr. Jekyll, and Captain Nemo, who have their own prototypes in the likes of Merlin and Aladdin, helped to establish the figure of the omnipotent man of science in the nineteenth century, but it was only near the end of the century that he begins to play a decisive role in speculative histories of the future. One stock personage, especially popular, is the scientist who uses his super-weapon to force mankind to abolish war and establish a world state. Richard Arnold, although he needs the collaboration of the anarchist Brotherhood, is such a man. Others are found in Hollis Godfrey's *The Man Who Ended War*, C. J. Cutcliffe Hyne's *Empire of the World*, and Arthur Train and William Woods's *The Man Who Rocked the Earth*, all first published between 1908 and 1914.[7]

But the same stock figure who saves humanity can also threaten it with destruction for less worthy purposes. The little known American writer William Henry Rhodes invented a character of this sort in his story "The Case of Summerfield," which first appeared in a San Francisco newspaper in 1871: Summerfield is a scientist who will destroy the oceans of the world unless he is paid a ransom. Robur, the somewhat unattractive hero of Jules Verne's *Robur le conquérant* (in English translation as *The Clipper of the Clouds*), completes his transformation into a world-defying villain in one of Verne's last works, *Maître du monde*. It makes an interesting companion piece to that other product of his final years, the novella *L'éternel Adam*, although *L'éternel Adam* is much more explicitly eschatological. Robert Cromie, a popular rival and contemporary of George Griffith, made his contribution to the tale of the scientist as terrorist in·*The Crack of Doom*, and Jack London published two short stories on the theme in 1908, stories that are mirror images of one another. In "The Enemy of All the World," London features an embittered and misunderstood genius who terrorizes mankind for eight years, and "Goliah" is the tale of a Berkeley-educated inventor who ruthlessly assassinates statesmen and blows up navies until he achieves his aim of worldwide disarmament under socialism. Emil Gluck, the evil wizard of "The Enemy of All the World," is London's Mr. Hyde; Percival Stutz, of "Goliah," his Dr. Jekyll. Still more terrible are the villains of J. B. Priestley, in *The Doomsday Men*, and Gore Vidal, in *Kalki*. The insane scientist of the first is prevented at the last possible moment from totally destroying the world with a doomsday bomb, and the false messiah of the second carries out his crazy scheme to kill everyone on earth with a bacteriological weapon of his own devising.

But there are relatively few such super-heroes or arch-villains in the speculative fiction of the last several decades. They seem to belong to an earlier era, when men like Edison and Pasteur captured the public imagina-

tion. Now that science is the collective achievement of anonymous technicians toiling in corporate and multiversity laboratories, the idea of the godlike
scientist imposing his sovereign will on a stunned humanity has become more
or less obsolete. Nevertheless, there are still many narratives of the world's
end in which science gets out of hand, through the accidents, miscalculations, or idiocies of its imperfect practitioners. The individual scientist has
been demythologized. But in an age of thermonuclear warfare, in an age of
atomic power plants and laser cannon and pilotless spaceships threading their
way through the moons of Jupiter, no one doubts that science still has the
power to bring civilization tumbling down.

One of the first writers to examine the theme of science running amok
was Karel Čapek. Nearly all his speculative plays and stories examine it,
whatever else they may have to say. His most famous work, *R.U.R.*, is the
classic drama of man's violent overthrow by his own brainchildren, the robots. Two novels of the 1920s, *Továrna na absolutno* (*The Absolute at Large*)
and *Krakatit*, offer inventors who wreak havoc unintentionally with their
inventions. In the more apocalyptic of the pair, *The Absolute at Large*, the
development of an unlimited power source leads to a world war that lasts for
nine years, in which hundreds of millions are killed and most of civilization
is destroyed. Stephen Southwold's *The Seventh Bowl*, published in 1930, ends
with an idealistic scientist using his invention to try to force an evil world
dictatorship to mend its ways, not unlike the hero of London's story "Goliah."
But Southwold's protagonist is no Goliah. The invention proves far more
powerful than he had calculated: its first test jolts the earth out of orbit, into
a collision course with the sun.

Since 1945 there have been dozens of such stories. The three disasters
that beset humanity in John Wyndham's *The Day of the Triffids*—blindness,
plague, and mobile killer plants—are all the result of research gone wrong.
The fabric of society disintegrates when the subjects of the experiments of an
animal psychologist escape and breed prolifically in J. T. McIntosh's *The
Fittest*. Nuclear bomb tests, in outer space and at the bottom of the Pacific
Ocean, respectively, destroy civilization in Brian Aldiss's *Greybeard* and Charles
Eric Maine's *The Tide Went Out*. A top-secret experiment in meteorological
warfare goes haywire in George Stone's *Blizzard*, plunging the earth into a
new ice age in a matter of days. Piers Anthony, in *Rings of Ice*, pictures the
drowning of the world after a team of single-minded government scientists
execute a dubious scheme to transform an "ice nebula" into orbiting rings
that will reflect enough sunlight to solve the energy crisis for "the next fifty
years." The rings melt prematurely and 2,000 feet of rain fall.

Recent fiction also features a fair number of generally well-meaning but
oblivious men and women of science whose efforts produce doomsdays remi-

niscent of the black comedies of Karel Čapek. In Ward Moore's unfairly neglected *Greener Than You Think*, a scientist who develops a process to enable food plants to thrive in deserts winds up being responsible for the death of the human race. Her process yields a monster mutant grass that soon chokes every square foot of the planet. But to the end she remains fatuously confident that she is on the verge of discovering the compound that will destroy mankind's gramineous foe. John Bowen furnishes a similar catastrophe, triggered by a similarly half-daft scientist, in *After the Rain*. The best-known example of tales in this vein is *Cat's Cradle*, by Kurt Vonnegut, Jr. The world's waters turn to ice with an abnormally high freezing point, ending all life, as the result of a ludicrous accident in the closing pages. But no world-wrecking accident would have been possible in the first place if Vonnegut's scientist, Felix Hoenikker, had been a complete human being instead of an autistic child-man.

Apprehensions of an ecological doomsday, which, as remarked above, began cropping up in significant numbers of stories after about 1965, are really only a variant of the theme of runaway science. In this case, technology and industry are the runaways, wasting, depleting, and poisoning the biosphere. For whatever reasons, few if any eschatological stories in this category reach the imaginative peaks of the best works in other major categories of terminal fictions. The real masterpieces are novels like Harry Harrison's *Make Room! Make Room!*, Stanislaw Lem's *Kongres Futurologiczny (The Futurological Congress)*, and John Brunner's *The Sheep Look Up*, or J. G. Ballard's story "Billennium," which deal not with the world's end but with a radical deterioration in the quality of life. But the eschatological possibilities are all there, waiting to be exploited—as in Stanley R. Greenberg's screenplay for *Soylent Green*. Greenberg takes unforgivable liberties with *Make Room! Make Room!*, the novel on which his film is based, but the story that results from those liberties is considerably more chilling, and, thanks to its added touches, a story with powerful eschatological implications.

All the same, there are a number of well-told novels and short stories that at least take ecological doomsdays as their points of departure. "Watershed," the last of the four pieces in James Blish's cycle, *The Seedling Stars*, is an early scenario, imagining an earth ruined by desertification. Jon Hartridge's *Earthjacket* envisages a future world in which pollution has made surface life all but impossible. A few degenerate savages roam the land, and under it, in subterranean habitats, a handful of technicians and bureaucrats rule over a wretched subhuman population kept asleep most or all of their lives because of dwindling supplies of oxygen. The world has not quite ended, but the human race has shrunk to a vestige of its old self, and for all but the fortunate few thousand members of the ruling class, civilization exists no more. In other works, such as Suzy McKee Charnas's *Walk to the End of the World*, Edmund Cooper's *The Tenth Planet*, Sheila Sullivan's *Summer Rising*, and Kate Wilhelm's *Where Late the Sweet Birds Sang*, the scene is a post-holocaust earth after civilization has destroyed itself by one or more of the varieties of ecological disaster catalogued for the Club of Rome in *The Limits to Growth* by Dennis Meadows and his colleagues. There is also a compelling story of the end of the world from the pen of a leading professional ecologist: "Eco-Catastrophe!", written in 1969 by Paul R. Ehrlich, author of *The Population Bomb*.

Ehrlich's story ends with the death of all marine life through pollution of the oceans by a pesticide invented in Soviet Russia, but then adds one more paragraph that lifts it out of the class of tales of purely ecological doom. Deprived of food from the oceans, the starving nations of East Asia blame Russia for the disaster, and World War Three begins with the Chinese invasion of the Soviet Union. In the real future, of course, this is the way in which ecological pressures are most likely to bring about the end of the world. Pollution, overpopulation, shortages of strategic minerals, and scarcity of arable land will not do the job alone, but they can exacerbate political tensions and lead, directly or indirectly, to armed conflicts big enough, in turn, to blow civilization to bits.

War is indeed the stratagem most commonly employed in the literature of Last Things. Of the terminal visions studied for the present work, some 35 percent make a great war or wars the principal or only cause of the world's end, in all more than one hundred short stories, novels, and plays, and our list is by no means exhaustive. As one might expect, the sort of war foreseen correlates closely in most instances with world events in the author's own present. But there is also a concern in speculative fiction with the effects of technological innovation on warfare that helps keep writers somewhat ahead of their counterparts in military science. If the gap in predictive power between fiction and non-fiction has tended to narrow in recent decades, one reason may be that many so-called experts have learned from the triumphs of speculative fiction to exercise their imaginations more boldly.

Before 1914, as noted in Chapter Two, the representative story of future war was neither apocalyptic nor critical of warmaking as such. Beginning with Sir George Chesney's novella, *The Battle of Dorking*, published in *Blackwood's Magazine* in 1871 in the aftermath of Prussia's blitzkrieg against France, scores of narratives of a future European war appeared over the next forty-odd years. In the great majority, the "lesson" of the Franco-Prussian War was endlessly repeated: any country that is unprepared for combat, whether politically or militarily or psychologically, will collapse just as Louis Napoleon's France collapsed before the war machine of the House of Hohenzollern. The lesson was well learned by all involved, and the result was World War One. For this outcome, novelists must share responsibility with politicians, journalists, military strategists, teachers of history, manufacturers of war matériel, and many others.

But such stories have little to do with secular eschatology. Our interest lies instead with a smaller group of fictions that anticipated far more than another Prussian blitz, fictions of a future world war engaging all or most of the Powers, fictions of grand-scale international or interracial struggle in which a fair percentage of humankind is annihilated and the civilization of the modern world is destroyed or radically transformed. Clearly, the authors of this smaller group come much closer to anticipating twentieth-century warfare than those who harped interminably on the prospects for a recurrence of *la Débâcle* of 1870.

A prime example of apocalyptic war stories from this period has already been discussed, Griffith's *The Angel of the Revolution*, which combines conflict among nations with the equally popular expectation of seizure of world power by a conspiracy of anarchists. None of Griffith's later novels of future war equals it, including *The World Peril of 1910*, in which he furnished the added thrill of earth's near-collision with a comet. The Kaiser's hosts besieging London are defeated by airships from the United States, as a single shot from a great cannon erected at Bolton disposes of the comet. But Griffith had taken his own best shot in *The Angel of the Revolution*.

Like most of his contemporaries, Griffith made much of the place of new technologies in future warfare. Aircraft, submarines, and mighty new explosives were his stock in trade. The coming importance of air power was stressed by many writers of the time, perhaps most comically (without any comic intent) by the American Stanley Waterloo in his 1898 novel, *Armageddon*. Despite its title, the book offers no scenes of mass destruction, but its events are otherwise eschatological, in much the same sense as *The Angel of the Revolution*. A world war of the near future is won when a single experimental American airplane arrives on the scene during a great naval battle, drops dynamite bombs on the Russian flagship of the European fleet, and then crashes into the sea. This fantastic apparition—bearing in mind that Waterloo published his novel in 1898, five years before Kitty Hawk—so astounds and demoralizes the Europeans that the Americans and their allies ultimately triumph. They impose global peace, guaranteed by the awareness of all concerned that if dynamite bombs can fall from the skies, no nation will any longer seriously contemplate loosing the dogs of war.

Not every vision of apocalyptic world wars and their super-weapons written during this period ends in some sort of victory for the forces of righteousness. Wells's *The War of the Worlds*, with its Martian invaders wielding invincible "Heat-Rays" rather like the laser and particle beam artillery now being developed by both the United States and the Soviet Union, is not a story of warfare between rival groups of mankind. But it issues an effective warning of the lethal capabilities of modern science. More to the point is Wells's later novel, *The War in the Air*, the most horrific of pre-1914 war novels, and the one that comes closest to anticipating the scenarios of future world wars that became standard after 1914.

In the great air war of Wells's prophetic imagination, a German armada bombards New York. Asian planes engage the Germans in a somewhat improbable armageddon of the air above Niagara Falls. But these are merely dramatic incidents in a conflict that has become worldwide and uncontrollable. Chaos, famine, pestilence stalk the planet. Civilization crumbles, and Wells's Cockney hero, back home in England after astonishing adventures, becomes a post-holocaust local chieftain. There are no victories of any kind for humanity in Wells's story. No scientists or anarchists or valiant statesmen spring to its rescue. As the hero's brother tells his young nephew in the Epilogue, the war may be going on yet, for all he knows. Travelers bring tales of sporadic fighting still in progress among desperate bands of men here and there around the world. Obstinacy is to blame, the old man says.

> "Everybody was getting 'urt, but everybody was 'urtin' and everybody was 'igh-spirited and patriotic, and so they smeshed up things instead. They jes' went on smeshin'. And afterwards they jes' got desp'rite and savige."
>
> "It ought to 'ave ended," said the little boy.
>
> "It didn't ought to 'ave begun," said Old Tom. . . . He sucked his old gums thoughtfully, and his gaze strayed away across the valley to where the shattered glass of the Crystal Palace glittered in the sun.[8]

Only a few months before the outbreak of hostilities in the real world of 1914, Wells published one more major novel of future war, which reverts to the Griffith model. *The World Set Free* recounts the history of a war that breaks out in Europe in 1958 and spreads throughout the world. The featured super-weapon this time is a devastating explosive manufactured from an artificial radioactive element known as Carolinum. The weapon itself is called an "atomic bomb." With hundreds of these bombs, airmen destroy the world's great cities. Millions perish. Starvation and anarchy ensue, but the statesmen of the broken nations come to their senses in time to prevent complete collapse. Meeting at a historic conference in Brissago, in Italy, they found a revolutionary world republic that will tolerate warfare no longer.

The World Set Free contains what is quite obviously one of the most incredible *coups de maître* in the history of scientific and technological forecasting. Its atomic bombs exploded in imagination more than a quarter of a century before the discovery of nuclear fission in experiments with uranium and before Einstein's fateful letter to President Roosevelt. But in other respects, *The World Set Free* is less daring than *The War in the Air.* The sudden reversal of humanity's decline after the Brissago conference and the whole second half of the novel, a synopsis of Wells's *A Modern Utopia,* gravely diminish its impact as a cautionary tale.

An important variation on the theme of apocalyptic conflict among the Great Powers in fiction before 1914 is the story of a coming *Rassenkampf,* a Darwinian battle to the death between the White Man and various contenders for his overlordship of the planet, chiefly the Yellow Man. Given the state of the sciences of life, culture, and society at the end of the nineteenth century, it is not surprising that men of color in pre-1914 fiction are often regarded somewhat like natural enemies of civilization, on a par with deadly germs and insects, and that race wars tend to be more eschatological than wars among "civilized" states. W. Delisle Hay, a nearly forgotten British futurist who wrote a novella about the choking of London by a poisonous fog entitled *The Doom of the Great City,* also published in 1881 a volume forecasting cold-blooded genocide "on a scale," I. F. Clarke observes, "that Hitler would have admired."[9] Hay anticipates the coming in the next century of a world government that will decree, in stern obedience to the law of nature, the thoroughgoing extermination of all the colored races. Bombers will pass over East Asia and a billion human beings will die. Hay notes that the yellow peoples, no matter how clever, are actually "mere anthropoid animals . . . incapable of lofty thought," characterized by "relentless cruelty, bestial vice, exaggerated animalism."[10]

Of course, if we adhere to our own working definitions, Hay's vision is not eschatological at all, since it was interpreted by the writer himself as simply an act of racial hygiene, embodied in a more or less utopian prophecy of the scientific, technological, and political wonders of the coming age. Standing much closer to eschatology are two early novels of race war in the United States, Pierton W. Dooner's *Last Days of the Republic,* about the Chinese destruction of America, published in 1880, and King Wallace's *The Next War,* an 1892 story of warfare between whites and blacks, won by the whites. For tales of worldwide devastation, for secular eschatology in the purest sense, one must consult above all the long out-of-print work of M. P. Shiel. His three novels *The Yellow Danger, The Yellow Wave,* and *The Dragon* (1898–1913) comprise a study in racism as vicious and apocalyptic as anything in modern literature. Shiel's gift for descriptions of psychopathic violence, well displayed in *The Purple Cloud,* is not wanting here, although it is difficult nowadays to empathize with his shining white heroes or enter into the world of ideas and imagination that gave rise to his gruesome Oriental villains.

But these were popular novels in their day, trading in the same stock notions of virtue and vice as the novels of George Griffith or George Allan England. *The Yellow Danger* establishes the pattern. Dr. Yen How, an evil Asian genius wracked with lust for an English woman who has rejected him, conceives the project of eradicating the white races. He rises to supreme authority in China, engineers a world war among the European Powers, and then joins with Japan in a surprise attack on the whole white race. Every white man in China is massacred. The Japanese navy batters what remains of Europe's fleets. A horde of four hundred million screaming Chinese, virtually the whole Chinese empire, hurls itself against the European mainland, raping and burning and killing as it goes, sparing no one. Europe dies, but naval forces under the command of Shiel's bluff hero, John Hardy, prevents the invasion of Great Britain. Hardy then turns the tables on the Chinese in Europe by infecting them with plague. The scorched and empty continent becomes British soil. The few surviving Chinese, whose "dark and hideous instincts" cannot be imagined even by "the vilest European,"[11] slink back to China, and it is now Britain's appointed task to rule the world.

The Yellow Wave and *The Dragon* are also novels of conflict between Asia and Europe, although neither reaches the peaks and depths of Shiel's first exploit in this vein. He was widely imitated by other writers, including Jack London in a short story written in 1906, "The Unparalleled Invasion," which ends like *The Yellow Danger* with the obliteration of the rampaging Chinese by bacteriological weapons. A *cordon sanitaire* established by an international army and navy seals off China from the outside world until every Chinese is dead and the land is clean and safe for re-settlement.

But the Great War that finally came in August 1914 did not turn out to be a racial conflict. As it ran its course over the next four years, it became apparent that no writer of fiction (and very few writers of non-fiction) had foreseen in more than the fuzziest outlines what would happen. The war of 1914–18 was not racial, aircraft and other super-weapons did not prove decisive, no worldwide revolution or world republic emerged from it, and it did not destroy or radically transform the civilization of white Western capitalism. The bourgeois and later Marxist leaders of the one major revolution precipitated by the war, the revolution that ended Tsarist rule in Russia, behaved more like conventional national statesmen than like tribunes of humanity.

All the same, the world had changed. Ten million people were dead as a result of the hostilities, and twice as many died in the influenza epidemic that radiated in all directions from the front lines in 1918. The war had involved most of the world's nations. Submarines, tanks, aircraft, and poison gas—if not decisive—made a good enough showing to persuade military analysts that with further technical progress they might still revolutionize future warfare.

Visions of a second and considerably more devastating world war began appearing in force within five years of the Armistice, and continued to appear through the late 1920s and 1930s. Practically all of these works have managed to drop out of sight. The branch of the publishing industry that specializes in reprinting "classics" of science fiction has mainly ignored them, perhaps in part because so many were written by mainstream authors or by trespassers from other genres. Few are works of towering literary significance, but this is likewise true of the tales of future wars written before 1914. At any rate, the output was brisk, and those titles that qualify as eschatological, or nearly so, follow much the same formula, volume after volume.

As before 1914, advanced weaponry, especially air power, counts for a great deal. In nearly every title of the 1920s and 1930s examined for *Terminal Visions*, the next world war features aerial bombardment of cities with apocalyptic consequences. The preferred super-weapon, used against cities and also troops, is poison gas. The gas attacks are almost always just as ruinously effective as nuclear strikes in stories written after 1945. Bacteriological warfare sometimes supplements or replaces gas, and there is also a fair amount of bombing with high explosives and incendiary devices. Atomic weapons appear now and then, but no narrative of a terminal war from the period compares in this respect with Wells's *The World Set Free*. Sometimes racial themes play a large role, or even dominate the story, although not as often as before 1914. In P. Anderson Graham's *The Collapse of Homo Sapiens*, for example, the last in a series of terminal wars that ends civilization is a massive racial conflict in which a coalition of the colored peoples strives to annihilate the white race and very nearly succeeds, before it breaks apart and the coloreds begin fighting among themselves. Philip Francis Nowlan's original Buck Rogers stories—not to be guessed from later uses of the Rogers character—tell of valiant white Americans rising up against a cruel Mongolian empire that had conquered the United States in the twenty-third century. The vile Orientals of Nowlan's imagination could have issued directly from the pen of M. P. Shiel or Sax Rohmer.

But the representative tale of terminal warfare in the 1920s and 1930s concerned itself with the menace of the armed nation-state, not with the Yellow or Black Peril. One quite typical work, which can speak for them all, is *1944*, a handsomely crafted novel by Hardinge Goulburn Giffard, second

Earl of Halsbury. Published in 1926, it based itself explicitly on forecasts by European military experts that any city in the world would be easy prey to poison gas attacks by bombers in a coming war. In Halsbury's scenario, world war breaks out in June 1944. Every Power is apprehensive about the designs of some other Power, but hostilities begin when Russia's charismatic dictator launches a surprise air attack on England and France only a few hours after attending an apparently successful disarmament conference in London. Germany is Russia's close ally in the new balance of power. The raids are devastating, but equally savage Western retaliation follows, Japan and the United States go to war, China and Russia destroy one another, and civilization falls apart. At the end of the story its protagonist, a Churchillian squire and M.P. who was alone among British leaders in foreseeing the holocaust, arrives in London with his family and a small party of confederates to try to establish some semblance of a national government. The city is empty, all its inhabitants having fled or died in the gas attack, but he will do what he can. The reader is left with the thought that in England, but perhaps nowhere else, regression to the Dark Ages is not inevitable.

Since Lord Halsbury's narrative breaks off at this point, with the war only recently ended, we do not learn how far back mankind will actually be driven, but the suggestion of a new Dark Age received elaborate treatment in other stories of the period. Many unfold in a relatively distant future when the Dark Age has already arrived, a post-holocaust setting nearly always reserved in the pre-1914 literature of Last Things for stories of natural disaster. Now that war is seen as a much greater disaster in and of itself, likely to inflict even more terrible wounds on civilization, the idea of a "return" to medieval or prehistoric conditions becomes correspondingly easier to swallow. One of the first was Cicely Hamilton's *Theodore Savage* (later revised and reissued under the title *Lest Ye Die*), a novel of tribal Britain after fire and gas wipe out her cities. The best in English is probably John Collier's *Tom's A-Cold* (in the U.S. as *Full Circle*), which could almost have been written by D. H. Lawrence. H. G. Wells's *The Shape of Things to Come*, and the screenplay he took from it, *Things to Come*, show scenes of a barbarous post-holocaust world, but in both the novel and the screenplay, Wells went on to rebuild civilization along utopian lines, exactly as in *The World Set Free*.

When the second World War actually arrived, it proved just as unlike the literary versions of it as its predecessor. Gas was not used after all, the bombing of cities had far less effect than the military experts as well as the writers had predicted, and once more civilization refused to sputter out, despite a fivefold increase in military and civilian casualties, and major shifts in the balance of world power. In fact, to judge from the plots of most of the

novels of future war published since 1945, the battles of the second World
War failed to seduce the eschatological imagination altogether. It was, so to
speak, a disappointment.

But I am exaggerating. The fact that there had been a major global war
at all, so soon after the first one, convinced writers and many others of the
virtual certainty of a third. When world power polarized at the war's end,
and a fierce rivalry developed between the United States and the Soviet
Union, no one had any doubts who the antagonists would be, next time
around. Finally, the nuclear devastation of Hiroshima and Nagasaki suggested
to writers how the next war would be fought and how, at long last, after so
many attempts, civilization would really succeed in demolishing itself.

There is as much similarity among the future war stories of the period
since 1945 as among those written in the 1920s and 1930s. A few broad
generalizations are in order. The end usually comes, once again, through the
total destruction of cities by airborne attack, except that now the super-
weapon is the nuclear bomb. In a sizeable minority of scenarios, about one
in five, the nuclear bomb is reinforced by chemical, radiological, or bacterial
weapons. In another sizeable minority, it takes two separate wars to accom-
plish the job. Racial conflict is rare, except in the outbreak of stories in the
late 1960s about race war in America's cities, which in any case affected only
America. Post-holocaust settings in a new Dark Age have become still more
popular than in the 1920s and 1930s; over half the narratives examined fit
this description.

But as with so many fictions of the endtime, stories of future nuclear
war are by no means all resolutely pessimistic. Even when the end is literally
the end, the mood is often one of bittersweetness rather than bitterness;
sorrow and compassion prevail over cynicism and misanthropic rage. Of the
more than sixty post-1945 stories of future war examined, about thirty-five
may actually be described as upbeat, with fundamentally happy endings. Of
the rest, only a dozen or so are wholly negative. In short, anxieties about
nuclear doom probably run no deeper than any other sort of anxiety treated
in secular eschatology. Moreover, the longer we live with the nuclear sword
over our heads, the stronger seems the thread by which it hangs. The proportion of future war stories in the literature of Last Things has dropped steadily
since the late 1960s.

A convenient illustration of the underlying optimism of many nuclear
fictions is John Wyndham's *The Chrysalids*, first published in 1955 and mar-
keted in the United States under the more obvious title of *Re-Birth*. Wyndham's story has all the now classic ingredients: a nuclear war that wiped out
civilization, scattered communities of farmers living like early nineteenth-
century American pioneers, mutants with radiation-damaged genes roaming

the wilderness, a new religion based on fear and persecution of genetic deformity. But one of the mutations is beneficial: several village children are born with telepathic powers. The child who has the loudest "voice" establishes contact across the world with a rising civilization in New Zealand, where all the people are telepaths. As a New Zealand aircraft rescues some of the fugitive mutant children in the nick of time during a battle between the farmers and the wilderness folk, Wyndham lets his readers know that mankind is on the way up again. A new world is in the making, and a new and higher race will make it.

Less simple-minded than *The Chrysalids,* but no less virile and life-affirming, Robert Merle's *Malevil* shows with stunning veracity how the best values of literary realism can be preserved in a novel that is also fully eschatological. What further enhances *Malevil* is that, unlike most authors of terminal war novels, Merle takes the time to paint a credible picture of the "real" world, the world before the holocaust, in two large opening chapters. Little by little, he carries us next through the terrible moments of the nuclear blast, as experienced by the hero and all his comrades, and finishes by recounting the pains and joys of survivorship in a ruined world without at any point violating the integrity of his characters, whom we have come to know so well. They change, or do not change, exactly as one would expect. The swift reversion to neo-feudal conditions among the few pockets of humanity that remain is plausibly developed, again through great richness of detail. There are also glimpses of the future after the future, a world to come that will probably restore the contradictions of modernity, at who knows what cost. One thing is quite clear: the men and women of Merle's future world will not be traumatized zombies or radiantly transformed saints. They will be simply human, with all the possibilities that "simply human" enfolds.

At the other end of the psychic and literary spectrum from the exuberant realism of *Malevil,* stands the gauntness and featurelessness of *Termush,* a novel in the mode of Kafka and Beckett by the Danish writer Sven Holm. It would be misleading to end our report from Cainsmarsh without a word or two representing the views of those secular eschatologists, like Holm, for whom nuclear war and heroics do not mix. Holm's setting is a hotel for wealthy survivalists, immediately after the holocaust. We learn next to nothing about anyone, not even the narrator. The disaster itself is barely mentioned, although it has been more or less totally destructive. At first only a few dying stragglers come to beg for help. But at the end of the novel, when armed men begin firing on the redoubt, the guests and staff flee in their Noah's ark, a motor yacht.

Where will they go? Do they care? Should even the reader care? The dust of the fallout, which the guests have carefully shielded from their bodies, seems to have penetrated their hearts. Even before the attack forced their departure, one of them had mysteriously left on his own initiative, another had committed suicide. A reconnaissance party sent out by the management had failed to return, for reasons unknown. The only issue that ever engaged the real interest of the guests was the question of how many outsiders could be fed and treated in the hotel without jeopardizing the dearly purchased "rights" of the guests themselves. But although everyone is now safely on board the yacht, no one feels a sense of relief. The weather is hot. The passengers are listless. "Outside the sea is still; there is no darkness and no light."[12]

Termush may not be typical of world's end novels, whether dealing with nuclear war or any other catastrophe. But it reminds us of something important, albeit obvious, that all of them share and that no amount of interpretation can argue away. They all concern the end. They concern a thinkable end of man's world, which he has well within his power to bring down on himself. To measure man only by the standard of the staff and guests of Hotel Termush, by the standard of what J. G. Ballard once called "*Homo hydrogenesis,*"[13] there may even be a sense in which such an end is devoutly to be wished.

In any event, long experience suggests that no country will be deterred from waging total war in the future by literary doomsdays. Before each of the great international conflicts of this century novelists and many others warned that the next war could not be won because of the inconceivable power of modern military technology. When the time for war came, they were all ignored. In all probability, they will be ignored again.

PART FOUR

◆

The War of
The World Views

11

$\blacklozenge$

Paradigms of Doom

THE INVASION OF all disciplines by the genetic obsession, the revolution of *Historismus* that occurred between the mid-eighteenth and mid-nineteenth centuries and at least for a time threatened to turn everyone into a historian, offered no grants of immunity. Thought itself, including the very ideas in which *Historismus* was rooted, belonged to the time-flow as much as any other doings of man. No scholar could stand "outside" the flow and peer omnisciently down into it. In this way, *Historismus* ingeniously provided for its own possible demise, but at the same time invalidated—or, as it were, booby-trapped—the claims to timeless truth of all its future rivals. The whole matter is a logician's nightmare.

At any rate, the heart of the historicist position with regard to thought, whether the thought of an Einstein or the thought of a hod carrier, is that every idea thinkable by every human mind owes much of its shape, color, texture, substance, and affective resonance to the collective mentality of the historical era in which it is thought. In a given age in a given culture, only certain ideas can be thought, and only in certain ways, no matter who does the thinking. For idealists like Hegel the collective mind of an age, the Spirit of the Times, represented a particular stage in the self-development of being, a process ultimately explicable as the working of the will of God in the world. For materialists like Marx the collective mind of an age was the complex of ideas serving concrete human needs and class interests appropriate to a particular stage in the history of the social relations of production. In either case, the collective mind is not a phantom. Difficult as it may be to define, it is something real, which keeps the boldest individual mind on a short and absolutely unbreakable tether.

Over the years this aboriginal historicist premise of a collective mind has taken many twists and turns. Intellectual historians have availed themselves of such variations of the premise as Carl Becker's climate of opinion, Thomas Kuhn's paradigm shift, the *mentalités* of Lucien Febvre and *les annalistes*, and, on the Germanic side, Wilhelm Dilthey's *Weltanschauung*, a word nearly spoiled by Adolf Hitler, who used it freely, but well worth salvaging as I have endeavored to do myself in my book *World Views*.[1] A *Weltanschauung* is, literally, a look at the world, best translated as "world view," a constellation of ideas, beliefs, and ways of knowing and feeling that, taken together, furnish a general understanding of the nature and meaning of reality. Individuals may have their own idiosyncratic world views, differing from one another in every sort of detail, but—if the historicist premise holds good—there are also collective world views. Such collective world views, belonging to particular cultures at particular epochs in their histories, establish the boundaries within which the thought of individuals of that place and time can unfold.

It follows that every product of culture, from a nursery rhyme to a symphony, from a teenager's diary to a treatise on metaphysics, bears the signature of the *Weltanschauung* of its age. Since *Weltanschauungen*, like all phenomena of history, keep changing and calling forth their opposites, more than one collective world view may be at work in a culture at any given time, or at least during periods of transition or "paradigm shift" from one to another. But a single world view will tend to dominate the thought and art of a culture for one or more generations at a time—the length of time depending on the velocity of social change in that culture. Just as a given style of dress identifies an age beyond possibility of error, so each age has its distinctive world view.

For students of intellectual history, it further follows, the story of the world's end holds a place of special interest. Terminal visions, like all artifacts, argue the premises of a given *Weltanschauung*. At the same time, they supply us with a glimpse of the *Weltanschauung* in what may be its darkest or its brightest aspect: when those whose minds it shapes imagine the end of the reality that it interprets, or look forward to an eschatological moment in which that reality may be gloriously and wholly transformed. Can there be a more strenuous test of what the world view means than occurs in the contemplation of the end of the world being viewed? At the very least, it will be worth our time in the next three chapters to investigate terminal fictions from the perspectives offered by a study of world views. Terminal visions are not just stories about the end of the world, or the end of the self. They are also stories about the nature and meaning of reality as interpreted by world views. They are propaganda for a certain understanding of life, in which the imaginary end serves to sharpen the focus and heighten the importance of certain structures of value. They are games of chance, so to speak, in which the players risk all their chips on a single hand. But games just the same.

Before defining the world views relevant to the terminal visions of the nineteenth and twentieth centuries, a few words of caution are imperative. It should go without saying, but probably does not, that although world views are "real," they are only real in the way that a law of nature or a volume of history is real. No matter how exhaustively verified the law or how scrupulously accurate the volume, both remain nothing more than images of a material reality infinitely more complex than any image can possibly be. Like the realistic painting of a pipe by Magritte—the canvas on which the artist himself wrote the words, *"Ceci n'est pas une pipe"*—they are just paintings. A world view is a heuristic device, an ideal type. It drastically simplifies the reality to which it points, slashing and trimming almost at will to make some aspect of the reality clearer and more comprehensible to the human mind. It also tends to ignore the many subtle changes in emphasis that occur as the reality behind the concept evolves through time, not to mention vital national and regional differences.

Another point to stress is that no world view has ever existed—even assuming it could have existed—in a chemically pure form in any individual human mind. In the simplest minds, residues of earlier world views linger on, thanks to exposure to works of art or craft or thought from earlier periods. In the most daring intellects, intimations of future world views are often detectable, or defiant regressions to a previous world view, seldom as free from contemporary influences, however, as the thinker himself may suppose. In one and the same work, a thinker or an artist may combine ingredients from two or three world views. Or he may switch allegiances in mid-career, as the Charles Dickens of *A Christmas Carol* became the Dickens of *Hard Times*, or the Igor Stravinsky of *L'oiseau de feu* became the Stravinsky of *Apollon Musagète*.

One last caveat must be issued. No one should confuse a world view with an ideology or any specific social or political doctrine, left, right, or center. Although world views nourish ideologies as generously as they nourish any other products of culture, the same broad assumptions can help lead one thinker to one system of political belief and another thinker to its exact opposite. The Christian world view of the Middle Ages, for example, was exploited equally to argue the rights of popes or emperors, kings or fractious nobles, rich men or poor, just as today it is invoked both to defend and to attack the fascisms of Latin America, or British rule in Northern Ireland.

We need concern ourselves in the pages that follow with only three

world views, which have arisen since the disaggregation of the Enlightenment near the close of the eighteenth century. A fourth, the world view of
the Enlightenment itself, inspired the production of few terminal visions—
perhaps none. The rationalism of the Enlightenment held that nature is a
logico-mathematical system which man, by virtue of his powers of sensation
and reason, can know without the aid of external authority. By knowing it,
he can also learn how to rationalize the human order, bringing it into harmony with the machinery of nature. Although it is false to assert, as some
have done, that the philosophers of the Enlightenment took no account of
historical development, their fondness for steady-state models of reality borrowed from mathematics and mechanics did militate against their construction of grand-scale theories of history, natural or human; and their passion
for reason clashed fundamentally with ideas of change through catastrophe,
even benevolent catastrophe. The closest any of them could get to a theory
of catastrophe, perhaps, was in the doctrine of the balance of nature expounded by Sade and Malthus, a balance that required small disasters to
prevent worse ones, although, as we have seen, this did leave the door open
for a fundamental reconception of the faith of the Enlightenment in the
inherent goodness of the natural order.

But the great rival and ultimately the successor of rationalism in the war
of the world views, the romantic *Weltanschauung*, proceeded along quite a
different path. All the terminal visons of the early nineteenth century surveyed in Chapter Two are steeped in romanticism. Elsewhere, I have defined
it as "the world view which holds that reality .·. . is fundamentally mindlike,
in process of organic development through time, and best reached by direct
intuitive perception rather than by measurement and analysis."[2] The romantic outlook is characterized by a profound anthropomorphism. It projects
human will and consciousness and feeling into the world order, as does, in a
much simpler way, the animism and totemism of primitive religion. The
romantics understandably took a renewed interest in varieties of mystical
religious experience ridiculed by the philosophers of the Enlightenment.
They were not all Christians or even theists, but they shared many values
with traditional faith, and Christian worship and piety benefited dramatically
from the romantic rebellion. Historical studies, too, benefited from the nostalgia of the romantics for the past. Romantics of every political persuasion
drew much of their inspiration from the pictures of an idealized distant era,
often an idealized Middle Ages, when hearts were warmer and minds purer.

But by the middle of the nineteenth century, and in some countries
sooner, another world view had crystallized which took the romantics to task
just as fiercely as the romantics had fought the *philosophes*. This new arrival
was positivism, the world view of Auguste Comte and John Stuart Mill, of

Charles Darwin and Herbert Spencer, of Karl Marx and Friedrich Engels, of realism and naturalism in literature and art, the world view that rehabilitated the scientific method of Galileo and Newton and looked to the models provided by natural science for the solving of all human problems. For the positivist

> the real, or at least the knowable, consisted of the data of sensory experience as verified, analyzed, and organized by the empirical sciences. . . . Positivism abolished metaphysics and theology or merged them with science; it denied or ignored the existence of supersensory reality, arguing that the world was not mindlike but on the contrary that mind was worldlike.[3]

Positivism was clearly the dominant world view of the Western world as a whole from about 1840 to about 1890. In the United States, it arrived much later and did not really begin to wane until after 1920. For students of speculative fiction, positivism has a unique importance, because it is also the world view of the "hard core" of the field, the world view of science fiction, with stress on the word "science." As a rule the term "speculative fiction" is preferable to "science fiction" because so much of what passes for science fiction has nothing to do with the methods and outlook and achievements of the natural sciences, and may even be violently anti-scientific. A good analogy is with the tortured phrase "classical music," the greater part of which is anything but classical. Still, there is an authentic fiction of science, true to the world view of modern science, which is to say, true to positivism. It originated in the fertile intellect and imagination of Jules Verne, flowered in the even greater genius of H. G. Wells, and continues on to the present day in the spiritual wake of two great editors, Hugo Gernsback and John W. Campbell, Jr., and writers of the caliber of Robert Heinlein, Isaac Asimov, and Arthur C. Clarke.

Already I may seem to be trapped in a flagrant inconsistency. How can there be science fiction, in its most rigorous sense, in the twentieth century—after the "waning" of positivism? The question can be answered in two ways, of roughly equal importance. First, the "dominance" of a world view in modern times, when social change is unprecedentedly rapid and indeed too rapid for culture to keep pace, is always much less than a monopoly. The decline of positivism has not meant its extinction. By the same token, romanticism lost ground among the avant-garde after the middle of the nineteenth century, but many writers, artists, and ordinary people in the second half of the century continued to embrace the syndrome of values associated with the romantic world view. Some still embrace it today, in whole or in part.

A second consideration is geographical. Although positivism has worn badly in major portions of the Western world, such as France and Germany, it has retained a relatively larger share of influence in the English-speaking countries. Britain and even more so America have not felt the full fury of world war, have not known totalitarian rule, have not submitted in less than a century to the traumas of social, economic, and political change from late feudalism to high capitalism experienced by most of the societies of Continental Europe. Britain effected the transition to capitalism earlier and more gradually, and feudalism—the real feudalism of Europe—had never existed in North America at all. As a result the pressures that compelled a premature end to the ascendancy of positivism on the Continent were at least partly avoided in the Anglo-Saxon countries. Positivist faith in the progress of man through science and technology continued to flourish with relatively little challenge well into the twentieth century. A tradition in speculative fiction of confident modernism and respect for dispassionate objectivity as a value in art as well as thought persisted despite the scorn of a growing Europeanized avant-garde.

But on the European mainland, change of a radical sort was noticeable in the climate of opinion as early as the 1880s, a change that began to touch Britain not long afterwards, and crossed the Atlantic in force by at least the 1920s. Eventually it shook speculative fiction in the Anglo-Saxon countries as well. In my book *World Views*, I call the new *Weltanschauung* "irrationalism," in full awareness of the hazards of choosing a term with so many pejorative connotations. But every term that intellectual historians have used to characterize this new world view, from "anti-intellectualism" and "anti-positivism" to "neo-romanticism," fails to give it any sort of real focus or substance.[4] Worse still, none of these terms has caught hold, so that they lack even the convenience of being generally understood and accepted.

Irrationalism is neo-romantic in many ways, to be sure, just as positivism revived the outlook of the eighteenth-century Enlightenment. But there are also significant differences between the two. The thought-world of such seminal irrationalists as Friedrich Nietzsche, Sigmund Freud, Herman Hesse, and Jean-Paul Sartre is not Goethe's or Wordsworth's or Chateaubriand's. At its center irrationalism holds "that man and the world . . . are not fundamentally governed by reason."[5] The world is not the coherent, reasonable, knowable, humanly meaningful order disclosed either by cold science or warm poetry, and man is neither machine nor angel. Beyond these negations, irrationalists agree on very little. Many make a faith of negation itself, others leap to a wide variety of structures of belief, from a desperate Christianity to mysteries of blood, spirit, earth, *Volk*, the life-force, the ground of being, or the collective unconscious. Some, like Freud, even make a virtue of reason. But the irrationalist leap is just that: a leap, even a leap in the dark. It may give to this or that adherent of the irrationalist world view the appearance of being a romantic, or a positivist, or a child of the Enlightenment, or a pious Christian of the Middle Ages, and sometimes the appearance has substance as well, but the problem with irrationalist man is that he no longer, in his bones, believes in the intrinsic correspondence of the external world and the world of ratiocination or consciousness. The gap between the two, requiring so many death-defying leaps, is uncomfortably wide and fearsomely deep.

But irrationalism shows signs of thinning out in recent decades. In its old strongholds, the French and German worlds, it has had little new to say for a long time. It has fared better of late in Britain and America, and especially America, where it is still almost a novelty. It also thrives in the Russian cultural underground, giving battle to a decadent official Marxism left over from the late nineteenth century. Nonetheless, I think the days of irrationalism as the preferred world view of the intellectual and artistic elites of Western civilization are drawing to a close.

In speculative fiction, and above all in the literature of Last Things, the contest of world views is everywhere in evidence, paralleling the larger struggles in thought and art generally. Positivism, as just noted, dominated much of the "golden age" of science fiction, and has preserved a great deal of its influence among writers, editors, and readers alike. Positivist terminal visions typically blame the world's end on the abuse of science and technology by irrational forces in society, on fanatical anti-positivist messiah-figures, on human error that can be rectified "next time," or on the blind workings of nature, which it is the glory of man to oppose and subdue, if he can.

Romantic and irrationalist terminal visions may blame the world's end on science and technology, viewed as evils in themselves. Or they may attack positivism directly. By its opponents positivism is routinely travestied as a mode of consciousness that reduces nature and man to objects fit only for manipulation by so-called experts, manipulation that is ultimately self-destructive. Or the end may be blamed on the sheer unreason, the sheer absurdity of the creaturely world. Romantic terminal visions often see the endtime as an opportunity to return to a bucolic past. Irrationalists may prefer something more exotic. At any rate, there is agreement that the modern world—the brave new world of science, mechanism, technocracy, industry, Taylorism, and what comfortable philistines smugly call "civilization"—will not do, and cannot fall apart soon enough. On the whole, and not surprisingly, the anti-positivist forces wield their greatest influence in speculative fiction among writers of the literary mainstream or of the "New Wave" of the 1960s, which hoped to bring ghettoized science fiction into the mainstream.

Anti-positivism has also long attracted writers of "soft science fiction," Peter Nicholls's catchall phrase for speculative fiction that stresses "human feelings" rather than future science.[6]

Thus are the lines of battle drawn. In the three chapters following, we shall have a look at a few choice examples of how each world view has inspired fictions of the world's end. In many of these works, the end of the world is only grist, albeit spectacular grist, for the mills of propaganda in a war of ideas as hard-fought as any war in modern history.

12

◆

Lest Ye Die

ALTHOUGH IDEAS OF the endtime owe much to the great myths of the endtime in antiquity, the myths of the beginning-time appear just as often—perhaps more often—in imaginative literature. The stories of Adam and Noah in Genesis reach deeply into the psychic underworld. They speak to the helplessness of childhood, the awful power of parents, and the pain of shame and guilt.

To some degree, romanticism was the outcome of a spasm of collective shame and guilt and fear that shook European culture during the late eighteenth and early nineteenth centuries. It originated among the peoples of the German-speaking world, searching for an identity of their own in the face of the challenge of the scientific rationalism and high sophistication and wealth and power of the West. As the West, which at this point means France and Great Britain, began to question its own values, especially in the aftermath of the French and Industrial revolutions and the jolts administered to the whole European state system by the exploits of Napoleon, romanticism also found a following in the innermost circles of the rationalist thought-world. The transition is well marked in such households as William Godwin's, where the rationalism of the father yielded to the romanticism of the daughter and son-in-law, Mary and Percy Shelley. The process was anything but clear or precise or straightforward; yet it unfolded by a remorseless logic of its own that nothing could obstruct. In the end, the climate of opinion in Europe had changed almost beyond recognition. It would never be the same again.

Some of the responsibility for the change must be borne by the brief revival of Christian faith that accompanied the romantic rebellion. Not all romantics were Christians, but the two world views stimulated one another profoundly. One of the results was a reawakening of what may be called the Edenic sensibility, a nostalgia for lost innocence, a recovery of the idea of sin, and dark suspicions of the place of science, learning, and industry and technology in the human scheme of things. The early chapters of Genesis teem with warnings against civilization: the taboo set on the fruit of the tree of knowledge, the corruptions of early human society that provoked the Deluge, the ill-fated building of the city with its proud Tower designed to reach all the way to Heaven. Many romantics struggled against the anti-intellectualism of the Biblical tradition, but they found it fearfully tempting, as it had not been for the philosophers of the Enlightenment.

In the literature of Last Things, the Edenism of the romantics is distilled, without enthusiasm but also without distortion or ambiguity, in an English novel of the 1920s, Cicely Hamilton's *Lest Ye Die*. Her text is Genesis 3:3, Eve's speech to the serpent, quoting God's commandment not to touch the forbidden fruit "lest ye die." In her Foreword, Hamilton reports that the "inward truth of the Eden legend" struck her one evening on a hill over Abbeville in the spring of 1918, as she watched the inhabitants of the town streaming out into the countryside to escape an expected German air raid. "In our wars," she adds, "the wars of the air and the laboratory," there is no safety for anyone. The only hope for man, if one may call it hope, is to heed "the prohibition laid upon Adam that he, the father of a combative race, should not eat of the fruit of the Tree of Knowledge."[1]

Lest Ye Die follows a familiar story line of the period: a world war is fought in the near future with fire and gas bombs dropped by aircraft, the cities are destroyed, and whole populations quickly revert to barbarism. A new religion arises, preached by a wild-eyed fanatic who "carried his gospel through a land left desolate, proclaiming his creed of salvation through ignorance and crying woe on the yet unrepentant sinners who should seek to preserve the deadly knowledge that had brought God's judgment on the world!"[2] Any scientist unlucky enough to have survived is caught and sacrificed to propitiate an angry Jehovah. When our hero, a young Whitehall bureaucrat, is forced to settle down with a tribe, he must prove that he knows nothing of science and technology despite his university education, and swear an oath against all "devil's knowledge." For some time, he nurses the hope that civilization will soon be restored. Eventually he comes to accept his fate. Centuries later, he reflects, man will eat the forbidden fruit again, but every time that he does, he will have to pay the same terrible price.

Although Hamilton adopts the Edenic view with a certain wistful fatalism—in itself a romantic gesture—her analysis of the evils of civilization, and her preference, when the chips are down, for rustic ignorance, are typical of how the romantic world view works in eschatological fiction. Her story is

propaganda: for simplicity, on the one hand, and against science and industrial civilization, no matter how devilishly attractive, on the other.

In the romantic era proper, from the 1790s to the 1840s, tales like
Hamilton's that restore man to the safety of Arcadia after a world-ending
catastrophe were few. But all the early nineteenth-century fictions discussed
in previous chapters bear the hallmarks of romantic consciousness in one form
or another. Shelley's *The Last Man,* for example, contrasts the pride and self-
confidence of civilization before the catastrophe with its helplessness in face
of the staggering power of nature. Science can do nothing. One of its spokesmen, the astronomer Merrival, loses his mind after the plague obliterates his
family. The last pages of the novel, as we have seen, furnish a moving study
in psychological estrangement and romantic melancholy, as one by one the
hero's loved ones perish. Among the terminal stories of Poe, "The Conversation of Eiros and Charmion" is a sardonic commentary on the failure of
science to foresee the apocalyptic force of a comet approaching the earth,
and "The Colloquy of Monos and Una" agrees with Genesis that "knowledge
was not meet for man in the infant condition of his soul," comparing industrialism to "some loathesome disease."[3]

The prototype of the romantic tale of the post-holocaust Eden is a short
piece by Poe's countryman and contemporary, Nathaniel Hawthorne. That
direst of hybrids, a romantic Puritan, Hawthorne has long been a favorite
subject of critics of "immanent" apocalypticism in American fiction, but in
his story "The New Adam and Eve," he also produced a literal apocalypse
that gives the wisdom of Genesis a fresh hearing. The premise is a sudden
end of all human life, decreed by God. A second creation of man ensues,
leaving the earth itself untouched, but the second holy couple is saved from
disaster when Eve persuades her spouse to abandon his blundering investiga-
tions in the most dangerous spot in the world: the great library of Harvard
University, whose books contain "the fatal apple of another Tree of Knowledge."[4] Whatever the future may hold in store, the new humanity has at least
resisted the damnable curiosity responsible for all the miseries of the first
world-cycle. Life will be simpler, and sweeter.

The integral romanticism of the age of Shelley and Poe and Hawthorne
passed, but the world view of romanticism underwent periodic revivals and
reaffirmations in the generations that followed. Neo-romantic values per-
vaded many of the finest terminal fictions of the late nineteenth and early
twentieth centuries. What deserves to be called the first major scenario of a
post-holocaust New Eden, William Morris's *News from Nowhere,* draws heavily on romantic fascination with the splendors of a half-mythical medieval
Europe. Even before Morris, Richard Jefferies had imagined a far rougher sort
of neo-medieval society in *After London;* but it suited his purposes no less

well, since what he had in mind was to provide a stage on which his autobiographical protagonist, the physically weak but intelligent Felix Aquila, could
prove his valor and win the fair heroine Aurora.[5]

Romanticism in a somewhat different guise, an attack on H. G. Wells's
vision of a worldwide technocratic utopia, dominates E. M. Forster's "The
Machine Stops," first published in 1909. Here, the post-holocaust Eden is
barely glimpsed; Forster's attention centers on the subterranean civilization
of the future, where a dehumanizing technology has robbed man of his kinship with nature. After the civilization self-destructs through sheer decadence
and incompetence, the only survivors are its "criminals," misfits exiled to the
surface who have managed to carve out a rude existence for themselves under
a natural sun, breathing unfiltered air and living natural lives. In their new
world, the folly of dependence on machine culture will never be repeated.
Man has learned his lesson once and for all.

The models furnished by Jefferies, Morris, and Forster live on in most of
the later fiction of speculative writers who adhere to the romantic tradition.
Once again, the post-holocaust Eden, whether described in detail or merely
foreshadowed, is not necessarily a utopia, but it is always a simpler, cleaner
place than the world of pre-holocaust modernity. Quite often, as in Forster's
influential tale, it is also a polemical retort to the vision of post-holocaust
civilization imagined by positivists, turning positivist values upside down.
For the neo-romantic, as for the positivist, civilization has been shattered by
one or more disasters, but the less sophisticated society that grows up among
the survivors is in all respects or in certain crucial ones superior. The disaster
itself is more frequently man-made, brought on or facilitated by modern
science and technology. If there are villains in the piece, they are men and
women trying to rebuild or clinging to remnants of the bad old civilization of
pre-holocaust days.

During the interwar period, a rich profusion of such stories appeared in
British fiction. The most purely Edenic are the first two volumes of C. S.
Lewis's "Ransom" trilogy, in which Lewis imagines glorious societies on Mars
and Venus, respectively. The only disasters involved are those plotted by the
arch-positivist earthling, Professor Weston (= Western Man), who fails in
both attempts, and is finally killed on Venus by his gallant Christian oppo-
nent, Elwin Ransom (= Christ, the Redeemer). But by our own working
definitions, neither novel is eschatological. Notable visions of post-holocaust
romantic Edens that do qualify as overtly eschatological appear in John Collier's *Tom's A-Cold*, Alun Llewellyn's *The Strange Invaders*, Frank Baker's *The
Birds*, Alfred Noyes's *The Last Man*, William Lamb's *The World Ends*, Dorothy
Stevenson's *The Empty World*, and many more, including the novel by Cicely
Hamilton discussed above, and two works by J. Leslie Mitchell and Stephen
Southwold that also make ideal subjects for closer study.

The books that Mitchell wrote under his own name are largely forgotten, but as "Lewis Grassic Gibbon" he published *Sunset Song* and other minor classics of Scottish fiction that still attract readers and a measure of critical respect. Two of his contributions to speculative literature also deserve attention. They have much the same message, the first a romance of prehistoric times entitled *Three Go Back,* and the other—almost a sequel—entitled *Gay Hunter,* in which the female protagonist travels into the far future and finds a post-holocaust Eden in the Chiltern Hills of Buckinghamshire. What she does find is, in fact, another prehistoric society, a happy Arcadian people living in a strangely warm England that is almost entirely deserted. The Chiltern folk know of only one tribe besides their own, the "Northern Folk," whose hunting grounds may lie in Scotland. When the tribesman who first discovered Gay escorts her to the dwelling place of his people, she learns with the help of the blind "Old Singer of the Folk" how civilization came to an end thousands of years ago. This latter-day Homer speaks archaic English, the language of the "Voices" heard in recordings from the old days that are stored in the ruins of a hydroelectric complex which the folk have made their home. The "song" of the Voices is mad, the Old Singer warns Gay. When she hears it, she is driven nearly mad herself.

The recordings were made for posterity in the Last Days. As Gay listens, they tell the whole dreary story of how mankind "rose" to tremendous heights in her own future. Science sent ships to the planets, created new life in test tubes, altered the seasons, and solved the labor problem by breeding a race of "sub-men" to act as the helots of the ruling class. But this proud Babel of the future was finally overthrown: by uprisings of the brutalized sub-men, by warfare between rival states, and by postwar plagues that dispatched most of the few survivors. What happened next, Gay can surmise from her own recent experiences. "Human life reached back to ancient days," she reflects, "to the way of the Cro-Magnard hunter twenty thousand years before Christ, and men found happiness and delight again, and ecstasy, simple and clean."[6]

But the Eden of neo-Paleolithic humanity is threatened with a new disaster. Two villains have accompanied Gay on her time-trip, members of the "Fascist Defence Corps," who do not share her innocent enthusiasm for the Old Stone Age. Persuading a number of foolish tribesmen to follow, they make their way to what is left of London in hopes of finding weapons and other useful impedimenta of civilization. They propose to bring civilization back, in all its Satanic splendor. Although London is a forbidden place, taboo to the tribe, the renegade savages are kept in line with the help of an occasional flogging and the fascists go about their sinister business.

They find the capital dominated, nowadays, by the loftiest architectural achievement of all history, a phallus-shaped tower that reaches the clouds, a full mile in height. Genesis 11:1–9 is the obvious reference. Sewer-rats grown to the size of lions prowl the empty streets, but the worst enemy of the conspirators is plucky Gay, who leads a band of loyal hunters to stop them before it is too late. Just as Gay and her party reach the outskirts, a mysterious explosion destroys the city and everything in it. The two villains may have quarreled, the wrong buttons may have been pushed in anger or in ignorance; no one will ever know. But mankind is once again safe. "The fevers of religion and science and civilisation had passed away," the heroine thinks to herself, "and out again, in the wastes of Time, spear in hand, [man] stumbled on a quest undying, with rain in his face and the wail of peewits to companion that endless trek."[7]

In a dedicatory note, Mitchell reports that his book "has no serious intent whatever. . . . It is neither prophecy nor propaganda. It is written for the glory of sun and wind and rain, dreams by smoking camp-fires, and the glimpsed immortality of men."[8] But in such a context, the glory and the dreams are patent metaphors for Edenic romanticism. Like all the fictions examined in this chapter and in the two that follow, *Gay Hunter* is propaganda from start to finish.

Another neglected romantic of the interwar period is Stephen South-wold, who wrote his speculative fiction under the pen names of "Miles" and "Neil Bell." He produced three eschatological novels in the early 1930s, a story of terminal warfare *(The Gas War of 1940)*, a dystopian history of the future *(The Seventh Bowl)*, and the engaging tale of an experiment in atomic physics that destroys the world *(The Lord of Life)*. The future war novel is much like others of the period, but *The Seventh Bowl*—in which the Gas War of 1940 duly appears, as only the first in a series of worldwide holocausts—is a vigorous satirical attack on the utopian thought of Wells and Shaw. It covers virtually all the ground traversed two years later by Aldous Huxley in *Brave New World*. Its secular Antichrist, the world dictator Burfleet, guides post-holocaust humanity through eugenics, state socialism, and environmental engineering into genocide and madness. Earth has become a well-manicured "garden" and men are like "gods," but life has lost its salt. The final accident that sends the earth crashing into the sun comes almost as a blessing.

In *The Lord of Life*, Southwold resumes his attack on positivism in a gentler mood. An eccentric scientist approaches the Prime Minister of Great Britain with the secret of atomic energy, which he offers the nation in exchange for an earldom, half a million pounds, and the legitimization of his seventeen children and four wives. When his offer is spurned, he conducts an experiment to show all the world that he is no charlatan. But the demonstration gets completely out of hand. His simultaneous annihilation of the atoms of ten different elements, from hydrogen to uranium, liberates so much force that the earth is literally stopped in its tracks. Most of its air and water and soil, and nearly all its flora and fauna, are whisked into outer space. The planet starts moving again a few seconds later, but the only human survivors are twenty dignitaries and crewmen trapped in a new submarine on its gala maiden voyage, and a single aviatrix testing an experimental high-altitude aircraft.

From these improbable materials, Southwold weaves an oddly convincing story of the slow revival of life. The dignitaries and naval officers in charge of things try to perpetuate the old society, but their ways lead only to injustice, bloodshed, and failure—as in the world already destroyed. In the end humanity carries on with just one man and woman and their children, who organize their own post-holocaust utopia on a beautiful island off the western coast of Asia Minor. They will need no church, no hierarchy, no civilization. The cockney hero, the butcher's son Sid Larkins, looks forward to a life of perfect contentment with his wife and his three little girls.

> Cripes! What a great life! Jam on both sides. This life of happiness that went on and on. His three babes and Elly. This was life and the key of the puzzle. There wasn't a puzzle at all, come to that. God? What about Him? What did it matter, anyway? There was or there wasn't. It was all the same. Elly and him and the three nippers. Gord! How great it was! All those books he'd read. What bunk they were. Dust and old bones. They didn't matter at all. What did matter was a wife and love and kids. His kids and his own woman.[9]

All that is required to round out the happy family is an equal number of little boys, whom Sid expropriates one evening from the declining rival settlement, which has no girls. He had been the nursemaid of the boys when he lived there himself, and they love him. Sid's dream of domestic bliss is complete. Under his lordship, the human race will go on, barefoot and pregnant, never missing the "dust and old bones" of civilization. Like *Gay Hunter*, Southwold's novel is an unblushing polemic for all the stock values of romanticism, set in the sharpest possible contrast with all the stock evils of modern science and technology and "progress."

Readers of Ray Bradbury's *The Martian Chronicles* will remember a comparable felicity in the last story, "The Million-Year Picnic." Atomic war has finished off the earth, and two families, one with sons, one with daughters, take possession of a deserted Martian town where they will replenish mankind. But the paterfamilias who is the author's spokesman has no intention of making the mistakes of old earth. He blows up the family rocket to eliminate any possibility of returning. Into the evening campfire he feeds a stack of papers symbolizing civilization. "I'm burning a way of life," he tells his boys, a life that had never "settled down to doing anything very good. Science ran too far ahead of us too quickly, and the people got lost in a mechanical wilderness." The men and women of Mars will make a fresh start, striking out "on a new line."[10]

Bradbury is representative of what might be termed the first "new wave" in postwar speculative fiction, one of the first writers to make a clearly romantic and clearly anti-positivist approach palatable to hard-bitten readers of science fiction as well as to readers of mainstream literature. That his work also happens to be sentimental and even a little meretricious is no doubt unfortunate, but what matters more is its appeal. It meets needs that writers of other persuasions cannot satisfy.

The Martian Chronicles is, in fact, a story about the evils of modern Western civilization from beginning to end. Most of it hinges on the contrast between the thousands of earthmen who preceded the families of "The Million-Year Picnic" and the culture of the now extinct native Martians. The first pioneers all returned to earth when war broke out, but during the few years of the great Martian land rush, they had threatened to turn the planet into a junk world, as far removed as possible from the serene wisdom and autumnal beauty of old Martian culture. Bradbury's old Mars was a utopia. The brown-skinned, golden-eyed natives had been declining in numbers long before a disease brought from earth wiped them out completely, but, like the American Indian (as portrayed by romantic anthropologists), their way of life was holistic, a seamless unity of art, religion, and science, in which nothing was allowed to fall out of balance, and nature was treated with reverence.

Bradbury's most succinct comment on the contrast between modernity and the good old days appears in another work, his short story "The Highway." The role of the Martians is played here by a Mexican peasant, Hernando, who watches a stream of cars heading north, gringo tourists all hurrying home. It must be something important, he tells his wife. The driver of the last car stops to ask for water for his boiling radiator. Hernando hospitably obliges, and learns from the man that "it's come, the atom war, the end of the world!" The car drives away. Picking up his plow, Hernando smells the sweetness of the jungle in the valley below his little farm. The jungle is green, the sky is warm and clean. He tells his wife that nothing has happened, and returns to work. " 'What do they mean, "the world"?' he said."[11] Long after "the world" has ended, aboriginal Mexico—and Mars—will live on, following the ways of the heart and the soil.

Very little in the romantic literature of Last Things published during the last thirty-odd years adds anything of note to the picture of the post-holocaust Eden already fully developed in works such as Gay Hunter, The Lord of Life, The Martian Chronicles, and all of their many predecessors. Clifford Simak's City, based on stories that began appearing even before Bradbury's, carries the same ideological freight, but without requiring a holocaust. Of later works that do require a holocaust or a world's end of some kind, all that usually distinguishes one from another is how far back in anthropological time each writer goes to find his model for Eden. In Brian Aldiss's *Hothouse*, it is the prehistoric rain forest, complicated by the efforts of two highly evolved beings with supernormal brains—a morel and a dolphin—to disturb the natural equilibrium of the endtime with grandiose schemes of world conquest. Both creatures are clever metaphors for modern Western civilization in all its self-congratulating guile and greed and folly. Stone Age models are also chosen by Piers Anthony in the three novels of *Battle Circle* and Arnold Federbush in *Ice!* For René Barjavel in *Ravage* and Doreen Wallace in *Forty Years On*, the New Eden is a second Middle Ages, and for Walter M. Miller, Jr., in *A Canticle for Leibowitz*, it is a neo-medieval institution, "the Albertian Order of Leibowitz." Barjavel, one should add, is also the author of two extraordinary anti-positivist dystopias that end with doomsdays, *Le Diable l'emporte* and *La nuit des temps*.

For obvious reasons most American writers choose settings for the post-holocaust Eden drawn from American history. A vaguely or explicitly Amerindian Eden crops up from time to time, as in Kate Wilhelm's *Where Late the Sweet Birds Sang* and *Juniper Time*—or, for that matter, in *The Martian Chronicles*. Steve Wilson, although English himself, makes a post-holocaust America the locale for his epic *The Lost Traveller*, pitting a romanticized Amerindian society against an evil neo-positivist superstate emerging on the Eastern seaboard. The Indians are reinforced by a convert, the hero of the novel, a Hell's Angel from California. Two counter-cultures, in short, combine to fight the Establishment. Another source is pre-industrial Yankee America, the "age of homespun" reconstructed with such success by Edgar Pangborn in various novels beginning with *Davy*.

The latest major exploit in romantic apocalypticism by an American writer, Russell Hoban's *Riddley Walker*, may also turn out to be the best eschatological novel of the 1980s. Hoban, a Pennsylvanian who has lived in London since 1969, hinges his story on the familiar contrast between lost innocence and the diabolism of modern civilization. His post-holocaust society, the English county of Kent in the third millennium after "Bad Time," is in most respects anything but utopian. The barbarians of this second Iron Age speak a corrupt Cockney dialect, and eke out lives of darkest superstition, cruelty, and petty tyranny. Worse still, they are making "progress" again. The vice known in neo-Kentish as "counting clevverness"—mathematics, and the arts and sciences of civilization in general—has re-entered their world. As it destroyed their ancestors, so it threatens to destroy them. Already, gunpowder has been reinvented. Rulers are emerging who will use the power it gives them to try to learn "the numbers of the 1 Big 1," the equations of nuclear weaponry. That ubiquitous figure of neo-Kentish folk legend, "Mr Clevver," with his horns, beard, red suit, and love of mathematics, the same Mr Clevver who inspired the building of the 1 Big 1 in the twentieth century, is about to score another triumph.

Or is he? Hoban holds out the faint hope that mankind will be spared the second time around. Legend preserves not only a garbled version of world history, but an enchanted picture of prehistory, the time "way back befor peopl got clevver [when] they had the 1st knowing. They los it when they got the clevverness." In those glorious days, "befor the iron ben and fire ben only littl," men put themselves right. Their knowing was not "in their heads" but an intuitive grasp of the way of things, acquired from their dogs as they huddled around a campfire at night. With the first knowing, men "dint have no mor fear in the nite they put ther self right day and nite that wer the good time."[12]

In new Kent, the first knowing has found a latter-day champion in the protagonist of the novel, young Riddley Walker. After almost succumbing to the wiles of Mr Clevver, Riddley renounces worldliness absolutely. As an itinerant puppeteer with a mystical Punch and Judy show, he embarks on a career of teaching his fellow men how to achieve oneness with nature. "Its the not sturgling for Power," he concludes, "thats where the Power is. Its in jus letting your self be where it is. Its tuning in to the worl its leaving your self behynt . . ."[13]

Whether Riddley's traveling show will help turn the tables on Mr Clevver, rescue the new Kentishmen from their delusions of pyrotechnic grandeur, and restore them to archaic rightness, Hoban does not reveal. The novel ends with a meditation by its hero on modern man's seemingly insatiable hunger for self-destruction. Riddley is resolved to stick to his sacred mission, come what may. But he knows the strength of his opponents only too well. From the standpoint of technique, *Riddley Walker* is one of the most original and masterful products of the contemporary literary imagination. Yet there is nothing original about its message. It adheres closely to the romantic formula of the antithesis between an ancient Eden of blessed ignorance and a doomed modernity lusting for science and power.

All in all, the persistence of romanticism in speculative fiction is impressive, even more so if one looks at the field as a whole, and not just at stories of the world's end. The continuing demand for "sword and sorcery" fiction, for example, which is little more than Scott and Tennyson and Wagner brought up to date and down to middlebrow tastes, speaks for itself. Gothic romance and horror have never been more popular. The quality of neo-romantic literature, in all fields, exhibits a slow and probably irreversible decline, but the enthusiasm of a generous segment of the reading public has not flagged.

But we cannot leave romantic and neo-romantic eschatology without at least a brief excursus on a further class of terminal visions in which writers fundamentally loyal to the Christian tradition have managed to interweave romantic and Christian values, producing work that conveys an almost mythological force. On the one hand, such work is far from secular in the strictest sense; on the other, it betrays the influence of secularism at every turn, and by the very nature of speculative fiction projects a future at odds in all sorts of ways with the *kirkliche Dogmatik* of official Christendom. To speak very generally, its ideational recipe is two parts romanticism, one part Christian doctrine.

The earliest example of a blending of romanticism and Christian faith in the literature of Last Things is the first of all stories of the world's end, Grainville's *Le dernier homme*. As we have seen in Chapter Two, Grainville concocts a narrative in which God hastens the end by sending Adam back to earth to persuade the Last Man not to sire children. When Omégare finally bends to the divine wish, the story—and the world—come to a swift conclusion. The dead leave their tombs, the sun and the stars disappear, the genie personifying nature is executed by his ancient rival Death, and eternity dawns. But Grainville finds it necessary to draw a veil over the final events, including the Judgment, a precedent honored by many of his pious successors, who thereby save themselves from getting into the hottest sort of theological hot water.

Among these successors was the philosopher Vladimir Solovyov, one of the high priests of the reaction against Western positivism in Russian thought in the late nineteenth century. In the year of his death, 1900, Solovyov published a novel of ideas, *Three Conversations on War, Progress, and the End of World History*, which includes a "short tale of the Antichrist." As in several later Christian fictions portraying the Antichrist, the enemy appears in the guise of a man of peace, reason, and civilization, a liberal humanist uniting in his person all the nefarious shams and self-deceptions of modernity. Solovyov imagines his arrival in the twenty-first century, when the European nations have joined together and all is apparently sweetness and light. The Antichrist is elected President of the United States of Europe after the success of his book, "The Open Road to Universal Peace and Well-Being." Later, he becomes emperor of a world state, with his court in Rome, and finally in Jerusalem. His chief lieutenant, Apollonius, is a brilliant scientist and progressive churchman.

But all this worldly tinsel is only a wile of Satan to seduce man from faith in God by tempting him with self-love. The new Emperor persecutes his enemies, Armageddon breaks out in Palestine, and the Antichrist, together with Apollonius and all his troops, are swallowed up by a crater of fire as Christ returns in glory to earth. As Czeslaw Milosz points out, Solovyov adheres to the nuclear Christian belief in "the tragic quality of human existence. Man wants to be good, but he is not good; he wants to be happy, but he is not happy; he wants to live, but he knows he must die."[14]

Milosz attributes the keenness of Solovyov's vision in unmasking liberal humanism to his peculiar position as a close observer of the Russian intelligentsia near the turn of the century. The stresses of Russian life forced changes of consciousness that happened only later and more gradually in the West.[15] But there was "unmasking" aplenty in progress even in the benighted West, as evidenced by the apocalyptic writings of Léon Bloy, the conversion of Jacques Maritain in 1906, the anti-positivist crusades of G. K. Chesterton and Hilaire Belloc, and a string of novels on the subject of the Antichrist and the end of time published just before the first World War.[16]

Of the novels, the best was the work of Robert Hugh Benson, a Roman Catholic convert and the youngest of three celebrated literary brothers who belonged to the same generation as H. G. Wells. Benson's *Lord of the World*, first published in 1907, is a powerful apologia for militant Catholicism which sees the Antichrist as a figure almost identical to Solovyov's. Again, he is every inch the angel, albeit fallen, a handsome young man of phenomenal intelligence, humanism, and charisma. He rises rapidly from obscurity in American politics, becomes the first President of Europe, establishes a life-worshipping state religion to supplant Christianity, and subtly manipulates public opinion to encourage the persecution of Catholics. The nations hail him as a prince of peace, who saved the world from certain war. To complete his infernal mission, the Antichrist decrees the euthanasia of all remaining Christian believers and personally leads an international airfleet to bomb Nazareth, where the last Pope lives in humble seclusion, awaiting the Day of Wrath. On the fateful last morning, the sun pales, the earth shakes, and in a flash "this world passed, and the glory of it."[17]

What distinguishes such works, and most of those that follow in the same tradition, is their venomous caricatures of the spokesmen of opposing world views, and in particular of positivism. For every page of piety, there are ten pages of partisan attacks on well-chosen enemies. Hugh Venning's *The End*, published in 1947, is a typical later work by a mediocre writer, presenting an Antichrist who becomes, like Solovyov's, the emperor of a new worldwide Roman Empire all of whose inhabitants are known by numbers, rather than by names. The personal number of the Emperor, of course, is 666. There has also been an outpouring in recent years of frankly commercial novels and films of the Antichrist in which the object is entertainment rather than conversion—works such as Stephen King's *The Stand* and Gordon McGill's *The Final Conflict.*

But some quite extraordinary and deeply felt fictions by mainstream writers have appeared since 1914 that rival Solovyov and Benson in their skillful fusion of romantic, irrationalist, and Christian thought. The most familiar to readers of speculative fiction is *That Hideous Strength,* a work of formidable polemic energy by C. S. Lewis bringing to a close the series of novels, noted earlier, in which he casts himself—or, at any rate, an Oxbridge don of the same age and specialty—as a Christ-figure with the suggestive name of Ransom. Thanks to Ransom and his unlikely ally, a re-animated Merlin, the world does not end in *That Hideous Strength.* But Lewis's scientist-villains do the worst they can. Their institute for applied science, nominally headed by the popular writer Horace Jules (a cartoon of H. G. Wells), engages in a program of coordinated experiments with far-reaching goals. As revealed one by one in the course of the narrative, the schemes of the conspirators begin with simple teamwork between government and science to solve national problems and climax with behavioral engineering on a massive scale, the eradication of all lower forms of life, and the eventual reduction of humanity itself to a single immortal brain.

Yet even the scientists are not the real masters of the institute. Behind the figurehead Jules, behind the experts, stands Hell and all its demons. They will use the institute to achieve incarnation and rule the planet in the service of an ultimate nothingness, the ruinous nullity of pure evil. Significantly, the technocrat who most completely embodies the dark spirits in charge of things is the most bland and inoffensive, the Deputy Director John Wither, whom we met in the Personal Preface of this book. Wither, alone, has no plans for engineering or controlling anybody. He believes, literally, in nothing. His only desire is for non-being, which in Lewis's chain of argument is the logical endpoint of modern thought, of its insane apotheosis of man and its willful severance of man from the love and grace of God.

Or, as Lewis argues in a volume of essays from the same period in his life as *That Hideous Strength,* science is bent on abolishing man.[18] It has given him not only power but the illusion that power is self-sufficient, that knowledge unrestrained by moral feeling can award him mastery of the universe. In reality this means that some men, the possessors of specialized technical knowledge, have won the chance to enslave and destroy other men, and bring civilization to a crashing end. As one of the villains explains in *That Hideous Strength,* when someone speaks of science "taking charge" of man, he is actually saying "that some men have got to take charge of the rest."[19]

A further example of Christian romanticism is *Présence de la mort* by the French Swiss writer Charles-Ferdinand Ramuz. Almost unknown to readers of speculative fiction, and not even mentioned in Jacques Sadoul's history of science fiction in *le domaine français*,[20] *Présence de la mort* is nevertheless an authentically eschatological tale, told in the author's terse, realistic style. Its romanticism is always one of thought, not of manner. In many ways, it belongs more to irrationalism than to romanticism, but overriding both is a commitment to the kerygmatic core of Christian apocalyptic. Ramuz shares Lewis's belief in the need for faith, and his fear of rampant intellectualism.

Brought up in an austere Calvinist home in the canton of Vaud, and nourished on large doses of the Bible, Ramuz was preoccupied throughout his life with the problem of good and evil, the struggle between modern science and tradition, and the terrors of judgment. One of his first works, *L'histoire du soldat*, was a fable about the Devil, written in collaboration with Igor Stravinsky. Another was *Le règne de l'esprit malin*, in which the Devil takes the form of a mysterious drifter and visits a Swiss village with disastrous results. But in *Présence de la mort*, published in 1922, there is no Devil, no Antichrist. There are many of each, perhaps. Evil is surely abroad in the land. But no supremely cunning serpent whispers obscenities in our ears. Evil takes care of itself.

The story opens with reports from America, heartland of modernity, that scientists predict the end of the world. The earth is falling toward the sun "through an accident to the law of gravity."[21] The time is midsummer, and the temperature rises higher every day. The water in wells, springs, and streams disappears, but despite all the signs of the approaching end, the Vaudois villagers and townsmen find it difficult to believe what they read. Who can believe anything from America? Are they not just trying to sell newspapers? But after the first week people begin to accept the truth of the prediction. Some drop dead in the streets, overcome by sunstroke. Ditchdiggers throw down their picks and shovels, invade a café, and help themselves to food and drink. After looting the place, they burn it down. Orgies become commonplace, banks are robbed, villages declare their independence and turn away strangers. A man who fears death commits suicide. News arrives of attempts to flee to the Arctic, but the ships have to turn back when great icebergs are calved by the intense heat. Alpine glaciers crack. A daring aviator who hoped to find coolness in the upper atmosphere fails miserably.

Then it is the last day. In Vaud, a few people are still alive, and they climb to a high mountain village, called by some unknown power. The grimness of the earlier chapters is left behind, and we enter a realm of mysterious spaces. A fierce wind rises. The bell ringer makes his way to the village church against its force. As the people arrive, time stops ticking away, and they stand forth "in their new bodies." Someone appears among them, "and He began to walk; He said: 'Come you?' And in their new bodies, they moved forward." A burning light melts their former eyes, but they have new eyes, new ears. Although at first they cannot walk, they learn all over again, and move forward, filled with wonder, and yet strangely comforted at the same time.

> Because, then, after all, they had not been deceived! Because they had not, then, done wrong in being attached to the earth, they were right in loving, in spite of all!
> And they said:
> "But we're home!"[22]

With the ascension of the elect to Paradise—not, of course, the words chosen by Ramuz—his novel ends.

One is reminded of another rapture, several degrees more sentimental, in a masterpiece of neo-romantic program music by Gustav Mahler. Just as Wagner's *Die Götterdämmerung* is a theatrical fiction inspired by Norse eschatology, so Mahler's Second Symphony, the "Resurrection Symphony" of 1894, is a fiction for orchestra, chorus, and soloists that culminates in the composer's rendering of the Christian myth of the Day of Judgment. Mahler goes so far as to provide a literal Last Trump. Four trumpets are directed to blow from opposite directions early in the last movement, and in the grotesque music that immediately follows, as the composer himself describes it, "the shuddering earth opens its graves and releases the endless, ghostly stream of the pious and the tortured, the once rich and poor, all raising their voices begging for mercy."[23]

But the choral finale, which begins with two stanzas of the ode *Aufersteh'n* by the pre-romantic poet Klopstock and concludes with verses of Mahler's own, dispels the terror. The composer resolves the old issue of whether God will eventually save all his children by depicting an immediate and universal redemption. Again, quoting Mahler, "the glory of God" appears to man.

> A wondrous, soft light penetrates us to the heart—all is holy calm!
> And behold—it is no judgment. There are no sinners, no just. None is great, none is small. There is no punishment and no reward.
> An overwhelming love lightens our being. We know and are.[24]

Not many Christian speculative visions of the endtime share the ingenuous faith of the Resurrection Symphony in a happy ending for the whole human race. But all are in tune with Mahler's essential insight, that the strife, anxiety, and confusion of modern life are passing evils, sure to give way in the Last Days to the primordial simplicity of Paradise. The key to bliss is not science and learning, or any worldly treasure that man can store up for himself, but childlike faith in the power of spirit. At bottom, purely secular visions of the end in the romantic vein purvey the same message. Modern man, like his Biblical parents, has earned death by rupturing his organic ties to nature and cosmos: after the holocaust, he may hope to find the garden-home of childhood once more.

13

•

Prometheus Unbound

THE PROMETHEUS OF Greek myth, like the Faust of Renaissance magic, may seem an unpromising choice to epitomize the positivist hero. Positivism by its very nature takes little pleasure in backward glances. Its focus is on fact, not legend; on the future, not the past. But the dauntless Prometheus and the redoubtable Dr. Faust foreshadow how positivism would later translate itself into the language of imaginative literature. Their appeal is much alike: they defy Heaven for the sake of enlightenment. In Biblical terms, they are Adams whose appetite for the fruit of the tree of knowledge is good, not evil; or, at least, worth the risk. In the literature of positivism, the cry is for Promethean daring and the Faustian gamble. Man must rebel against Zeus, even negotiate with the Devil, for the sake of understanding and controlling his world. In short, positivism vindicates Adam. The original "sin" was a declaration of independence, a coming to manhood, a decision for truth, strength, and danger, over against the security of the womb.

In terminal visions, positivism reads the endtime as a unique opportunity for modern man—with his science, his technology, his engineering, his Promethean courage, and his Faustian ambition—to prove himself. It is a time of testing. It is a time for confounding the enemies of reason and renewing the compact of civilization. That romantics like Percy Shelley also found Prometheus an irresistible figure, or that romantics like Goethe felt the same attraction to Faust, speaks as much to the powerful residues of eighteenth-century rationalism in the poets as it does to the metaphorical ambiguities of Prometheus and Faust. The heroes that Shelley and Goethe chose for their epic verse were not only proud rebels. They were champions of the arts of civilization, striving to enlarge the empire of man.

155

But if romantics can sometimes make a virtue of science, many positivists through the years have smuggled romantic values into their propaganda for science. This is especially true of positivist art and literature, which has never succeeded in inventing a wholly independent positivist aesthetic. Even Emile Zola, the beau ideal of a ruthless naturalism in fiction, was often as sentimental, as hero-worshipping, and as unclinical as any romantic who ever set pen to paper. If he had written speculative fiction, the temptation to "romanticize" would have no doubt carried him still further. In fact Zola did write a little speculative fiction toward the end of his life, his unfinished tetralogy *Les Quatre Evangiles,* his poorest work, yet in some ways his most romantic. F. W. J. Hemmings argues not only that "the romantic poet survived in Zola" but also that "little of him that is worth having could have existed if the poet had died."[1] The same could be said of the great majority of positivist masters, both in the nineteenth century and in our own.

Positivism in speculative fiction begins, unmistakably, with Jules Verne, who did much to excite public confidence in man's future progress through science and technology. In the main, as we have seen, Verne did not exploit the eschatological possibilities of speculative fiction, but the generation that immediately followed him, the second positivist generation, plunged into them with enthusiasm. The simplest formula called for science—usually mediated by a hero—to restore civilization after a great cataclysm inflicted by nature. The opportunities for a modern Prometheus, with or without benefit of romantic touches, are obvious. The original Prometheus defied Zeus, which is to say, the forces of nature; he also saved mankind from extinction by warning his son Deucalion, the Greek Noah, of Zeus's plans to send a world-destroying flood. A representative modern Prometheus is Cosmo Versál, the wealthy scientist of *The Second Deluge* by Garrett P. Serviss. We rehearsed Cosmo's adventures in Chapter Nine. All that need be added here is the emphasis that he places on rebuilding civilization after the Second Deluge with the aid of science. Not only is Cosmo himself a distinguished scientist and inventor: he fills his ark with like-minded people. A full one-fourth of those he selects are scientists, "the true leaders" of mankind, "trained in the right method."[2] Even more places are reserved for mechanics and agriculturists. Of other workers the best represented are doctors, teachers, and architects. But there will be only one lawyer, only one philosopher, and nobody at all from "society." As Henri de Saint-Simon, one of the great informing spirits of the positivist world view, said a century before, the future belongs to *les industriels,* not *les oisifs.*

George Allan England in *Darkness and Dawn* offers a still more glamorous version of the scientist-hero of the endtime. Consulting engineer, erstwhile lecturer in anthropology at Harvard, inventor of a "terrible explosive," and apostle of "scientific materialism," his protagonist Allan Stern is a brawny fighter and devoted lover to boot. Waking up in the devastated world of the far future, he vows "to keep the fires of science and of truth alive, and, if that be possible, to start the world again on a higher plane." No easier said than done. By the novel's end Stern has organized the few hundred barbarous survivors of the cataclysm into a nation of 100,000 thriving Yankees, with air and monorail service, wireless sets, and the promise of a world to come where "idleness" has vanished forever and "nature's forces have by science been enslaved."[3]

In two earlier stories, an already perfected scientific society responds to the challenge of disaster by escaping underground. Gabriel Tarde's *Fragment d'histoire future* tells of Miltiades, hero of a utopian world state, who proposes the excavation of deep caverns after the surface of the earth becomes too cold to support civilized life. The saved remnant of "neo-troglodytes" use their knowledge of biochemistry to synthesize nutrients, and they establish a great museum of artifacts, books, and treasures of art to preserve the best of the old surface civilization. In the end, a scientifically planned, regulated, balanced society emerges. When it discovers a rival subterranean community of Chinese, who have no museums and libraries, who breed indiscriminately, live in filth, and feed on the thousand million human corpses frozen in the eternal snows above, it prudently blocks off all contact with these degraded folk, preferring its own higher ways. In George Griffith's *Olga Romanoff*, as reported in Chapter Ten, the scientists of utopian Aeria construct a shelter in which the best of their kind can weather the fall of a comet.

The models supplied by Serviss and the other members of his generation have continued in use through the decades, with various twists and turns. J. J. Connington's Promethean industrialist Nordenholt, of *Nordenholt's Million*, saves mankind with science, technology, and pitiless survivalism. John Wyndham, a typical latter-day positivist and champion of the fundamental decency of man, views a world united in heroic self-defense against alien monsters in *The Kraken Wakes*. When an ultrasonic weapon is finally developed that wipes out the enemy in its ocean refuges, a large part of mankind is already dead, but the survivors will pick up the pieces and soldier on. The heroine reminds her husband that there were "only five million or so of us in the first Elizabeth's time—but we counted."[4] Wittingly or not, Keith Roberts puts an almost identical speech into the mouth of his hero Bill Sampson in *The Furies*. England is reduced to a population of just two million by another alien horde, but Sampson reflects that "we shall make out. After all there weren't many more of us in the time of the first Elizabeth."[5] The image of plucky Renaissance man, small in numbers but great in culture and courage, celebrates the modern world by singling out what even its detractors might be willing to call a golden age.

Despite the preponderance of writers drawn to irrationalism in the "New Wave" science fiction of the 1960s, there is one considerable New Waver who uses eschatological situations to promote a point of view that comes perilously near positivism. The man in question is Michael Moorcock, editor from 1964 to 1971 of *New Worlds*, which became during those seven lively years the company journal of the New Wave in Great Britain. A master of several styles and genres, Moorcock is difficult to pin down, and no doubt prefers it that way. His photograph in *The Science Fiction Encyclopedia* shows only his abundant beard, and above it, a mask. "Michael Moorcock," the caption reads, "an author of many faces, is here appropriately enigmatic."[6]

To judge from his eschatological fictions, however, the "real" Moorcock is not far removed in world views from that stylistic *bête noire* of all self-respecting New Wave writers, John Wyndham. He preaches a similar gospel of tolerance, reason, and humanism, deepened by a sense of irony and humor missing in Wyndham, not to mention an altogether higher order of technical literacy. But the humanism is much the same. Indications of Moorcock's perspective appear in two relatively early novels of the world's end, *The Shores of Death* and *The Ice Schooner.* Both exploit post-holocaust situations, in which cults of unreason lead to self-destruction but science saves the day. More convincing are the volumes of Moorcock's trilogy, *Dancers at the End of Time (An Alien Heat, The Hollow Lands,* and *The End of All Songs),* and its companion works, *Legends from the End of Time* and *The Transformation of Miss Mavis Ming,* the last of these published in the United States under the eminently Johannine title of *A Messiah at the End of Time.*

The "End of Time" books are bona fide frolics, whose humor turns chiefly on the contrast between Victorian earnestness and the innocent amoralism of the Dancers, a handful of superfolk whose omnipotent technology allows them to lead lives of pure freedom in the final centuries of the universe. When one of them, Jherek Carnelian, falls in love with a housewife mysteriously abducted from H. G. Wells's hometown of Bromley in 1896, the story gets under way, "the story of Jherek Carnelian, who did not know the meaning of morality, and Mrs. Amelia Underwood, who knew everything about it."[7] The age of the Dancers is surely Moorcock's metaphor for the best of all possible worlds, from the point of view of positivist humanism. The Dancers enjoy perfect freedom because they finally enjoy the limitless power first glimpsed by Francis Bacon in *The New Atlantis* and celebrated by every apostle of progress through science since the Marquis de Condorcet. Although they can do virtually anything they please, they love each other and quarrel like lovers and play like polymorphously perverse children—and why not? They belong to an age, foreseen by Moorcock in another work, when the world "will no longer need martyrs."[8] Mrs. Underwood, by contrast, is an exquisitely beautiful moralist of an age of scarcity, when self-sacrifice and self-discipline were essential to civilization. Moorcock seems to mock her, but he does not. She is right for her time, as Jherek is right for his.

The problem is that, owing to the unfathomable abduction of the fair Amelia, she and Jherek find themselves together, at the end of time. Later in the story, they meet in 1896 as well. In either era, one or the other is a hopeless anachronism. But they have a common destiny, which the reader learns near the end of the trilogy. Jherek's natural father Lord Jagged, a scientist of daunting powers, emerges as Amelia's abductor. He had combed through history to find the perfect genetic mate for his son. Now that the cosmos is coming to its entropic end, he offers to send them forward into the next world-cycle. They agree to make a one-way journey to the dawn of time, where they will resume civilization as the Adam and Eve of the next Palaeozoic era, starting at the point already reached by the humanity of their own world-cycle. Amelia's sense of duty, joined to Jherek's love of freedom, will strike a perfect balance between order and chaos. Without Jherek's superpowers, they will eventually die of old age, surrounded by their children and their children's children, the harvest of their indissoluble love, after a life of honest Victorian toil.

As for the rest of the Dancers, Lord Jagged contrives a seven-day loop in time that will enable them to continue their merrymaking forever, using the last week of the expiring world-cycle over and over again. Jagged himself, the eternal Faust, will disappear into the time-stream, pursuing his researches into the nature of being. Morality and amorality are both satisfied; and the unquenchable mind of science, which has made this happy ending possible in the first place, will find satisfaction in never being satisfied.

Moorcock's "End of Time" novels are happy fabulations, not realistic fictions, but his message comes across no less clearly for it, and the message is one of exoneration. Man is cleared of the charges against him in both Christian and romantic propaganda. He is not incorrigibly evil, and the power that flows from knowledge does not corrupt or debase him. Lord Jagged is the Faust of Lessing and Goethe, not the legendary swindler who went to Hell. Faced with the horrors of the endtime, man will use his human strength to outwit nature and survivors will be found to populate and civilize the postholocaust world. Notice that the price paid by Jherek (whose initials are those of Jesus Christ—and of Jerry Cornelius, Moorcock's most famous literary hero), the price for leaving the revels at the end of time and setting up housekeeping in the Palaeozoic, is the same as the "punishment" meted out to Adam and Eve by God in Genesis. He must give up immortality and he must exchange a life of play for a life of labor. But Jherek is not being punished. He is making a voluntary sacrifice for the sake of a higher good: the survival of civilization, and the love of Amelia, who is herself the delightsome embodiment of civilization.

The theme of man's heroic survival after the entropic decay of the present universe, a survival made possible by science, is actually quite common in speculative fiction of the positivist persuasion. Isaac Asimov, a positivist *par excellence*, was among the first writers to advance the concept in his short story "The Last Question," published in 1956. He postulates a universe running down to a final and irreversible end. But mankind, surviving now only as a cosmic super-mind of incalculable intelligence, discovers in the black and silent endtime how to reverse entropy. The cosmic mind gives the command, "Let there be light!", and the universe is reborn. The creature of one universe has become the creator of the next. It would be difficult to imagine a more blasphemous tale, in terms of traditional Jewish and Christian theism, but then Asimov is not, to say the least, a traditional theist.[9] There are roughly comparable dénouements, proceeding from somewhat different ground assumptions, in James Blish's *The Triumph of Time* and Poul Anderson's *Tau Zero*.

The best recent example of survival beyond the entropic doomsday is supplied in George Zebrowski's novel *Macrolife*. Most of the book deals with the replacement of the planets as homes for mankind by mobile space habitats, but in Part III, "The Dream of Time," the author addresses the problem of entropy. At the end of the cosmic cycle, after aeons of scientific and cultural progress, much of life manages to survive the implosion of the universe by passing through the black hole at the end of time, into which all creation has collapsed and from which it will re-emerge. Mankind reaches the next cycle, meeting and fusing with a still higher form of collective being from earlier cycles. Together, the old and new minds will continue life's exploration of a reality that has no end.

Other stories imagine a new cycle of life, but not of the whole cosmos, thanks to the survival of a single human being. Alfred Bester's "Adam and No Eve" was analyzed at the beginning of Chapter Seven, but for a statement of heroic positivism, a better source is James White's short novel *Second Ending*. White explains in his introduction that he rose to the challenge of writing "a Last Man on Earth story" when a friend suggested that he could not do it "because all my stuff was upbeat."[10] The result, of course, is an "upbeat" Last Man on Earth story—not such a contradiction in terms as White's friend supposed.

In *Second Ending,* the catastrophe is man-made. Nine out of ten human beings are killed in a nuclear war that starts by accident and lasts for three weeks. In the twenty-first century, another nuclear war annihilates all life on earth, sparing just one man, who had been cryogenically preserved in an underground hospital pending the discovery of a cure for his rare disease. Restored to health, he directs a program of research by robots to rejuvenate the planet. The program continues for millions of years, nearly all of which he spends in suspended animation, awaking for brief periods to check on the robots' progress and to give more orders. Despite all his efforts, the restoration of animal life on earth turns out to be impossible. In any case, the sun will soon become a nova, making life of any kind impossible. But the robots have meanwhile pursued an alternative project of their own. Guiding evolution on the unspoiled planet of another solar system, they have managed to produce humanoids so similar to *Homo sapiens* that the two species can interbreed. The hero is transported to the new earth by his robot allies, meets its people, and finds them pleasing. "You wouldn't mind if your sister married one of them," he reflects. "Come to think of it . . . you wouldn't mind marrying one yourself."[11] He will be a new Adam, mingling his aboriginal genes with those of an alien Eve, and mankind will rise again. Science has once more saved the day, despite a series of calamities as awful as any in the literature of Last Things.

The rhetorical thrust of nearly all the texts cited thus far is unambiguously positivist, but they tend to avoid confrontations with other world views. Science, reason, and human decency stand up to catastrophe, and snatch some sort of victory from its jaws. Although this strategy can lead to work of considerable evangelical force, the opportunity to face and refute the intellectual opposition is missed. Such is not the case with another large category of positivist terminal visions, in which the catastrophe serves only as the backdrop for a dramatic struggle between the forces of science and anti-science, or, in a more general way, between the values of modern civilization and those of pre-modern culture.

One formula that positivist writers have employed time and again, especially since the 1940s, is an inversion of the romantic tale of the post-holocaust Eden. In the positivist variant, mankind has also returned to savagery, barbarism, feudalism, or whatever, and blames the catastrophe that ended the old world on science. In the endtime, the survivors regard the arts and sciences of the past as dangerous, to be proscribed altogether or at least carefully regulated. The survivors often adhere to a religion that inveighs against positivism and all its works. But the new world is a Hell of darkness and cruelty, not an Eden of purity and love. Enlightened heroes come forward to challenge the anti-positivists and restore modern civilization, with perhaps a few improvements to avoid errors that may have been committed before. The romantic prescription for utopia is neatly turned upside down.

Of works whose plots we have already briefly analyzed in other contexts, the device of the post-holocaust contest between positivism and romanticism appears in several: in H. G. Wells's *The Shape of Things to Come*, for example, and also in John Wyndham's *The Chrysalids*, Robert Merle's *Malevil*, and Larry Niven and Jerry Pournelle's *Lucifer's Hammer*. The opponents of scientific salvation in *The Shape of Things to Come* consist of a miscellaneous array of recrudescent reactionary elements from the pre-holocaust society, including Fascists in what remains of Italy, royal families exhumed from retirement, romantic littérateurs, and the Catholic Church. The villains of Wyndham's novel are the preachers of a fundamentalist Christian sect who interpret the third World War, which they call "Tribulation," as a punishment sent by God because of man's "irreligious arrogance."[12] The opposition party in *Malevil* is headed by the false priest Fulbert, and in *Lucifer's Hammer* by the television evangelist Henry Armitage.

One writer, the English novelist Edmund Cooper, has made the post-holocaust positivist utopia his chief stock in trade, in a variety of muscular novels depicting duels between the endtime enemies of scientific civilization and its champions. The struggle is one that seems hopeless for the forces of enlightenment, but ultimately they prevail, and the modern world—in a suitably chastened higher form—supplants neo-medieval obscurantism and tyranny. We have already examined *All Fools' Day*, a thoroughly typical Cooper novel, as an illustration of the psychology of survivorship. It also illustrates his approach to the war of the world views.

Two sets of enemies of civilization are featured in *All Fools' Day*. One is a bizarre homicidal cult known as the Brothers of Iniquity, who believe that God has punished man for trying to create a rational society, and that his deepest wish is for men to destroy each other. The Brothers plan to slaughter all the survivors of the catastrophe and then gain admission to "some indescribably psychotic heaven until God should choose to have more interesting nightmares and clothe them with substance in some far and infinitely absurd anti-Eden"[13]—perhaps a sarcastic allusion to the terminal visions of J. G. Ballard. Another set of villains is headed by a mad squire, Sir James Oldknow, whose very name is a Dickensian parody of reaction. Oldknow has restored a brutal feudalism in Leicestershire with himself as lord and master. Our hero survives both challenges, and leads a successful effort to rebuild modern civilization.

In another representative work by Cooper, *The Last Continent*, superstitious white barbarians discover, with the help of civilized black emissaries from a former earth colony on Mars, that their community of "Noi Lantis" has grown up around an ancient scientific research station, whose occupants were the sole survivors of a cataclysmic world war. The scientists proudly christened their station New Atlantis, but little by little their descendants had degenerated. Now, with help from the Martians, civilization will return to a reformed earth, and science will flourish again.

Of all Cooper's post-holocaust novels, the most explicit tract for positivism, and perhaps his finest work, is *The Cloud Walker*, first published in 1973. The time of the story is the twenty-eighth century, after civilization has fallen twice in the aftermath of world wars. Throughout the world science and machinery have been renounced in favor of early medieval simplicity. In England Christianity has given way to a new religion based on legends surrounding the life and times of Ned Ludd, the mythical "king" of the Luddite bands who systematically destroyed industrial machinery in England in the early nineteenth century as a protest against unemployment. Elevated to divine status, Ludd is now worshipped as the true savior of mankind. The Luddite Church keeps careful watch to make sure that no machine is used or invented except the few authorized by the Church itself. Inventors are burned at the stake as heretics. What follows is the story of Kieron Joinerson, a young apprentice who defies the authorities, invents a flying machine, discredits the Luddites, and becomes one of the founding fathers of a new world civilization linked by helium-filled dirigibles. Kieron, the Cloud Walker, is honored just before his death at a great international festival in which four thousand aeronauts from all over the globe participate. Mankind is on the march once more.

In American speculative fiction, the prototypical story along these lines is Stephen Vincent Benét's much acclaimed "By the Waters of Babylon," first published in 1937 as "The Place of the Gods." The hero is a young man, a priest's son, who is slated to become a priest himself some day, in a tribal society of upstate New York after "the Great Burning and the Destruction." Somewhere to the east of the tribe, across the Hudson, lies the Place of the Gods, now a forbidden city of the dead. The young man defies the death penalty prescribed for such visits, and goes there to see it for himself. He learns that the "gods" were only men, like those of the tribe. His father spares his life, but warns him not to speak to the folk of his expedition. "Truth is a hard deer to hunt," he tells his son. "If you eat too much truth at once, you may die of the truth. It was not idly that our fathers forbade the Dead Places." But the spell is broken for the young man. Although he agrees with his father that the ancients may have eaten knowledge "too fast," he vows that when he becomes chief priest, "we shall go beyond the great river. We shall go to the Place of the Gods—the place newyork—not one man but a company. . . . We must build again."[14]

Benét's influence on postwar American speculative fiction was considerable. Many American examples of the post-holocaust tale reinforce the positivist side with a secret organization of scientist-survivors who aid the rebels in their struggle against unreason. In Leigh Brackett's classic novel *The Long Tomorrow*, the contest is between the New Mennonites, a sect that condemns machinery as devil's work, and Bartorstown, a onetime federal research center located underground in the Rocky Mountains, which has survived "the Destruction." Michael Kurland's *Pluribus*, which pits the people of the "enclaves" (actually former universities) against the Simples, the know-nothing followers of the superstitious Brother Simon, follows Brackett's formula closely. On a galactic scale, the same story line dominates the novels of *The Foundation Trilogy* by Isaac Asimov.

In still another post-holocaust story with an American setting, *The Masters of Solitude* by Marvin Kaye and Parke Godwin, a tribe of pagan telepaths joins forces with the reclusive people of City, the New York City of old, where science and technology flourish. Each will learn from the other, and progress will go forward as never before. But an important episode of the novel before this happy ending is the salutary extermination of the Kriss—a dour, cruel, puritanical tribe descended from the pre-holocaust Christians, a people with a "dead god," who love death and "sing about death like it was a woman."[15]

This less than flattering reference to Christianity as a religion consecrated to the death-wish calls to mind a relevant theme in eschatological fiction that American writers have treated with special vigor since the 1950s. We touched on it in Chapter Eight, in examining stories that viewed the endtime as a metaphor of the urge to self-destruction buried in the psychic underworld. Many of these stories are also positivist propaganda, implicit defenses of science, reason, and secular humanism against death-wishing cults traceable in their spiritual origins to Christianity and other traditional faiths. None of the authors concerned had the advantage of knowing what would happen in Jonestown in November 1979, but Jim Jones is very much like a character from their works. I am thinking, in particular, of Gore Vidal's mainstream novels *Messiah* and *Kalki*, Bernard Wolfe's *Limbo*, and D. Keith Mano's *The Bridge*.

The Bridge is the least well known of the four, but it illustrates their point of view no less forcefully. As in the others, the emphasis of the story falls on the anti-positivists and their nefarious cults of death and mutilation, far more dangerous than the ills of modern civilization they may hope to cure. Mano's point of departure is the coming of the Age of Ecology. The United States of the relatively near future has submitted to the tyranny of a governing council of monomaniacal ecologists, so disturbed by the ruthlessness of technology that they have decreed an end to all killing of life, in a Western version of the discipline of Jain monks. People are fed a chemical diet, containing a drug that renders them docile. Insects swarm, animals run wild, plant life is destroying the cities. Nearly all medical procedures have become illegal, since they kill "unconscionably high numbers of bacteria." Even tumors have the "right to life" and must not be excised by surgery. Finally, the Council proclaims that because the mere act of breathing harms "innumerable forms of microscopic biological life, we of the Council . . . have decided that man in good conscience can no longer permit this wanton destruction of our fellow creatures, whose right to exist is fully as great as ours." The Council calls for the contrite termination of the human species by universal suicide and sets an early deadline for compliance. The corpses will help fertilize the earth, so that "the heinous crimes of murder and pollution committed by our race throughout history may in some small way find redress."[16]

The Council manages to enforce its will by a mixture of persuasion and coercion, anticipating the methods of the Reverend Jones, but one man holds out savagely against the tide of self-destruction. He, along with ten women, elude their persecutors and become the Adam and Eves of the post-holocaust America. Centuries later, a new world has emerged, which is more or less the exact opposite of the Age of Ecology. A level of industrialism has been reached that allows the mass production of black Model T Fords. Defectives and criminals are killed in public, as part of the Feast of Eater, the chief holiday in the calendar of the new state religion. Its motto is "All things eat or are eaten." Its communion meal is human flesh and blood, taken from the bodies of the executed, and it remembers the hero not only as Adam but as a redeemer who "made man lord again over all things of the earth."[17]

The faith of Mano's robust new America is clearly not positivism in any formal sense, but the villainy in the drama is a syndrome of values that secular humanists of all stripes oppose. As one of the characters remarks in the Epilogue, the fatal flaw in civilization is the cancer of guilt, which leads ultimately to senile self-loathing and self-destruction. Between savage youth and suicidal old age, man enjoys only "a few moments—no more, a few—when the balance is held, when he is a god."[18] Some day, he suggests, the death-wish will return, and the love of life will wither again. But Mano's sympathies lie with that brief historical moment of vital divinity, before the thanatotic decline sets in. Life is good. Meat is good. The "blue haze of factory smokestacks active even on the Feast of Eater" is good.[19] The world is man's to enjoy, for as long as his courage holds.

What can happen if man renounces science and reason and the relentless conquest of nature is also the object of several standard short stories in the literature of Last Things. John W. Campbell, Jr., later the editor for twenty-four years of the most fiercely pro-science of genre magazines, *Astounding Science-Fiction* (after 1960, *Analog*), published two signally Wellsian stories in the 1930s under the pseudonym of Don A. Stuart that portray a bankrupt mankind near the end of time. "Twilight," the first, takes its readers to the far future. In man's progress he has cleared the planet of all other life except for ornamental plants and a few pets, but now he is bored with his existence and he is dying out. The one essential quality missing is the "instinct of curiosity," which had driven the scientists and inventors and explorers of the past, and has now faded in the twilight of man's day. The sequel, "Night," takes place much later still. The sun is red and cold. Only a few stars remain in the sky. All life on earth has finally ended, but on Neptune a moribund civilization of machines feebly carries on, machines designed by their human makers "to be eternally curious, eternally investigating." As it turns out, curiosity is not enough, after all: there also has to be purpose, a goal beyond mere survival, which man has not been able to program into his robots.

Arthur C. Clarke engraves a comparable epitaph on the tombstone of mankind in "The Awakening," a story in which history has reached a dead end. Having failed to conquer interstellar space after colonizing the solar system, mankind grows senile and is conquered, or replaced, by a race of intelligent insects. By contrast, in Clarke's "Rescue Party," the human race evacuates the solar system in a fleet of starships when the sun is about to become a nova, and goes on to amaze the galaxy with its scientific prowess and imperial exploits.

In the last few years, a further argument has arisen in the pages of speculative fiction mirroring the debate in future studies over the relative merits of "hard" and "soft" (or "appropriate" or "intermediate") technology. This sometimes reduces to a struggle between positivism and a new romanticism of mindless attunement with nature, but many of the advocates of soft technology retain important elements of the positivist credo. Solar energy systems, electric cars and trains, and diversified organic farming scarcely constitute a formula for escaping back to the tenth century. The fact that so staunch an anti-positivist as J. G. Ballard has furnished a brilliantly contemptuous parody of the soft technology movement in his 1976 story "The Ultimate City" suggests just how close to classical positivist values that movement often hews. It is not so much a question of attacking science, technology, reason, or secular humanism, as bringing them into line with the dangers and possibilities of the late twentieth century.

In terminal fictions, two quite recent novels occupy the middle ground between the extremes of old-style Wellsian propaganda for industrialism at open throttle and the dream of a new Eden. One of these is Douglas Orgill and John Gribbin's *The Sixth Winter,* a novel of the return of the ice age which ends with a plea for cooperation between modern science and Arctic folk wisdom, to permit civilization to continue in a radically modified form in an icebound world. The other is *Summer Rising,* by Sheila Sullivan.

Published in 1975, *Summer Rising* is one of the first works of fiction inspired by E. F. Schumacher and his case for an "intermediate technology" in *Small Is Beautiful.*[20] Sullivan transports her readers to the middle of the twenty-first century, after the gradual winding-down of modern civilization and the restoration of a medieval society and economy. "No abrupt or dramatic event," she notes,

> had accounted for the collapse. There had been no war, no bomb; only a remorseless gearing down, from a humming urban prosperity to a life so cold and threadbare that those bewildered people who had survived the decline sometimes wondered if they still lived on the same planet.[21]

In any event, the cities are deserted, and the pits and factories stand silent. Post-modern Britain is divided into various small polities, including a new kingdom of Cornwall, where Cornish has been resuscitated and all speakers of English are hanged from the nearest tree.

The novel rises to its climax after a difficult journey to Ireland by the hero, the heroine, and her child. Two factions contend for power in an Ireland restored almost to the Stone Age by civil war. The positivist faction demands an end to poverty, disease, ignorance, and dirt—through the fullest possible use of science and technology. Its opponents warn that "we must not destroy—we dare not destroy—for a second time that relationship with the earth" achieved by the ancients. But there remains a third option, for whom the chief spokesman is the wise old Lord of Ireland, who turns out to be the heroine's grandfather. "We must have bricks and cement and ships and looms and metal," one of the Lord's loyal supporters proclaims. "We've got them in a basic form already and we must keep them and perhaps develop them a little further—an intermediate technology."[22] The "new Luddites" who want to destroy all machinery are just as dangerous as the advocates of total commitment to technological solutions. The middle-roaders prevail, and a bright future seems assured.

Such compromises, however, are not especially common in eschatological fiction. The endtime is a time for dramatic choices between life and death, good and evil, right and wrong. Most texts that carry any intellectual freight at all lean heavily to one side or another in the war of the world views.

14

◆

Follies and Mysteries

W HATEVER POWERS OF ensorcellment romanticism and positivism still wield—and they should never be underestimated—our report on the war of the world views in eschatological fiction cannot end here. Especially on the European mainland, but increasingly in the Anglo-Saxon world as well, the world view of the cultural avant-garde in this century is irrationalism. It would be odd, even incredible, if speculative literature had contrived to dodge its influence. Such a feat would throw serious doubt on the thesis that irrationalism really does enjoy a pre-eminent position in twentieth-century Western thought.

As it happens, the thesis is in no trouble because of the performance of speculative fiction, including even its science-fictional hard core. There has been a steady drift of serious writers of speculative fiction into the irrationalist camp, clear to anyone by the end of the 1960s, but starting decades earlier. The chief interpretative difficulty arises in trying to separate the threads of the newer irrationalism from those of the older, but still living romanticism. One of the works discussed in Chapter Twelve, Ramuz's *Présence de la mort*, was described as perhaps belonging more to the former than to the latter, if only because it refuses in any way to romanticize its characters or inject romantic feeling and sentiment into its narrative of events, except in the final scene in the mountains. Even there, the culminating mystery of the endtime is mysterious in a way that sets it apart from both Christian and romantic tradition.

The mystery, one cannot help but think, is something of a mystery to Ramuz, too, something not merely ineffable and intangible, but also problematic. The rights and wrongs of the story, not to mention the cause of the

169

disaster that ends the world, are all tantalizingly vague. One is left with a sense of longing for revelations, of longing for faith and truth; but the revelations never quite come. A good parallel might be drawn with the life's work of Ramuz's fellow Swiss, Carl Gustav Jung, a thoroughgoing exponent of the irrationalist world view. Jung called for a return to the saving inspiration of the eternal pre-rational archetypes buried in man's ancient religions and literatures, but it was a matter of indifference to him which myths, which symbols, which gods we invoked for our therapy. The secret of life is that we are creatures who need secrets.

Another characteristic of *Présence de la mort* that smacks of irrationalism is its sheer disjointedness. The details in and of themselves are nearly all realistic, but they do not hook together to form a coherent drama following the conventions of classicism, romanticism, or realism. Irrationalist culture dwells on the random, the dreamlike, and the fragmentary as a way of underscoring its perception of the fundamental irrationality of human existence or of being itself.

At the apex of irrationalism in apocalyptic literature are such works, evaluated in Chapter Eight, as Beckett's *Endgame* and Ionesco's *Le piéton de l'air.* The less the irrationalist knows or claims to know, the more absurd the universe in which he sets the fruits of his imagination, the more fully he embodies the irrationalist world view. But the difficulty with the endtime is the way in which it compels the writer to draw boundary lines. He must say: it is finished. On *this* day the world ends. On *that* day it may begin again. Knowledge of the end of the world is a gnosis, a secret pointing to salvation. The purest irrationalism shies from such ambitious claims. To be sure, as Frank Kermode argues, the endtime can be radically immanentized, so that it reduces merely to an individual's death or to a time of personal crisis or of waiting for crisis, a waiting for Godot. But the story of a literal public endtime, which is our subject in *Terminal Visions,* does not choose this route, and thus it is not surprising that the purest irrationalists are reluctant to imagine literal public endtimes. They prefer limbos to heavens and hells.

All the same, there is a stream of stories, trickling out of the 1920s and 1930s and swelling much larger in the last few decades, in which writers present comedic, fabulous, absurd, or mystical ends that betray at many points the influence of the irrationalist world view. One sees more than a touch of irrationalism, for instance, in the work of Karel Čapek. His villains, like the giant amphibians of *War with the Newts,* are clearly enough vehicles of protest against various evils of modern civilization, but Čapek does not put too much stock in any of the usual formulas for combating evils. His heroes are anti-heroes, well-meaning blunderers, and mankind scrapes by, if at all, with little help from anything or anybody. Nor does he lay claim to any sort of private pipeline to the Absolute. On the contrary, as the industrialist G. H. Bondy laments in *The Absolute at Large,* the trouble with God is the size of him. "He is infinite. That's just where the trouble lies. You see, everyone measures off a certain amount of Him and then thinks it is the entire God." People will never learn that none of them has more than "a few wretched metres or gallons or sackloads of divine truth."[1] Bondy does not add that the value of all fractions of infinity is the same, no matter how big their numerators, and evades entirely the issue of how to assay the contents of the sacks, but his epistemological relativism is disturbing enough, without pushing it further.

Of the various terminal stories since Čapek that traffic in misanthropic black comedy, absurdism, and the like, it is often difficult to be sure whether a given text harks back in all innocence to the satirical tradition perfected by Swift and Voltaire, or whether it disavows the faith of reason itself. There are even doubts about some of the texts of Swift and Voltaire, for that matter. But the most plausible construction of the great eighteenth-century satirists is that they habored a profound belief in reason and commonsense, together with a rationalistic theology, and scolded man from a schoolmasterish impulse to correct him, however low their opinion of his corrigibility may have sometimes dropped. In the irrationalist world view, man and universe are either meaningless, or open to many meanings; a joke or a mystery. Reason is a useful tool for certain kinds of mental exercises, not an open sesame or the straight and narrow path to the good life. Reason may also be far more dangerous, and hence more crazy, than honest craziness.

F. Wright Moxley, a Brooklyn-born lawyer of forty when he published his eschatological novel *Red Snow* in 1930, was perhaps more of a Swiftian than an irrationalist. But this unique foray into speculative fiction, his only one, is also one of the few from Čapek's generation that compares favorably with anything by the Czech master. Its grand terminal event is the instant sterilization of the human race by a red snow that falls for ninety seconds all over the planet on August 17, 1935. The snow vanishes without a trace after it falls, and no attempt to discover its origin or its nature succeeds. The churches blame the disaster on human wickedness, but the first response of mankind to its loss of a future is to engage in fierce wars of religion. The same Protestants who deplore human wickedness go on a rampage in America, killing many Jews and expelling the rest, persecuting Catholics, and sending an army of holy crusaders to China to hunt down a pagan Antichrist supposedly headquartered in Tibet.

The 1940s are a decade of war throughout the world. The blood flows freely. European and American armies are soundly defeated by the Asians, and the entire population of Japan, which had attacked China, is wiped out by a bacteriological weapon. Arabs assail Jews in Palestine, and a Jewish army of revenge is lost in the desert. So it goes. Eventually, the wars peter out, but mankind's behavior does not improve. Science fails in all its efforts to restore human fertility. People turn to art and sex for relief, with predictably idiotic results. A female Pope sends a fleet to convert America, but her ships are sunk. Dissipation, idleness, the breakdown of hygiene, and indifference to the plight of the aged produce many more needless deaths. The last man, Phaeton Andrews, dies on Easter in A.D. 2027, after a lightning bolt has killed all his cronies. Or does he die? According to a rabbit who saw everything, a golden chariot with magnificent horses descended to earth, a being—not human—gave Phaeton the reins, and the two of them rode, laughing heartily, up into the sky. The events of Greek mythology are adroitly reversed.

Red Snow, as suggested, may be more Swiftian than irrationalist. At all odds, it is not romantic. Moxley represents man as inherently cruel and foolish. Nor is any help to be expected from the no less absurd devices of his civilization, from religion, government, science, or art. The only sane response to the human predicament is the laughter of the Olympians.

Moxley's gift for black comedy, one of the special blessings of American literary culture, is shared by many of his successors, often American, in the speculative fiction of the era since 1945. The list is led by Kurt Vonnegut, Jr., and his eschatological chef d'oeuvre, *Cat's Cradle*, a work whose irrationalism, one might say, is almost too obvious. Vonnegut first came on the scene in 1952 as the author of *Player Piano*, a fairly conventional, if unusually well-written, rehash of the dystopian themes of *Brave New World*, with the same pungent assault on scientism and the enslavement of modern man by technology. Comedic elements appear, but do not quite take over. Seven years later, he published what is probably his best speculative novel, *The Sirens of Titan*, a manifesto of comedic absurdism, an outrageous spoof of science fiction, and a sermon against the follies of religion and metaphysics still more effective than his earlier indictment of science and the machine. Saying just what J. G. Ballard, his irrationalist contemporary in Britain, was saying at just about the same time, Vonnegut uses *The Sirens of Titan* as his soapbox for proclaiming that the universe (= outer space) is nothing but "a nightmare of meaninglessness without end," and that only inwardness (= Ballard's "inner space") remains to be explored.[2]

Cat's Cradle, which followed in 1963, is Vonnegut's one major apocalypse. Here, he returns to his quarrel with science and technology, but from a more sharply absurdist perspective. The story pits the scientist as antivillain against the absurdist prophet as anti-hero. Felix Hoenikker is the stereotypical absentminded scientist, one of the "fathers" of the atomic bomb and the inventor—on a whim—of "ice-nine," a modified water with a melting point of 114.4° F. When a piece of ice-nine, in a scene out of the slapstick cinema of the 1920s, falls into the sea by the sheerest chance, a chain reaction occurs that congeals all the water in the world, rendering life impossible. Only ants, who have learned how to survive by an ingenious system of cooperative suicide-cum-cannibalism, are likely to keep the world going—to no conceivable purpose.

The absurdist prophet Bokonon who serves as the novel's anti-hero is not actually met in the flesh until the end, but the religion he has invented plays a prominent part in the story throughout. It is Vonnegut's own credo, for all practical purposes: the belief that God is completely indifferent, that the world is meaningless, that man must accept his fate as he finds it, and satisfy himself by loving his fellow man in a spirit of cheerful resignation. The contrast with the anti-villain Hoenikker, on these points, is absolute. Hoenikker was too preoccupied all his life with the games of reason and invention to love anyone, and the only attempt he ever made to entertain his son, a midget somewhat reminiscent of Oskar in Günter Grass's *Die Blechtrommel*, ended in disaster. Hoenikker horrified the little boy by making a cat's cradle out of string and thrusting it in his face. As the story goes on, the cradle becomes an unobtrusive but powerful symbol of the illusions of reason and faith alike. Just as there is no cat in the cradle that is not there, so there is no God in the universe and nothing but game-playing, alternatively useful and deadly, in the science that pretends to understand it. In *Cat's Cradle*, as in all his work, Vonnegut stands convicted of a certain deep-down sentimentality, a flaw that he freely confesses himself,[3] but it is an absurd sentimentality, in Camus's sense, not romantic tenderness. All hope of a coherent universe is dead.

The lunacies of science out of control are the stuff of a number of other apocalyptic black comedies of the postwar epoch. As noted in Chapter Ten, Ward Moore's *Greener Than You Think* and John Bowen's *After the Rain* use the theme of the silly scientist whose inventions take a catastrophic wrong turn. Peter George, with invaluable help from Terry Southern and Stanley Kubrick, converted his straightforward novel of nuclear suspense, *Two Hours to Doom* (in the U.S. as *Red Alert*), into the screenplay for Kubrick's film *Dr. Strangelove,* and later wrote a novel based on the film that features the same inimitably mad German scientist planning the same eugenic dystopia for a selected group of survivors in the bowels of a mine-shaft. Stanislaw Lem's *The Futurological Congress*, although its apocalypse turns out to be a drug-induced fantasy, supplies evidence that the spirit of Karel Čapek survives in Marxist Poland. As Darko Suvin notes, Lem's parables argue that "no closed reference system is viable in the age of cybernetics and rival political absolutisms; the protagonists are redeemed by ethical and aesthetic insight rather than by hardware, abstract cognition or power."[4]

In some stories of the endtime that display an irrationalist slant, the place of black comedy is filled by ironic detachment or simple whimsy, with science once again under attack for its impotence or its threats to human self-determination. In one variant, we witness the extinction or degeneration of an alien species whose fate has a lesson for mankind, in works such as John Brunner's *Total Eclipse* and Herbert W. Franke's *Der Orchideenkäfig*. In another, man provides for his survival from disaster in a technologically marvelous sheltered habitat, but leaves something out of his calculations, the situation in J. Jefferson Farjeon's *Death of a World* and Sven Holm's *Termush*. D. G. Compton in *The Silent Multitude* and Arthur Sellings in *Junk Day* survey an ambiguous post-holocaust world through the eyes of misanthropic rebels against the old civilization who, themselves, are tainted by its romantic egoism.

For sheer whimsy, nothing is quite equal to the English writer Ronald Duncan's short novel, *The Last Adam*. After a mysterious explosion lifts the planet's atmosphere, everyone on earth dies of asphyxiation before it has time to rush back. Everyone dies, that is, except an effete poet who dotes on Dryden, Gluck, and the *Gita* and who happens to bear the name of Ronald Duncan. The poet was in an operating room, under oxygen, just before the surgeon's knife descended. He does all the usual things that last men do, including a spot of arson: he burns down what, to Duncan's taste, is London's most detestable edifice, the Royal Albert Hall. Pangs of loneliness finally compel him to tour Europe in search of another survivor. He finds his Eve in Italy, a beautiful young archeologist from Boston earnestly engaged in re-search on underwater ruins as if the world had never come to an end. But she recognizes her "duty to the race." Attired in a fetching negligee, she tries one evening to seduce him, with all the plastic ardor of someone following a manual on lovemaking by a professional sex therapist. Her villa is scrupu-lously clean. Everything is tidy, her desk is stacked with legible neat notes. Duncan feels his blood running cold. After dinner, in this "clinical Garden of Eden,"[5] the archeologist offers him an apple for dessert, which he declines. He quietly leaves. The round of history will not begin again, and Duncan is off and away, tempted by the fruit of the tree of knowledge—but not enough to eat it.

At the other pole from whimsy stands obsession. In many irrationalist apocalypses, the writer seizes the opportunity of the endtime to send his protagonist on journeys into the subconscious. A generous sampling of such works was treated in the discussion of the psychology of terminal visions in Chapter Eight. But a few supplementary points are in order, to clarify the relationship between psychological analysis in fiction and world views. The stories examined in Chapter Eight were chosen for their method, not for their structures of value. In all of them the end was a time for plumbing the depths of the id. But the id can also be a homeland, a center radiating goodness, and worthy of celebration just like the science and reason of the positivists or the love and simplicity of the romantics.

Not that all explorations of the sub-rational are necessarily irrationalist. Bernard Wolfe's *Limbo*, for one example, is a story of global ruin and renewal that focuses on the interaction of sado-masochism and militarism, but from a view of the world that is resolutely positivist. He takes the position championed by Freud himself in his more hopeful moments, the Freud who was a nineteenth-century man of science as well as a twentieth-century man of doubt and anxiety. Wolfe's chief spokesman in the novel, a neurosurgeon, reaches the conclusion that the urge to self-mutilation and the urge to give battle are two different aspects of the same madness, "a horror of things physical, the things of the material world and of the body—a moralistic, puritanical need to lash and lacerate thingness." The search for mystical transcendence belongs to the same syndrome of flesh-fearing neurotic perfectionism. "The romantic-poetic cry for the oceanic is only a thirst for oblivion."[6] In place of the manias of the death-wish, Wolfe's heroes offer rational self-understanding through psychoanalysis, a humanism of sanity and balance and wholeness, acceptance of modern science and technology without divinization of either, and an enthusiasm for change and progress, which they call "joining history." In the story, the greater part of mankind, committed to irrationalist philosophies, destroys itself in wars. But on the Isle of the Mandunji in the Indian Ocean, the foundations of the sane society of the next century are being firmly laid.

From Wolfe's island to the demented landscapes of J. G. Ballard, the distance is best measured in parsecs. Both writers explore the id, but just as the world view of *Limbo* is positivist, the world view of all of Ballard's work belongs wholly to irrationalism. In a representative exegesis of his own fiction, Ballard admits that the world he destroys so often "is in fact an image of the writer himself," which makes the writing of terminal stories an act of symbolic suicide. But he denies that such suicides are "negative."

> On the contrary, I believe that the catastrophe story, whoever may tell it, represents a constructive and positive act by the imagination rather than a negative one, an attempt to confront the terrifying void of a patently meaningless universe by challenging it at its own game, to remake zero by provoking it in every conceivable way.[7]

It would be difficult to imagine a better statement of the task of the literature of Last Things from the irrationalist perspective. When reinforced by his view, quoted in Chapter Eight, that the challenge of the "void" is also a kind of experiment in psychospiritual transformation, by which characters divest themselves of the illusions of the external world, his definition of catastrophism is entirely consistent and comprehensive.

All the "good" and "bad" guys in a Ballard eschatological story behave as one would expect. His villains, as H. Bruce Franklin has observed, are sometimes caricatures of the heroic men of action in the rituals of adventure fiction.[8] They stand up to chaos, and try to "conquer" it with science, technology, engineering, and the will to power—figures such as the industrialist Hardoon in *The Wind from Nowhere*, the pirate Strangman in *The Drowned World*, and the journalist and self-appointed messiah Ryker in "A Question of Re-Entry." More often, Ballard does not take the trouble to introduce villains at all. Or he substitutes colorless and ultimately pitiable defenders of the old pre-holocaust rationality, people deaf to the song of the endtime sirens, like the expedition commander, Colonel Riggs, in *The Drowned World*, and the tedious vegetarians of the soft-energy community from which the young hero flees in disgust in "The Ultimate City." The heroes, for their part, are one and all seekers of inwardness, conquerors of the self, supermen in the Nietzschean sense, who dare to live dangerously even if it kills them, as it usually does.

The fact that most of the heroes of Ballard's later fiction exhibit a fascination with cities and industrial hardware, such as automobiles, instead of wilderness, marks no fundamental change in their consciousness. They were never nature-lovers in the romantic sense in the first place, and their obsessive interest in the debris of industrialism is anything but an enthusiasm for progress. As before, their fascinations are intensely private, and what draws them is the city as junk, as ruins, as something desperate and collapsing and dangerous, not the city as a symbol of advancing rationality.

The question of whether Ballard's final literary destination may be a kind of bisexual mysticism, after the intensely heterosexual and homosexual manias of the fiction of his early and middle periods, is raised by a quite recent novel, which seems to open a new phase of his work, *The Unlimited Dream Company*. The hero is a 25-year-old drifter who dies in an air crash and is reborn to become the magical messiah of Shepperton, London's Hollywood. He incorporates everyone in Shepperton into his being, and plans a universal fusion. The dead will be raised, and all men and women and children in the valley of the Thames will merge. They will reach out to absorb the people of all the world, and finally all of creation, trees, stones, everything, "happily dissolving ourselves in the sea of light that formed the universe."[9] Presumably the mystical fantasy is just another metaphor for inward transformation, but Ballard's work has always verged on mysticism, in more or less the same way as Samuel Beckett's has done, differing from traditional mysticism only in its thoroughly solipsistic inwardness, which is to say its lack of any acknowledged belief in an "ultimate" reality transcending the self.

In speculative fiction, Ballard's peculiar blend of irrationalism and secular eschatology turns up in a number of works by other writers, with or without any direct influence from Ballard: in Anna Kaven's *Ice*, in Angela Carter's *Heroes and Villains*, in M. John Harrison's *The Committed Men*, and, from the other side of the Atlantic, in Samuel Delany's enigmatic and interminable novel *Dhalgren*. The discussion of mysticism in Ballard also brings to mind one last important group of irrationalist terminal visions that must not be neglected. Whatever one makes of a mysticism without transcendence, several writers of eschatological fiction have produced texts that expound mysticism in a more traditional sense. They give their expositions a characteristically irrationalist and Jungian twist, which prompts suspicions that their mysticism is more hypothetical than real. But every serious intellectual who makes the leap to any sort of faith nowadays risks the same accusation.

The beginnings of mysticism in fictional scenarios of the world's end may be traced to works of the late nineteenth and early twentieth centuries under the influence of theosophy, spiritualism, vitalism, and other similar movements of quasi-religious thought rising up to do battle with positivism during that period. Camille Flammarion imports spiritualist ideas into the closing fantastic pages of *La fin du monde*. The ghost of Cheops appears to the last man and woman at the end of terrestrial history, revealing to them some of the secrets of the spirit world. After they die in the flesh, Cheops transports their spirits to Jupiter, where a new civilization flourishes. An epilogue offers a poetic vision of the cosmos as an eternal realm of rising and falling worlds, endlessly self-renewing. Flammarion's spiritualist interests may seem incongruous in a professional scientist, but he was not alone in his enthusiasms. They were shared by many in his day, including the occasional fellow-scientist, such as Oliver Lodge and Alfred Russell Wallace, not to mention the good friend of Flammarion's old age, Sir Arthur Conan Doyle. The spirit world also figures in the writings of William Hope Hodgson, *The Night Land* among them, and there is a mysticism of sorts in various works by J.-H. Rosny aîné. In a careful study of Rosny's fiction, J.-P. Vernier shows that the pitiless vision of nature in *La mort de la terre* holds a higher significance for its author, a glimpse—vague as it may be—of the ultimate oneness of all being. Cosmic unity is symbolized by the last man's voluntary surrender of his body to the mysterious mineral creatures who will replace mankind, after his battle to preserve the human race is finally and irrevocably lost.[10]

In the interwar years the mystical path in speculative fiction was taken by Olaf Stapledon and Aldous Huxley, two British writers of the first rank who attempted to bridge the world views of positivism and irrationalism. In essence, however, both were irrationalists making a "place" for positivist values in a larger scheme of things in which mysticism is the orchestrating principle.

Stapledon's mysticism was, to say the least, wildly eclectic, somewhat in the manner of his equally isolated French contemporary Pierre Teilhard de Chardin. In his major works of speculative fiction, *Last and First Men* and *Star Maker*, he represents the final goal of evolution as the self-perfection of the cosmic mind. Through dialectical change within history, the consciousness of the universe will mature and ultimately fuse with its other self outside of space and time, the "Star Maker." Stapledon clothes traditional mysticism, Spinoza, Hegel, and evolutionary cosmology in the spangled dress of speculative fiction.

The case of Aldous Huxley is perhaps even more complicated. Raised in a home bristling with memories of one of the greatest positivists of them all, his grandfather Thomas Henry Huxley, the young Aldous passed through a series of rebellions that led from mocking skepticism to an infatuation with the vitalism of D. H. Lawrence to the syncretic mysticism of his mature years. At the time of the writing of *Brave New World*, first published in 1932, he was near the end of his Lawrentian phase. His *confessio fidei* as a mystic is *Eyeless in Gaza*, in 1936, followed by *Time Must Have a Stop*, *The Perennial Philosophy*, *Ape and Essence*, and his last novel, a mystic's vision of utopia, *Island*. *Brave New World* and *Island*, like all utopian fiction, are caustic critiques of the present-day world, in this instance critiques of the science, technology, and ruthless imperialism of modern Western positivist civilization. Huxley's only contribution to the literature of Last Things is *Ape and Essence*, the scenario of a post-holocaust Hell in which the outcome of the misdeeds of modern man is not the dehumanizing technocracy of *Brave New World* but simply universal destruction, accompanied by the transformation of most of the survivors into a dwindling race of mutant beast-men who worship Satan—under his apocryphal name of Belial.

In the propagandistic heart of the novel, the shrill diatribe of the Arch-Vicar of Belial, Huxley lays all the responsibility for the world war that devastated civilization on civilization itself. The tide turned early in the nineteenth century, the Arch-Vicar explains, with the rise of the machine, the population explosion, and the abandonment of faith in the spiritual ground of being for a faith in man's capacity to wring infinite riches out of nature through science and technology. The world became a single interactive community, but Western man expropriated the worst aspects of Eastern culture and Eastern man expropriated the worst aspects of Western. Instead of a new order in which Eastern mysticism and Western science could temper and enrich each other, there arose a gang of despotic national states with teeming populations and no respect for life or liberty, engaged in a vicious armed struggle for the treasures of the earth. Inevitably, they clashed once too often. The result was World War Three, a holocaust fought with nuclear and bacteriological weapons that eliminated most of the world's people and led to the monstrous devolution of most of the rest. In the battle between ape and essence, between essenceless ape and man's better self, the forces of Belial triumphed.

Huxley drops a few hints toward the end of the novel of how the disaster may be reversed. His hero and heroine flee to join forces with a band of surviving "normal" human beings, believers in the mystical Order of Things who are pledged to fight the Belial in all of us and build a higher society. But the outlines of that society are left quite vague. Huxley did not get around to drawing them until 1962, in *Island*, the crown and summing-up of his life's work.

More recently, patches of eschatological mysticism may be found in some of the novels of Colin Murry (writing as Richard Cowper), the son of the erstwhile British mystic and pacifist John Middleton Murry; his best effort is *The Twilight of Briareus*, published in 1974. But the main event of the 1970s in such matters was the emergence of the mainstream novelist Doris Lessing as a critically acclaimed laborer in the vineyards of speculative fiction. She gave warning signs of her intentions in 1969 in *The Four-Gated City*, an otherwise conventional novel set in the present, whose "Appendix" carries the story forward from the late 1960s into the last five years of the twentieth century, by means of a series of imaginary documents composed after "the Epoch of Destruction." The post-holocaust world is in chaos and turmoil, but children are being born, superhuman children with psychic powers who are the forerunners of a new and higher race.

The Four-Gated City was followed by *Briefing for a Descent into Hell*, a further report on the author's spiritual progress, which contained science-fictional elements but nothing overtly eschatological. In *The Memoirs of a Survivor*, however, which appeared in 1974, Lessing assembled the materials of speculative fiction, secular eschatology, and a mysticism inspired chiefly by her studies of Sufi masters, into a coherent synthesis. The scene is a half-deserted post-holocaust city in England. Life meanders very much as in Delany's Bellona in *Dhalgren*. But the external events, the comings and goings of street gangs, the establishment of a commune to care for stray children, the inexorable decline of public services, the enigmatic news reports on the radio, all matter very little except to establish a kind of background noise representing the slide of modern civilization into chaos. The central events are the internal ones, as the memoirist—a clearly autobiographical figure—pursues her explorations of consciousness and transcendence in her flat. In the final episode, the wall through which she has viewed many scenes from her own past opens one more time. The memoirist beckons the young friends who are staying with her, and together they step through the wall, following a mysterious female figure, "who went ahead showing them the way out of this collapsed little world into another order of world altogether."[11] They do not return.

"The ending of *The Memoirs of a Survivor*," writes Roberta Rubenstein, "is a rendering into language and image of the essentially ineffable experience of transcendence—the state of elevated consciousness characteristic of the mystical experience."[12] As with most attempts to render the "ineffable," it reads like solemn gibberish to the uninitiated, but there is no reason to question Lessing's sincerity. Since *The Memoirs of a Survivor*, she has embarked on the most far-reaching project of her career, a series of speculative novels roughly analogous to the "Ransom" stories of C. S. Lewis, with the covering title of *Canopus in Argos: Archives*. The first, published in 1979, is *Shikasta*, a laborious history of the world from the age of the Giants of Biblical times to the period just after World War Three, which killed all but one percent of earth's people. As in *The Four-Gated City*, much of the interest of the novel toward the end centers on the imminence of better times, as utopian communities of survivors begin to form. Faith in the creative power and unity of the cosmos returns to mankind, after millennia of depravity under the malign influence of beings from the "criminal planet" of Shammat. Lessing follows Lewis in attributing the perennial struggle between good and evil to cosmic forces, but her theology is Jungian and Sufi, not Christian.

In all this work, Lessing not only runs up against the problem of capturing in words experiences that by their very nature transcend the categories of rational discourse: like most would-be modern mystics, as they make their various "leaps" to faith, she is plagued by the demons of cultural relativism. Wherever we turn, to Aldous Huxley, or Ramuz, or Lawrence, or Hesse, or Jung, or the forerunner of them all, Friedrich Nietzsche, there clings to all these leaping, plunging imaginations in quest of higher truths and deeper faiths, a tentativeness that is quite the opposite of the transforming spirituality they seek. Always self-conscious, hesitant to stake claims that may limit their future freedom, torn in too many directions by knowledge of too much history and religion and philosophy, they bring us a truth that is subtly undermined by the incorrigible relativizing intellectualism of its own messengers.

As Robert Galbreath observes, in a comparative study of Lessing, Hesse, and Isaac Bashevis Singer, the saving knowledge of modern gnosticism is a "problematic gnosis."[13] The phrase is self-contradictory in terms of traditional mystical thought, but it expresses well the unique nature, and dilemma, of the larger movement of ideas in which Lessing now works. The problematic gnosis of her mysticism is only a special case of the still more problematic quality of irrationalist thought in general, gnostic or agnostic. Of all modern world views, irrationalism is the most strenuously ambiguous. Inevitably, it imagines ambiguous apocalypses.

PART FIVE

◆

Aftermaths

15

◆

Blind Alleys and Return Trips

THE TOUGHEST QUESTION, which we have saved until last, is whether in stories of the world's end, the world really ends. That is, in how many scenarios of the endtime has the author in fact set aside the "world" that he knows, abolished it in his imagination, and moved on to something qualitatively new—or at least brought his readers to the point where they can move on by themselves?

Our concern in this final part of *Terminal Visions* is not with pre-modern archetypes that supply inspiration (as in Part Two), not with psychic or historical events that ignite fears of disaster (as in Part Three), and not with world views that furnish propaganda for deliberate preaching (as in Part Four), but with the underlying meaning of the world's end tale for the culture in which we live. Such meaning is ordinarily hidden from the author. It is not really his business.

Clues abound, but the best of them turn up in the aftermaths of world-ending calamities. In what the author sees happening after the end we often discover what the end was all about, and whether it really took place, or was only the occasion for a lesson, a judgment, a critique, or a commentary on the passing show. By this criterion, endtimes come in three varieties: ends without aftermaths, because the end is final and absolute; ends that curve back on themselves, in a pattern of cyclical return; and ends that liberate. The first two varieties will occupy our attention in this chapter, and the third in Chapter Sixteen.

Modern stories of the world's end that lead into blind alleys or take their readers on round trips to doomsday carry, in most cases, the same hermetic message. They reflect a conserving temperament and an ironic sensibility that may wear the ideological armor of any of the great world views. Their posture may be defensive, censorious, didactic, regretful, or whatever, but the point is that the world of the author's experience does not end in his consciousness or in his loyalties. He does not escape its boundaries. The future he envisages is either empty or an empty repetition, because he is firmly attached to the present order of things. He fits the classic Marxist analysis of eschatology offered some years ago by two Soviet futurists: "Every class or social group doomed by history to early extinction or departure from the stage usually produced or recruited ideologists who projected the gloomi-est pictures of mankind's early end."[1]

Positivists may succumb to this kind of eschatological conservatism al-most as readily as romantics or irrationalists. The positivist who believes fervently in the mission of science and modern civilization, but who writes a cautionary terminal tale about the foul play of its enemies, is writing defen-sively, hoping to conserve a scheme of things just as surely as the romantic who wants to restore the organic wholeness of various imaginary "good old days." By the same token, there are terminal visions centered in romanticism or irrationalism that do look forward to a new world, transformed beyond recognition. The new world is seldom seen except in metaphor by any writer—and seldom understood for what it is. No doubt that is the best way to ensure that it will be new, and not just a paraphrase of the familiar. But there are no new worlds in endtimes that simply end, and none in endtimes that bring us round to our starting points.

The dead end, paradoxically, is the least eschatological of all ends imag-ined by writers of terminal fiction. It fulfills better than all others the literal requirements of eschatology. It seems to foreclose hope. It condemns without mercy and without possibility of appeal. Nonetheless, in almost every story of a dead end studied for this book, the upshot is not so much destruction as a desperate clinging to the life being destroyed. The author has found a way of confessing his allegiance to the world, and a strategy for telling us of its fragility. The more hopeless the situation, the fiercer his allegiance and the stronger his determination not to let the world go. Since the beginning of the nineteenth century, about one terminal fiction in six has required such a final, irreversible end. Of these, no matter what the world view of the writer, only a few are serious exercises in prediction. Time and again, they reveal a conserving impulse, which does not necessarily carry with it a conscious wish to warn of troubles ahead, but does indicate the writer's emotional attach-ment to an established order of things.

The end as blind alley is illustrated quite well by such romantic stories as Mary Shelley's *The Last Man*. As in so many "last man" fictions, she uses the terminal situation to comment on the toppling of the mighty, but in a

mood of regret and sadness, with little deliberate ironic intent. Her protagonist is left alone and lonely; the whole attention of the novel falls on a fondly
remembered past. It is much the same with Byron's "Darkness." Hood's poem
"The Last Man" is a sardonic comment on the class war, which continues
between the two last survivors of a world-wide disaster, and Wells's *The Time
Machine* laments not only the failure of life on an exhausted earth but the
degeneration of mankind when class conflict is not resolved. Although Wells
was a socialist, an atheist, and a positivist, and Shelley a Christian romantic
with conservative instincts, their two novels reek of *Weltschmerz* and nostalgia. Wells moved on to a different kind of eschatological vision in the work
of his maturity, as Shelley did not, but *The Last Man* and *The Time Machine*
are both melancholy countdowns to oblivion.

Many other later works that we have already examined in other contexts
emit the same affective signals. From the 1930s come the two Campbell
stories, "Twilight" and "Night," Moxley's *Red Snow*, Southwold's *The Seventh
Bowl*, and Spitz's *La guerre des mouches*. All are critical of various ills of
modern times, and all have their axes to grind, but they share a bleakly
retrospective mood. Among still later fictions, there is the black humor and
sentimental humanism of Vidal's *Kalki*, Vonnegut's *Cat's Cradle*, and George's
Dr. Strangelove; the sense of man's helplessness before a nature raging out of
control in Moore's *Greener Than You Think*, Disch's *The Genocides*, and Stone's
Blizzard; the bittersweetness of Shute's *On the Beach* and Roshwald's *Level 7*;
and the savagely morbid "Among the Dead" by Edward Bryant.

A few other stories of dead ends, not previously discussed, display conserving impulses that are at least as powerful as any displayed in these works.
Donald Wandrei's first published story, "The Red Brain," and its sequel, "On
the Threshold of Eternity," are examples of pure nostalgia, tales of the end of
the universe and the death of its last beleaguered inhabitants after eons of
stupefying grandeur; they recall the poem of another Shelley, Percy's "Ozy-
mandias of Egypt." Amelia Reynolds Long's "Omega" and Edmond Hamilton's "In the World's Dusk" are similar pulp-fiction tales of the 1930s, and
Ray Bradbury contributed two others in the early 1950s, Bradburian sentimentality at its excruciating best, "There Will Come Soft Rains" and "The
Last Night of the World."

Just as sentimental, but with a heavy coating of simulated fin-de-siècle
decadence and sadomasochistic horror, respectively, are Harlan Ellison's stories "The Wine Has Been Left Open Too Long and the Memory Has Gone
Flat" and the much reprinted "I Have No Mouth, and I Must Scream." The
protagonist of "I Have No Mouth" is a computer, the Allied Mastercomputer
("AM" for short), a fusion of all the computers that planned the third World
War. Seizing control of the world in the final stages of the war, AM had

finished the job by eliminating every one of its despised human masters except five specimens. Consciousness and intelligence are intolerable to the computer, trapped in its immobile electronic body. As talion punishment for having belonged to the race that created it, AM keeps the specimens alive to be tortured for eternity. The future will be an interminable drama of pointless recrimination and revenge—not unlike the idea of Hell in Christian teaching.

The late 1950s and early 1960s were a particularly rich time, as we have seen, for novels of nuclear war, many of them adopting the formula exploited so effectively by Shute in *On the Beach*. The lives of selected survivors are followed down to the time when they have become last men and women. The mood is generally one of sadness and regret, contrasting the beauty of the world as it is, or could be, with the universal blight of atomic war.

Helen McCloy's *The Last Day*, which she published in 1959 under the pseudonym of Helen Clarkson, carries out the formula to perfection. Divided into six chapters, one for each of the last six days of life on earth, the novel takes as its protagonists Lois and Bill Cobbett, two ordinary Americans in middle years, who have journeyed to a New England fishing village to spend their summer vacation. The first day is uneventful, but at dawn on the morning of the second day, war comes. The nearest nuclear bomb blows out the windows in the Cobbetts' cottage. All the radios go silent, and the villagers dig in, following the instructions for sheltering against fallout supplied by a nuclear physicist on holiday. Despite the sandbags and other precautions, the survivors begin to die one by one of radiation poisoning. Their silent radios testify that the calamity has been worldwide. On the last day, Bill dies in the arms of Lois, and she alone remains of all the people in the village. She finds one bird miraculously alive, a small brown bird, making its home on the beach in a hollow shielded from the worst effects of radiation. The bird has no mate, no nest, no eggs. "The last bird of all singing to the last human being. . . . As I listened to his innocent joy," Lois confesses, "slowly, for the first time since the bombs fell, tears began to slip down my cheeks." She feels shame and guilt for all mankind, as she lies down to sleep "in the only place I knew in the whole world that was windless and clean."[2]

The novel ends at this point, but the reader knows what lies in store for the heroine. Her last resting place will be the beach, a favorite zone for secular eschatologists, marking the point of transition from land to ocean, from man's active life as an air-breather to amniotic unconsciousness and oblivion. In McCloy's vision, the mother-ocean, too, has been sterilized by radiation poisoning. All life on earth is dead. A world, in itself whole and sound and beautiful, has been blasted to nothingness by man's "runaway technology."[3]

Regret is rendered more bitter still in *The End of It All* by the Belgian novelist Camille A. M. Caseleyr, writing as Jack Danvers. Set in Caseleyr's adopted home country of Australia, *The End of It All* destroys the world not with nuclear bombs but with an omnipotent bacteriological weapon used after the bombs had failed to give either side victory. The author's spokesman is an Aussie scientist who has just invented a process that will triple world grain production. But suddenly there are no people to eat his grain. Hunger no longer exists, as pestilence stalks the last few survivors in the dry hills west of Alice Springs. The scientist curses man for his stupidity, "a stupidity which nothing could cure but death."[4]

The other major strategy for creating scenarios of the world's end that foreclose the future borrows the ancient idea of cyclical time, doing for fiction what Oswald Spengler did for historiography in 1918 in *The Decline of the West*. There are no cyclical visions in the literature of Last Things comparable in imaginative power to Spengler's masterpiece, but a few notable writers of every recent generation have tried their hand, with many others hinting at a cyclical view of history even if it is not explicitly argued.

Actually, cyclical fictions come in two distinct varieties, of which only the first displays the purity and logical rigor of the Spenglerian approach. One might even say, only the first is cyclical. In pure cyclicism, every culture on the great wheel of history is equal to every other, and there is no such thing as mankind in the abstract, recording cumulative progress as the wheel turns. But in the variant of cyclicism set forth by the English scholar Arnold J. Toynbee in the twelve ponderous volumes of *A Study of History*, published in 1933–61, net gain does occur. The dialectics of civilizational rise and fall are simply part of the wise economy of world history. The future is open. Endtimes come, but they do not compel, or necessarily compel, the re-setting of the cosmic clock.

In fiction the two undoubted classics of this cyclical progressivism, which took their inspiration from speculative metaphysics rather than from Toynbee himself, are Olaf Stapledon's *Last and First Men* and *Star Maker*. Neither book trades in relativism or fatalism or retrospective melancholy. In Stapledon the cycles of history are means to the higher end of the transcendence of man by superman, and of life itself by absolute spirit. Cycles also figure prominently in Isaac Asimov's *Foundation* novels and in Michael Moorcock's *The End of All Songs*, but science comes to the rescue, as mankind learns to outfox the cyclical process.

Spenglerian cyclicism, of course, is an entirely different matter. Outfoxing does not occur, or at any rate not by acts of mortal man. In the preeminent work of science fiction that adheres to a pure cyclicism, Walter M. Miller's *A Canticle for Leibowitz*, the ancient doctrine of the rise and fall of states is harnessed to the propagandistic purposes of an Augustinian view of history, with stunning effect. At one point in the last part of the novel, Miller's spokesman, the abbot Zerchi, asks the rhetorical question, "Are we doomed to it, Lord, chained to the pendulum of our own mad clockwork, helpless to halt its swing?"[5] The time is A.D. 3781; the civilization rebuilt from the ashes of World War III is about to be incinerated in World War IV. Miller surely wants his readers to answer Dom Zerchi's question with a re-sounding "Yes!" Mankind is chained to its man-made pendulum, cursed by original sin, destined to repeat the same crimes over and over again. The Church also goes on, through the cycles, charged with her holy mission until the Last Trump. As the novel ends, a starship blasts off for Alpha Centauri, to continue the rounds of history under a new sun. Good and evil are locked in mortal combat, and there can be no victory for either side.

A Canticle for Leibowitz is open to other interpretations. It hints of man's coming redemption, and perhaps even progress of a sort. Robert Scholes and Eric S. Rabkin compare its closing pages with Arthur C. Clarke's Childhood's End, a much less ambiguous forecast of good things to come.[6] But on balance, I suspect that Miller's message is essentially the same as that of C. S. Lewis. The promises of redemption refer to the time beyond time, not to a higher life under any sun known to astronomers. Miller's world view is the cyclicism of orthodox Christianity, neither hostile nor friendly to science, but con-temptuous of all utopism. As he writes in the opening paragraph of Part III (subtitled "Fiat Voluntas Tua"), it is inevitable that man should conquer the stars and make after-dinner speeches celebrating his victory. "But, too, it was inevitable that the race succumb again to the old maladies on new worlds, even as on Earth before. . . . Versicles by Adam, Rejoinders by the Crucified."[7]

Miller's story, like most cyclical fiction, is placed in the relatively far future. A few cyclical romances, not the least interesting, occur in imaginary remote pasts. A favored location is Atlantis, following the example set more than two thousand years ago by Plato in two famous dialogues. In "one grievous day and night," he reports, the whole great island with all its people vanished beneath the waves. The sad ruins of Atlantis were identified by Verne's Captain Nemo in Vingt mille lieues sous les mers, and her civilization has been brought back to life again and again, always with the same lugub-rious finale, and sometimes with clearly drawn implications for the future of our own world. A memorable early example is C. J. Cutcliffe Hyne's The Lost Continent.

But for the cyclical implications of the Atlantis legend, a far better early source is Verne's own posthumously published novella, L'éternel Adam. As we noted in Chapter Ten, Verne's positivism faltered in his last years. But in L'éternel Adam, Verne did much more than cast doubt on the benevolence of science. He composed one of the most sternly fatalistic stories in the history of speculative fiction. It amounts nearly to a repudiation of all the hopes and visions with which Verne was associated in the public mind.

L'éternel Adam tells the story of a monster earthquake causing floods that engulf the whole world in the twenty-first century. Every continent is submerged, but the Atlantis once visited by Captain Nemo miraculously returns from the deeps, the only dry land available to the single shipload of human survivors. From their offspring, who at first degenerate into savages, a new race arises. Drawing on both the archeological evidence of the original Atlantis and a recently discovered memoir of one of the few survivors of the deluge of the twenty-first century, a savant of the new Atlantis brings the story to a close with a world-weary meditation on the cycles of history. Civilization, fallen twice before, will fall again. "Bending under the weight of those vain efforts piled high in the infinity of time," the savant comes with reluctance to "an intimate conviction of the eternal return of all things."[8] His last thoughts may well have been Verne's too; they are a far cry from the boyish exuberance of the author of the *Voyages extraordinaires*.

Verne's countryman René Barjavel has recently given the old Atlantis legend a provocative new twist in *La nuit des temps*, a neo-romantic story told in a spirit of ironic resignation that differs hardly at all from the disillusioned positivism of *L'éternel Adam*. As the narrative begins, French scientists conducting subglacial tests in Antarctica uncover evidence of a city buried deep in the polar ice cap. An international team of experts thaws out the last Antarcticans, a man and a woman preserved at absolute zero in a golden sphere full of scientific marvels suggesting a civilization higher than that of the twentieth century. Using a device that projects the woman's memories on to a television screen, the scientists are able to watch the last days of her quasi-utopian homeland, Gondawa.

Utopian or not, Gondawa was totally destroyed by something far from mysterious to the woman's twentieth-century rescuers. A series of four world wars (the same number as in *A Canticle for Leibowitz*) fought between the superpowers of 900,000 B.C., Gondawa and Enisor, left the planet all but lifeless. The third, a nuclear exchange prompted by Enisorian aggression against Gondawan lunar bases, had killed 800 million people alone. In the fourth, Gondawa used a doomsday weapon that obliterated Enisor, sinking much of it under the Atlantic Ocean, and tilting the earth's axis so drastically that Gondawa, also wasted, was now located at the South Pole, where its ruins soon disappeared under thousands of feet of ice. Despite vehement peace demonstrations led by students, Gondawa (= Western Europe and North America) was prepared to risk world annihilation rather than submit to the ruthless collectivism of Enisor (= Soviet Russia or Maoist China).

"They're us!" cries the American scientist Hoover after he witnesses the final hours of Gondawan history. The few dozen survivors of the fourth war had somehow scratched their way back up to civilization in nine hundred millennia. "They've repopulated the world, and now they've achieved the same state of idiocy they were in before, ready to blow themselves up all over again. Great, isn't it? That's the human race!"[9]

At the end of the novel, the Antarctic expedition no longer dominates the world's headlines, thanks to the sabotage of all its secrets by a scientist who had plotted to sell them to parties unknown. Elsewhere, it is business as usual. Crises roil Asia, South Africa, the Middle East, Berlin. Student protesters shout in the streets, demanding peace. The world dangles on the brink of war. The distant heirs of Gondawa and Enisor gird themselves for yet another cataclysm. Barjavel has made his point, skillfully if not with any excess of subtlety, that *Homo belligerans* is doomed to repeat his follies as long as he lives.

Oswald Spengler himself could hardly have said it better. But on occasion the German philosopher has wielded a direct influence on the writing of cyclical stories, as in the tetralogy *Cities in Flight* by the late James Blish. Spengler is cited twice in the tetralogy, along with other cyclical philosophers of history, and the history of the future imagined by Blish corresponds closely to the pattern of the past expounded in *The Decline of the West*, a point well made by Richard D. Mullen in his study of the uses of Spengler in American science fiction.[10]

Blish was something of a religious philosopher and amateur historian as well as a writer of matchless speculative fiction. His other work includes *Doctor Mirabilis*, based on the life of Roger Bacon, and *A Case of Conscience*, whose Jesuit hero struggles with the theological implications of the future. *Cities in Flight* began its publishing history as the "Okie" stories in the pages of *Astounding Science-Fiction* in 1950. The first of the four novels to be published as a book was *Earthman, Come Home* in 1955, which became the third volume in the tetralogy. The others appeared between 1957 and 1962, rounding out a galactic history some twenty-one centuries in length.

Blish's account of the rise, fall, and rise again of human civilization in outer space, together with brief allusions to earlier and later non-human empires, is clearly Spenglerian. At the same time, Blish cannot resist the Asimovian touch of building into his future the heroic, essentially modern Western theme of men who are affected but not dominated by the cyclical rhythm of galactic history. For Isaac Asimov in *The Foundation Trilogy*, the heroes are the masterminds of the First and Second Foundations; for Blish in *Cities in Flight*, they are the flying cities themselves, and above all Mayor John Amalfi and his peripatetic Manhattan. Strong traces of the paradigm of cumulative progress mark the millennial career of Amalfi and his city, although nothing so forthright as the progressivism of the Asimov novels.

But the cyclical paradigm returns in triumph in the last volume of the set, when the cosmos comes to an abrupt end in A.D. 4104 as the result of a stupendous collision of the realms of matter and anti-matter at the exact midpoint of the cyclical histories of both. Our champions, the leading citizens of Manhattan, fly a planet to the hub of the universe, where the molecules of each will ingeniously survive the cataclysm to become the world-stuff of new universes. At the very moment of the Big Bang, "Creation began."[11] Blish's combination of almost Wild Western titanism and Spenglerian fatalism is unique, held in balance only by the imaginative energy, no less unique, of this distinguished novelist.

At all odds, the point has been made. In the doomsdays of cyclicism, life is constrained by the shape of time to repeat itself. As with fictions of the dead end, the writer's attention centers on the past and present, not the future. He may be angry, resigned, or enthralled. In any case, he borrows an ancient wisdom, most often for the sake of expressing present-day anxieties. In the process—again just like the writer of fictions of the dead end—he gives testimony favorable to the prosecution, testimony that the end of the old world-order is near, but he is a reluctant witness, whose sympathies lie with the defense.

His outlook is encapsuled in that shortest of all cyclical tales, James Thurber's wistful cartoon history of the future, *The Last Flower.* Wasting no time, Thurber starts off with World War Twelve, which, "as everybody knows, brought about the collapse of civilization." A young woman restores love to the world, by her tender affection for its last surviving flower. From such simple beginnings, the race regenerates. Towns grow, troubadours sing, workmen work. Demagogues return, too, fanning the fires of discontent, until mankind goes to war again. "This time the destruction was so complete . . . that nothing at all was left in the world . . . except one man . . . and one woman . . . and one flower."[12]

Which was probably enough.

16

•

The End of First Things

J. G. BALLARD has a story, "The Venus Hunters," about a strangely rational lunatic of middle years by the name of Charles Kandinski. The man works as a waiter at a local café and has published a hackneyed book at his own expense relating an encounter with inhabitants of the planet Venus. The Venusians, he says, have warned mankind not to leave earth. An astronomer, Ward, befriends Kandinski, not crediting his wild story, but fascinated by his sane demeanor, his quiet charisma, his perfect sincerity. Eventually Ward comes to believe in him, although he knows that Kandinski is a victim of delusions. He ruins his career by trying to help Kandinski approach the United Nations.

The key to the story, perhaps the key to all of Ballard's work, and to much of the eschatological fiction studied in *Terminal Visions*, comes into view near the end, when another astronomer at the observatory, Professor Cameron, tries to explain what this Venus-hunting is all about. Kandinski has told the truth, he says. Cameron quotes Jung on the imminent change in Platonic Great Years, the transition at hand from the Christian epoch to a new age marked by "confusion and psychic chaos." Kandinski is someone who senses the transition intuitively, but cannot express himself without resorting to mythogeny. Nonetheless, he is telling the truth, in his own way, and performing "one of the most important roles in the world today, the role of a prophet alerting people to this coming crisis." His fantasies reveal "the immense psychic forces stirring below the surface of rational life, like the isotactic movements of the continental tables which heralded the major geological transformations."[1]

Of the many narratives of the world's end studied for *Terminal Visions*,

194

well over two-thirds foresee no blind alleys, and no return trips. In this great majority, there are survivors, with a future that may be better or worse than the era just ended, but a future that will be different, because the endtime came. Obviously some writers anticipate much greater qualitative differences than others. There is no agreement among writers on the world view of the future society, or on its dominant ideology, or on anything else. In many instances, the expected endtime and its survivors are transparent metaphors for a wide range of either subjective or objective experiences in the writer's own life or world. But all of these fictions of the end, and perhaps even a few of those examined in the immediately preceding chapter, perform the same role in modern Western culture that Charles Kandinski performed in Ballard's story. Whatever else they do, as art or as entertainment, they speak the sibylline truth that the world is coming to an end.

There must be no mistake on that point. The "world" we see around us, which has been changing at such breakneck speed since the late eighteenth century, the modern world of capital, labor, nationalism, empire, and the historic ascendancy of Western Europe and her children, both west of the Atlantic and east of the Oder, is coming to an end, and quite possibly to a pyrotechnic end. The great majority of terminal fictions, those in which the end liberates writer and reader from childlike belief in the granitic permanence of the world-as-it-is, display Kandinski's intuitive sense of an approaching change of epochs; and, again, it matters not at all whether the author knows what he is doing. "When you are living in a period of destructuring," writes William Irwin Thompson, "the unconscious projects mythologies of destruction."[2] Myths of destruction symbolize the "destructuring process" whereby one civilization is replaced by another.

I agree. Although a certain amount of violence and upheaval may well accompany the fall of our world, the literal end foreseen in eschatological fiction is vastly improbable. We are not headed for absolute black oblivion, through the doings either of man or of nature.[3] Even a full-scale thermonuclear third world war would very likely leave enough of South Asia and the Southern Hemisphere intact to enable a high civilization of some kind to carry on, as in Syd Logsdon's recent novel *A Fond Farewell to Dying*.

But the modern world-order is falling apart, destructuring itself, from within. Its malaise is not bodily. It may lurch on for another century. Nevertheless, its political and economic institutions are obsolescent, its traditional systems of faith and value are no longer credible, and its heart is cold. The shape of the new planetary civilization that will replace it can only be guessed at, as Thompson has tried to do in his book *At the Edge of History,* and as I have tried to do in my own *Building the City of Man.*[4] In any event, it will effectively supplant what now exists: a confused mass of disintegrating local civilizations which have penetrated one another's living space much like the plant-life of a jungle.

To return to our mythologies of destruction, the best historical analogy is with the early Christians who wrote the New Testament and the non-canonical prophetic books of the first and second centuries A.D. In their own minds, the end of time drew near. The destruction of all created being was at hand. But the meaning of their testimony for the culture in which they lived is something quite different. What they sensed, but could express only in mythic imagery, was the imminence of the end of an epoch, the epoch of Helleno-Roman paganism. They knew in their bones that something was awry, and so it was. The Roman imperium still had a few centuries of fading life to live in the West, and many more in the Greek East, but the civilization that had given rise to the imperium in the first place was already in steep decline during the Apostolic age of the Church. Paganism had exhausted its creative possibilities. The economic and political institutions of imperial Rome were foundering. The end was near. Somehow, in their own way, the Christian apocalyptists knew.

But like the great majority of modern writers of eschatological fiction, they were not content to wring their hands and predict universal doom or eternal return. To a man, they foresaw, like John in Revelation 21:1, "a new heaven and a new earth." The endtime would be followed by a radically different order of things, good for some, bad for others, yet absolutely distinct from the old order of things now sentenced to destruction. Again, the apocalyptists were right—if we can agree that Western Christendom, as it took shape during the Middle Ages and as it evolved into modern civilization between the fifteenth and eighteenth centuries, was a "new earth," quite unlike any civilization of antiquity.

Proving beyond all doubt that fictions of the world's end are encoded prophecies of a new world civilization still to emerge from the toils of history is something obviously that we cannot do. The new civilization has not yet arrived. Perhaps it never will. In any event, modern writers are in many ways unlike their Christian forerunners: better schooled in history, more worldly, driven by a different mixture of motives, and less sure of what they believe.

But the two situations do not have to be just the same, to yield roughly comparable outcomes. We must hope with some passion that the two situations are not identical, and that the aftermath of our own endtime will be as unlike the aftermath of the Helleno-Roman endtime as the civilizations of Christendom and paganism were unlike. To hope otherwise would be to succumb to the fatalistic cyclicism explored in the preceding chapter, or in Chapter Four.

One difference between the Christian apocalyptists and modern writers of eschatological fiction strikes the reader almost immediately: at least some of the modern writers know perfectly well that they are writing in code, although they vary considerably in their perceptions of how their codes should be deciphered. But this is not a serious problem for the historian, whose chief concern in interpreting texts is to identify their relevance to the times and to the cultural matrix. Writers of fiction may have no idea—or an imperfect or erroneous idea—of the forces at work in their lives, the forces that shape their thought and determine how their writing will affect others. They can take the possibility of world-wrecking disasters quite seriously, or weave their imaginary disasters into a fabulation that conveys no eschatological message, and it is all the same in the final showing. What matters is that eschatological props are wheeled on to the stage; eschatological strings are pulled; eschatological hopes and fears are fed.

But in one sense, the inclination of many writers of eschatological fiction to fabulate does help to strengthen our thesis. No matter what the author's purpose in encoding his message, the fact that he may not take his disasters "seriously" gives us all the more license to dig below the narrative surface for subterranean meanings. Whether satirical (as in *War with the Newts*), indeterminate (as in *The Memoirs of a Survivor*), or pseudo-scientific or pseudo-mythic (as in *Hothouse*), the non-realistic endtime directs attention away from this or that cause of disaster toward larger prospects, such as epochal change.

Writers of every persuasion have indulged in eschatological fabling, although for obvious reasons those drawn to irrationalism contribute the largest share of the black comedies. Among positivists, a perhaps surprisingly rich source of fabulations is H. G. Wells. "Surprisingly," because Wells is best remembered for his many realistic novels and stories, works that we have examined in a variety of contexts in earlier chapters. Some of these would be appropriate material for consideration here, too, and in particular three of his novels of future war, *The World Set Free*, *The Shape of Things to Come*, and *The Holy Terror*, in each of which a scientifically managed world civilization becomes possible only in the aftermath of a great planet-wide conflagration.[5] War as the midwife of a new world, as we know, is a pervasive theme of speculative fiction. Whether meant to be taken literally or not, it makes a plausible agency of transition, and its ravages divide old orders from new in the most dramatic possible way.

But not all of Wells's fiction is realistic, by any means. In an exceptionally long literary career, he produced at least seven novels and dozens of short stories that qualify as either fantasies or fabulations. Several of these are plainly eschatological, or incorporate eschatological materials. In almost every instance, the point—and in the case of Wells at least, the point is seldom hidden from the author—is the imminence of world transformation. In "The Story of the Last Trump," for example, a pseudo-mythic tale of a celestial accident, the trumpet created for use on doomsday is dropped to earth by a careless "blessed child." Found by two Londoners who manage to blow one half-blast on it before a fiery hand snatches it back to Heaven, the instrument gives men and women all over the world one brief thrilling prevision of the Day of the Lord. But they refuse to believe their eyes, and attend to their business like rabbits "who go on feeding in their hutches within a hundred yards of a battery of artillery."[6]

Much closer to Robert Scholes's concept of a fabulation is *The Food of the Gods*, a novel first published in 1904 that starts out like Wells's earlier scientific romances, and grows little by little into a Swiftian fable about things to come. It is only marginally eschatological, but enough so to warrant our attention. In its opening chapters, *The Food of the Gods* belongs in fact to the familiar sub-genre of disaster stories that call for murderous attacks on screaming human victims by giant insects and what not. Two scientists develop a miracle food that gets loose and causes a plague of just such creatures. A particularly atrocious film visited on the world by Bert I. Gordon in 1976, and billed as "H. G. Wells's *The Food of the Gods*," draws only on these opening chapters for its story line. But up to this point Wells has just been trying to get his readers well hooked. By 1904 they had come to expect realism in his speculative fiction. The main part of the novel is still to come.

As time goes on, a number of children receive the Food of the Gods, by design or miscalculation. They grow into giants six or seven times normal height. In the end war breaks out between the two races, the pigmies and the giants, Wells's metaphors for the old traditional civilization and the new world of his prophetic imagination, built to the bigger scale of possibilities opened up by science and technology. The giants are presented with a "reasonable" compromise by the leader of the pigmies, a reservation of their own where they can live in peace, agreeing to manufacture no more Food. But they spurn the offer bravely, and the conflict resumes. The giants—young Gods—will not stop until the Food is available everywhere, and the old humanity and its small-scale world have disappeared forever. "You cannot have pigmies and giants in one world together," say the Gods. "It is one thing or the other."[7] As Wells himself wrote of his novel, *The Food of the Gods* is not a disaster story but a "dream version" of his thesis that "the most complex and extensive readjustments in the scope and scale of [human] ideas" are demanded by the "profound change in conditions" that has overtaken the modern world.[8]

A second novel published just two years later, *In the Days of the Comet*, exploits eschatology in the same fabling way, with the same realistic opening

scenes. This time, the eschatological events are a set of three disasters occur-
ring simultaneously, any of which could lead to the collapse of civilization or
even the destruction of mankind: labor unrest and violence, the outbreak of
a general European war, and the arrival of a comet that envelopes the earth
in a miraculous green mist. But when the protagonist awakens the next
morning, everything has changed. The strikes are over, the war has been
called off, and the comet, far from causing any destruction, has modified the
nitrogen in the atmosphere to transform all mankind into a reasonable,
unselfish, and peace-loving race for the first time in its tragic history. The
glimpses of the collectivistic utopia that arises in place of the old society are
among the most convincing that Wells ever wrote, with a luminous beauty
that sometimes recalls William Morris. But the bathing of the planet in the
green magic of the comet is sheer moonshine, clearly intended to be viewed
by the intelligent reader as a metaphor for world-historical processes.

Wells's imaginative energies ebbed in his later years, as the *idée fixe* of a
new world-order absorbed more and more of his attention. The problems that
beset the rest of his fiction at this time also diminished the effectiveness of
his fabulations. The most successful of the later efforts, *Mr Blettsworthy on
Rampole Island,* is only intermittently eschatological. One of the less successful, although fully eschatological in its thrust, is *All Aboard for Ararat.* The
title is superb—but not much else. The protagonist, Noah Lammock, makes
his selection of inhabitants for the new Ark, and the result is a pale shadow
of Wells's thoughts in earlier prophetic tracts on the kinds of men and women
required to guide the world through revolution to a scientific new order. Here
and there, gleams of the old genius still shine through. They fail to save the
book.

A far superior fabulation with a neo-positivist slant, Moorcock's *The End
of All Songs,* was discussed in Chapter Thirteen. But it is Moorcock's New
Wave colleague J. G. Ballard who has been the most consistent producer of
pure fabulations in the Scholesian sense during the past quarter of a century.
We have returned to Ballard's work several times, as an important source for
studying the psychopathology of terminal visions, as an arch-irrationalist,
and just a few pages ago, as the author of "The Venus Hunters." Despite the
message of "The Venus Hunters," most of Ballard's work veers inward. Yet it
is conceivable that his foremost contribution to twentieth-century fiction
will turn out to be somewhat like Wells's—the prophecy of an epochal change
in public consciousness, prelusive to a new and radically liberated world-
order.

The problem in interpreting Ballard is simply that although his literary
range is narrower than Wells's, he makes a more convincing sibyl. He is much
better at keeping his visions sibylline, in the sense of more scrupulously

enciphered. All the same, the explanation that he uses myths of universal disaster to symbolize private experience does not tell the whole story. For one thing, there is an evangelical quality about his private experiences. Although they are intensely private, they have a way of spreading from one character to another. They are also experiences in which the author takes unconcealed delight.

In short, Ballard has something to sell. The obsessed figures in the parched landscape of *The Drought* or the urban desert of "The Ultimate City" each follows his own obsession, but in various ways they reinforce one another, weaving in and out of one another's dream-lives rather like lovers. In *The Crystal World,* various characters submit to crystallization in turn, as the zones of frozen time slowly expand from their original centers to engulf the world. The reason for the failure and recall of the scientific expedition in *The Drowned World* is that most of its members are hearing the siren song of sea and jungle, the fatal southward pull back to prehistoric times. Each man flees individually, but in response to the same primordial call. In *High-Rise,* Ballard's novel of the disintegration of law and order in a tower of luxury flats, all the inhabitants suffer from the same inscrutable malady and become much more of a community than they ever were in the old days of industrial anonymity. *The Unlimited Dream Company* takes the process to its ultimate conclusion: one man's psychic space enlarges until he can engulf a whole town, and eventually a whole planet.

All this suggests that Ballard is describing not only personal transformation but the epochal shift analyzed by Professor Cameron in "The Venus Hunters." Self and world are changing together, in answer to world-historical signals—like the massed humanity that marches into the sea in "The Reptile Enclosure," a death march triggered by an obscure configuration of infrared light emitted by space satellites. The scientific explanation, as almost always in Ballard, is poppycock, and deliberately so, in keeping with his irrationalist bias against the vanities of modern science. But the epochal change is real.

What, then, of the nature of the transformation? Why does it usually consist of people committing mass suicide by drowning or wandering off to certain death from heat stroke or turning into living sculptures of polychrome crystal? Earlier, in Chapter Eight, we wondered if Ballard's sadomasochistic fantasies symbolize psychic transformation, as Ballard insists, or merely cater to the death-wish lurking in all of us. Perhaps both views are correct. But taking Ballard at his word, we can argue that his sadomasochistic fantasies are symbols of transformation, private and public, in the same way that his worldwide natural disasters are symbols of the invalidity of bourgeois culture. Images of destruction, in this reading, are chosen not to whet the carnal appetites of unwary readers or to give the author himself perverse thrills, but to stress that authentic transformation is not liberal reform. Authentic transformation demands risk, sacrifice, suffering, loss, and even death, in the sense of the death of the old self, following the Nazarene's injunction to give up one's life in order to receive it back again.

This still leaves the nature of the transformation vague. It will be drastic, we may assume, but then Auschwitz was drastic, too. All we can say on Ballard's behalf is that he is something of a mystic, but like Doris Lessing and the other contemporary irrationalists discussed in Chapter Fourteen, he deliberately avoids attachment to specific programs and formulas that might put his imagination on too short a tether. Meanwhile, he is sure of one thing: the comfortable, tidy, proper, and rational world of today, the middle-class world of the garden city and the luxury apartment and the smug expert, does not work.

Typically, the escape that Ballard selects for his heroes is an escape from the hurry-scurry of time into a realm where time has congealed. The way to prevent crystallization, in *The Crystal World,* is to keep moving. When someone is ready to join the crystal world, all he has to do is come to rest, and the process painlessly lifts him across the threshold into eternity. The characters of *The Drowned World* flee southward, but only to reach the womb of prehistory, where all motion will become superfluous. In *The Drought,* Ransom and the others live in a "timeless world" of self-abstracted indifference, on a changeless beach and a changeless desert. The wastes of sand recall Ransom's favorite painting, Yves Tanguy's "Jours de Lenteur," a canvass filled with "smooth, pebble-like objects, drained of all associations, suspended on a washed tidal floor . . . drained beaches, eroded of all associations, of all sense of time."[9]

Sometimes Ballard supplies one more inkling of the nature of the transformation in store for new-world man. It is not found in every example of his work. But in episodes here and there Ballard seems to look beyond psychic revolution, to a more concrete aftermath in which time has started up again. The last lines of *The Drought* report an astonishing change in the changeless world: after ten dry years, clouds form again. Ransom's shadow disappears, "as if he had at last completed his journey across the margins of the inner landscape he had carried in his mind for so many years." Darkness covers the dunes, but it is the darkness before a storm. "It was some time later that he failed to notice it had started to rain."[10]

Ransom may have failed to notice—for the moment. Ballard has not. Time, and with it the possibility of life and history, has returned with the first rainfall, and the future once again stands open. In another story, "Chronopolis," the hero escapes from the suburbs, where the survivors of a bizarre social revolution against urbanism live in "a zone of endless afternoons." He returns to the deserted inner city to carry out his desperate plan of starting up the clocks all over London. Since timepieces were outlawed nearly forty years ago, his acts are criminal, and he goes to prison, sentenced to twenty years of clock-watching. Similar "crimes" obsess Ballard's hero in "The Ultimate City," after he makes his escape from the tedium of a solar-powered utopia. In two other stories, "The Garden of Time" and "A Place and a Time to Die," the protagonists are stereotypical reactionaries, clinging to a sterile timeless past, who cannot prevent the overrunning of their villa, in one instance, or their town, in the other, by mysterious ragtag armies of marching masses. The reader sees the stories in both cases from the point of view of those overrun, but clearly it is the masses who will make the future, and their relentless movement is like the swinging of a pendulum, a sign of the restoration of time.

One more image of a revolutionary future beyond modern civilization occurs in "Low-Flying Aircraft," a story first published in 1975. Early on, Ballard seems to be telling another one of his familiar tales about preoccupied stragglers at the end of time. During the last forty years, the earth's population has dwindled alarmingly, although the threat of extinction leaves the survivors strangely unmoved. Europe is down to 200,000 people, the United States to 150,000. Only one live birth in a thousand yields a normal child; the rest are deformed and must be destroyed. Our protagonists are Forrester and his pregnant wife Judith, vacationing lazily on a nearly empty Costa Brava, and Gould, a physician of uncertain mental health, who is also a pilot. From time to time Gould makes crazy flights low over the hills, spraying them with phosphorescent paint. When Judith's baby is born, it is another blind monster.

But Ballard does not furnish his patented ending. Forrester, Judith, and Gould do not simply go their separate ways, falling deeper and deeper into meditative trances. In the dénouement, we learn from the doctor-pilot that he sprays the hills with a special paint to provide trails for blind mutant cattle, whose blindness is only relative. They can see, but their eyes receive light from "a different section of the electromagnetic spectrum." Following Gould's trails, the cattle learn to escape the local farmers who would have slaughtered them. The blindness of Judith's child is of the same order. Forrester turns it over to a young mutant woman to raise, rather than letting it be destroyed. Gould explains that a new race is arising, which will supplant mankind, and nature has made it easier for Homo sapiens to fade away gracefully, by depriving it of feelings of despair. Instead of the end, it is the beginning.

To be sure, such moments are not common in Ballard's work. It is also true that he prefers to see the new world in good measure through the eyes of the old. H. Bruce Franklin faults him for his bourgeois dandyism, his indifference to working people, his hedonism. "What could Ballard create," he asks, "if he were able to envision the end of capitalism as not the end, but the beginning, of a human world?"[11] The answer is that Ballard has shown that ability many times. But he usually prefers to keep the future veiled, perhaps for some of the same reasons that led Karl Marx to avoid explicit utopographic prophecy. In any case, Ballard insists on remaining faithful to his craft by writing about only what he knows. A former medical student, military airman, media specialist, and now free-lance writer, what he knows is the urban middle class. But what of it? Why attack writers for being true to their own experience? What matters is that they tell whatever truth they do have. Not many producers of speculative fiction have told as much truth as Ballard, not only in his eschatological work but in such brilliant exercises in anti-capitalist dystopian fiction as "Billennium," "Build-Up," and "The Subliminal Man."

At any rate, fabulations in which the world's end becomes a symbol of world transformation offer one invaluable set of clues for understanding the cultural significance of the literature of Last Things. Another clue may be found in the tendency of authors to invent many different ways of ending the world. It is like the liar who gives himself away by offering too many excuses for the same offense. Some of the abundance, to be sure, is only the result of commercial pressures, the public demand to be frightened in as many ways as possible. Such an explanation works especially well for disaster films, where legitimate artistic and prophetic values rarely come into play. But it does not work for every writer by any means. The variety of world's ends in the output of an H. G. Wells or a J. G. Ballard cannot be explained solely in terms of market forces. The same is true of other major writers of eschatological fiction such as Karel Čapek, Olaf Stapledon, John Wyndham, Brian Aldiss, René Barjavel, John Christopher, and Michael Moorcock—each of whom has ended the world several times in a variety of entirely different ways. The sense of an impending end is stronger in all of them than fear of this or that specific threat to the survival of civilization.

Now and again, a writer brings the world to an end in two or more ways in the same work. Anna Kavan's *Ice* represents the endtime as a race between encroaching glaciers and spreading wars, and shows little interest in either. Her attention centers on private matters, but these in turn may symbolize larger processes of transformation active in the world-order. One of the first of all terminal novels, Richard Jefferies's *After London,* advances a number of possible explanations for the collapse of civilization, and reaches no firm conclusion about any of them. What really concerns the author is to discredit the civilization of his own time and move on in his imagination to a fresh new world in which life once again offers a chance for personal heroism. In Alun Llewellyn's novel of the 1930s, *The Strange Invaders*, the endtime includes a second world war, a second ice age, neo-Stalinist barbarian tyranny, and attacks by giant lizards.

There are, it goes without saying, many other examples, but the story to end all others in this special category is Robert Heinlein's "The Year of the Jackpot," a whimsical piece about a statistician who keeps track of the known waves of human and natural disaster, and computes that in a single year they will all crest with catastrophic results. In the fateful year, everything happens as he knew it would, from an epidemic of compulsive undressing in public, through volcanoes, earthquakes, air crashes, and epidemics, to floods, nuclear war, and the conversion of the sun into a nova. The world has about thirty minutes left when the story ends. Heinlein's yarn is more likely a spoof of disaster stories than a fable about world regeneration, but it establishes a point.

Lest we lose sight of the bigger point, however, it should be made once again. The bulk of eschatological fictions—not just a few fabulations or tales of multiple calamity—can be read as indicators of a growing consciousness within modern Western culture that its end is in view and that a new, higher, or radically different civilization and public order will replace it during the next century. Any work that shows prescience of an approaching collapse of the existing cultural, political, and socioeconomic world system, and some awareness of an aftermath among the survivors that is qualitatively different from the prevailing system, deserves to be registered as a work of prophetic insight. The insight may, of course, be entirely wrong. In the early 2080s, our descendants may be living with the same chaos of Coca-Cola, fundamentalist Islam, suburban shopping malls, starving East Africans, Eurocommunism, and H-bombs crouching in their silos that we know so well in the early 1980s. But it is not bloody likely.

Thus it is not just the odd short story by Ballard or fable by Wells that looks forward to world transformation, but a considerable array of eschatological fictions already studied in several contexts in this book. Shiel in *The Purple Cloud*, Forster in "The Machine Stops," Ramuz in *Présence de la mort*, Stapledon in *Last and First Men*, Bradbury in *The Martian Chronicles*, Wyndham in *The Chrysalids*, Christopher in *The World in Winter*, Moorcock in *The End of All Songs*, Lessing in *Shikasta*: these, and a great many others, are signposts to new times, after the endtime. Signposting also occurs in works of speculative fiction that fall outside our definitions of eschatology, but offer transformational scenarios just the same. Utopias, dystopias, stories of the superman, and sagas of the colonization of space can all double as visions of a new and higher life for mankind, without the stresses of the endtime. Works such as Arthur C. Clarke's *Childhood's End*, Robert Heinlein's *Stranger in a Strange Land*, and Ursula K. Le Guin's *The Left Hand of Darkness* may have done as much as any world's end story to advertise the possibility of epochal change.

Nevertheless, it remains undeniable that terminal visions bring emphasis of a special kind to the prophet's cry of woe and warning. They attack us at our most vulnerable point: our sense of mortality, and our fear of nonbeing. They take us to the outer limits of despair before raising us, if raise us they do, to the uplands of life and hope. They tell us that first things, the period described by Marx as "the prehistoric stage of human society"—the stage before man is liberated from the natural laws of jungle and marketplace and balance of international terror—are drawing to a close. History, in the sense of a destiny made by man himself, will soon begin.

Or so we dream. But for now, in the "meanwhile" of a faltering civilization, thoughts of ending come more easily to mind. The end of anything, whether a term of imprisonment, a love affair, a fellow man, or a book, is a time when memories fall into sharp focus. Creation pauses in its tracks. The vision of the end of the world chills the heart. Never so much as then, do we cry out for the warming breath of new life.

NOTES

A Personal Preface

1. C. S. Lewis, *That Hideous Strength* (New York: Macmillan, 1946), p. 420.
2. See W. Warren Wagar, *The City of Man: Prophecies of a World Civilization in Twentieth-Century Thought* (Boston: Houghton Mifflin, 1963), and *Building the City of Man: Outlines of a World Civilization* (New York: Grossman, 1971).
3. For K'ang, see K'ang Yu-wei, *Ta T'ung Shu: The One-World Philosophy of K'ang Yu-wei*, ed. and tr. Laurence G. Thompson (London: Allen and Unwin, 1958), p. 104.
4. See W. Warren Wagar, "The Bankruptcy of the Peace Movement," *War/Peace Report*, 9:7 (August/September, 1969), 3–6.

Chapter One

1. The phrase is H. Bruce Franklin's. See his "Chic Bleak in Fantasy Fiction," *Saturday Review*, 55:29 (July 15, 1972), 42–45.
2. See Hal Lindsey, *The Late Great Planet Earth* (Grand Rapids, Mich.: Zondervan, 1976), and *The 1980's: Countdown to Armageddon* (New York: Bantam, 1981). Another representative work in the same vein is Bill Petersen, *The Last Days of Man* (New York: Warner, 1977).
3. See John Wesley White, *World War III: Signs of the Impending Battle of Armageddon* (Grand Rapids, Mich.: Zondervan, 1977).
4. Gordon Rattray Taylor, *The Doomsday Book* (New York: World, 1970); Fred Warshofsky, *Doomsday: The Science of Catastrophe* (New York: Reader's Digest, 1977); Gerrit L. Verschuur, *Cosmic Catastrophes* (Reading, Mass.: Addison-Wesley, 1978); and Isaac Asimov, *A Choice of Catastrophes* (New York: Simon and Schuster, 1979). For the younger reader, there is Daniel Cohen, *How the World Will End* (New York: McGraw-Hill, 1973). See also Charles Berlitz, *Doomsday 1999 A.D.* (Garden City, N.Y.: Doubleday, 1981), an agitated pastiche by the author of *The Bermuda Triangle*.
5. See, for example, Paul R. Ehrlich, *The Population Bomb* (New York: Ballantine, 1968); Donella H. Meadows, Dennis L. Meadows, et al., *The Limits to Growth* (New York: Universe, 1972); and Garrett Hardin, "Living on a Lifeboat," *Bioscience*, 24:10 (October, 1974), 561–68.
6. Representative titles include John Gribbin, *Forecasts, Famines, and Freezes: Climate and Man's Future* (New York: Walker, 1976); Reid A. Bryson and Thomas J. Murray, *Climates of Hunger: Mankind and the World's Changing Weather* (Madison, Wis.: University of Wisconsin Press, 1977); Howard A. Wilcox, *Hothouse Earth*

(New York: Praeger, 1975); and D. S. Halacy, Jr., *Ice or Fire? Surviving Climatic Change* (New York: Harper and Row, 1978).

7. Louis René Beres, *Apocalypse: Nuclear Catastrophe in World Politics* (Chicago: University of Chicago Press, 1980), and General Sir John Hackett, et al., *The Third World War: August 1985* (New York: Macmillan, 1979). See also Shelford Bidwell, ed., *World War 3* (New York: Prentice-Hall, 1978), and Nigel Calder, *Nuclear Nightmares: An Investigation into Possible Wars* (New York: Viking, 1980).

8. "The Deluge of Disastermania," *Time*, 113:10 (March 5, 1979), 84. See also Andrée Conrad, "Beyond the Panic Principle: Disaster and the American Imagination," *Book Forum*, 4:2 (1978), 204–54; James Cornell, *The Great International Disaster Book* (New York: Scribner's, 1976); Jay Robert Nash, *Darkest Hours: A Narrative Encyclopedia of Worldwide Disasters from Ancient Times to the Present* (New York: Nelson-Hall, 1976); and David Annan, *Catastrophe: The End of the Cinema?* (New York: Crown, 1975).

9. Roberto Vacca, *The Coming Dark Age*, tr. J. S. Whale (Garden City, N.Y.: Doubleday, 1973); Robert Heilbroner, *An Inquiry into the Human Prospect*, rev. ed. (New York: Norton, 1979); William Irwin Thompson, *Darkness and Scattered Light: Four Talks on the Future* (Garden City, N.Y.: Doubleday, 1978); and Christopher Lasch, *The Culture of Narcissism: American Life in an Age of Diminishing Expectations* (New York: Norton, 1979).

10. See, for example, Bruce D. Clayton, *Life after Doomsday: A Survivalist Guide to Nuclear War and Other Major Disasters* (Boulder, Colo.: Paladin, 1980).

11. Walter E. Westman, "Doomsday Expectations," in *Science*, No. 4255 (August 27, 1976), 720.

12. See, for example, Fred L. Polak, *The Image of the Future*, 2 vols. (New York: Oceana, 1961); Koenraad W. Swart, *The Sense of Decadence in Nineteenth-Century France* (The Hague: Nijhoff, 1964); Chad Walsh, *From Utopia to Nightmare* (New York: Harper and Row, 1962); Ernest Lee Tuveson, *Millennium and Utopia: A Study in the Background of the Idea of Progress* (Berkeley and Los Angeles: University of California Press, 1949); Melvin J. Lasky, *Utopia and Revolution* (Chicago: University of Chicago Press, 1976); Harold L. Berger, *Science Fiction and the New Dark Age* (Bowling Green, Ohio: Bowling Green University Popular Press, 1976); I. F. Clarke, *The Pattern of Expectation: 1644–2001* (New York: Basic Books, 1979); Frank E. and Fritzie P. Manuel, *Utopian Thought in the Western World* (Cambridge, Mass.: Harvard University Press, 1979); Robert Nisbet, *History of the Idea of Progress* (New York: Basic Books, 1980); and W. Warren Wagar, *Good Tidings: The Belief in Progress from Darwin to Marcuse* (Bloomington: Ind.: Indiana University Press, 1972).

13. Herbert Marcuse, *One-Dimensional Man: Studies in the Ideology of Advanced Industrial Society* (Boston: Beacon, 1964), pp. 254–57. This is not to imply that all, most, or indeed more than a few secular eschatologists would be likely to agree with Marcuse's reasons for "refusing" modern civilization.

14. See David Ketterer, *New Worlds for Old: The Apocalyptic Imagination, Science Fiction, and American Literature* (Garden City, N.Y.: Doubleday, 1974), pp. ix and 50.

15. See Immanuel Wallerstein, *The Capitalist World-Economy* (New York: Cambridge University Press, 1979).

16. Robert Heinlein, "Science Fiction: Its Nature, Faults and Virtues," in Basil

Davenport, et al., *The Science Fiction Novel: Imagination and Social Criticism* (Chicago: Advent, 1959), p. 28.

17. Frank Kermode, *The Sense of an Ending: Studies in the Theory of Fiction* (New York: Oxford University Press, 1967), p. 27. Bultmann does not exhaust the possibilities of modern theology. In the "theology of hope" of Jürgen Moltmann and others, the future is once again taken with the utmost seriousness. But when Kermode was writing *The Sense of an Ending*, Moltmann was little known outside Germany, and Bultmann's demythologized eschatology dominated lay discussions of the subject.

18. John R. May, *Toward a New Earth: Apocalypse in the American Novel* (Notre Dame, Ind.: University of Notre Dame Press, 1972), p. 38.

19. David Ketterer, *New Worlds for Old*, p. 15.

20. Ibid., pp. 7 and 14.

21. See Robert Scholes, *Structural Fabulation: An Essay on Fiction of the Future* (Notre Dame, Ind.: University of Notre Dame Press, 1975), and *Fabulation and Metafiction* (Champaign-Urbana, Ill.: University of Illinois Press, 1979).

Chapter Two

1. Brian Aldiss, *Billion Year Spree: The True History of Science Fiction* (Garden City, N.Y.: Doubleday, 1973), ch. 1, "The Origin of the Species."

2. Jane Dunn, *Moon in Eclipse: A Life of Mary Shelley* (New York: St. Martin's, 1978), pp. 134 and 274.

3. Mary Shelley, *The Last Man* (Lincoln, Neb.: University of Nebraska Press, 1965), p. 76.

4. Ibid., p. 159.

5. Hugh J. Luke, Jr., "Introduction," in ibid., p. xvii.

6. Ibid., p. 342.

7. Ibid., p. 290.

8. See, for example, the lines of Perdita, ibid., p. 97; and of Lionel, ibid., p. 231.

9. A. J. Sambrook, "A Romantic Theme: The Last Man," *Forum for Modern Language Studies*, 2:1 (January, 1966), 25–33; and Henry F. Majewski, "Grainville's *Le Dernier Homme*," *Symposium*, 17:2 (Summer, 1963), 114–22. See also Jean de Palacio, "Mary Shelley and the 'Last Man,' " *Revue de Littérature Comparée*, 42:1 (January-March, 1968), 37–49.

10. See Burton R. Pollin, *Discoveries in Poe* (Notre Dame, Ind.: University of Notre Dame Press, 1970), ch. 5, "The Role of Byron and Mary Shelley in 'The Masque.' "

11. See I. F. Clarke, *The Pattern of Expectation*, ch. 1, "The Discovery of the Future."

12. Friedrich Meinecke, *Die Entstehung des Historismus* (Munich: Oldenbourg, 1936), available in English as *Historism: The Rise of a New Historical Outlook*, tr. J. E. Anderson (London: Routledge, 1972).

13. I. F. Clarke, *Tale of the Future*, 3rd ed. (London: The Library Association, 1978).

14. See Bernard Bergonzi, *The Early H. G. Wells: A Study of the Scientific Romances* (Manchester: Manchester University Press, 1961).

15. There is also a very little tale, written as part of an unpublished appendix to *Mind at the End of Its Tether*. Entitled "The Culminating Man," it concerns a plutocrat who remains safe in his "central strong-room" after the world's end. He has bought biological immortality by endowing a research institute, but to no avail. A heavenly exterminator flushes him out. "The cold air of righteousness blew in upon him, and forthwith he and all his gettings and belongings shrivelled into a slimy powder and evaporated to nothing." Manuscript in the H. G. Wells Archive, University of Illinois, reprinted in W. Warren Wagar, ed., *H. G. Wells: Journalism and Prophecy, 1893–1946* (Boston: Houghton Mifflin, 1964), pp. 441–42.

16. The original edition was published in London by Eveleigh Nash. Hyperion Press of Westport, Connecticut, reprinted the Nash edition in 1976. The novel is also available in Hodgson, *The House on the Borderland and Other Novels* (Sauk City, Wis.: Arkham House, 1946), pp. 307–637, and in a two-volume edition published in 1972 (New York: Ballantine). The Ballantine edition suffers from some allegedly "judicious" pruning.

17. Jules Verne, *Hier et demain: Contes et nouvelles* (Paris: Hetzel, 1910), p. 213 fn.

18. An English translation is available under the title *Omega: The Last Days of the World* (New York: Cosmopolitan, 1894; and New York: Arno, 1975).

19. Robert Louit, in Peter Nicholls, ed., *The Science Fiction Encyclopedia* (Garden City, N.Y.: Doubleday, 1979), p. 231. Cf. Jacques Sadoul, *Histoire de la science-fiction moderne* (Paris: Albin Michel, 1973), ch. 8, "Hier (1905–1949)."

20. The original edition was published in Paris by Plon. An English translation by George Edgar Slusser is available in J.-H. Rosny, *The Xipehuz and The Death of the Earth* (New York: Arno, 1978), pp. 51–183.

21. See Dale L. Walker in Walker, ed., *Curious Fragments: Jack London's Tales of Fantasy Fiction* (Port Washington, N.Y.: Kennikat Press, 1975), p. 6.

22. I. F. Clarke, *Voices Prophesying War, 1763–1984* (London: Oxford University Press, 1966), p. 131.

23. See, for example, Jacques Sadoul, *Histoire de la science-fiction moderne*, and Manfred Nagl, *Science Fiction in Deutschland* (Tübingen: Tübinger Vereinigung für Volkskunde, 1972).

24. J. G. Ballard, "Some Words about *Crash*," in *Foundation: Review of Science Fiction*, 9:1 (November, 1975), 46.

25. The last two novels were first published in the United States under the titles *Out of the Deeps* and *Re-Birth*, respectively.

26. The titles of these novels also underwent sea-changes: in the United States they first appeared as *No Blade of Grass*, *The Long Winter*, and *The Ragged Edge*.

Chapter Three

1. Frank E. Manuel, *Shapes of Philosophical History* (Stanford, Cal.: Stanford University Press, 1965), pp. 2–6.

2. See Grace E. Cairns, *Philosophies of History: Meeting of East and West in Cycle-Pattern Theories of History* (New York: Philosophical Library, 1962).

3. Mircea Eliade, *The Myth of the Eternal Return*, tr. Willard R. Trask (New York: Pantheon, 1954), p. 88.

Chapter Four

1. Seneca, *Questions naturelles*, tr. Paul Oltramare, 2 vols. (Paris: Société d'Edition "Les Belles Lettres," 1961), 1:157.
2. Ludwig Edelstein, *The Idea of Progress in Classical Antiquity* (Baltimore: Johns Hopkins Press, 1967), pp. 167–77; cf. Eric R. Dodds, *The Ancient Concept of Progress and Other Essays on Greek Literature and Belief* (Oxford: Clarendon Press, 1973), pp. 21–23.
3. Seneca, *Questions naturelles*, 1:159.
4. Lucretius, *The Way Things Are*, tr. Rolfe Humphries (Bloomington, Ind.: Indiana University Press, 1968), p. 85.
5. See Heinrich Zimmer, *Myths and Symbols in Indian Art and Civilization*, ed. Joseph Campbell (New York: Pantheon, 1946), pp. 15–19.
6. Mircea Eliade, *The Myth of the Eternal Return*, p. 114.
7. See Eric R. Dodds, *The Ancient Concept*, pp. 3–4; cf. Ludwig Edelstein, *The Idea of Progress*, p. 8 and fn 16.
8. See Fung Yu-lan, *A History of Chinese Philosophy*, tr. Derk Bodde, 2 vols. (Princeton, N.J.: Princeton University Press, 1952–53), 2:469–74.
9. *Li Chi: Book of Rites*, tr. James Legge, 2 vols. (New Hyde Park, N.Y.: University Books, 1967), 1:364–67.
10. Fung Yu-lan, *A Short History of Chinese Philosophy*, ed. and tr. Derk Bodde (New York: Free Press, 1966), p. 159.

Chapter Five

1. See, for example, John Baillie, *The Belief in Progress* (London: Oxford University Press, 1950), pp. 57–87, and the "secular theology" discussed in Wagar, *Good Tidings*, pp. 257–66. A representative text is Arend van Leeuwen, *Christianity in World History*, tr. H. H. Hoskins (New York: Scribner's, 1966).
2. Mircea Eliade, *The Myth of the Eternal Return*, pp. 111–12.
3. Arnaldo Momigliano, *Essays in Ancient and Modern Historiography* (Middletown, Conn.: Wesleyan University Press, 1977), ch. 12, "Time in Ancient Historiography."
4. Jürgen Moltmann, "Eschatology," *Encyclopaedia Britannica*, 15th ed., 30 vols. (Chicago: Encyclopaedia Britannica, 1974), *Macropaedia*, 6:960.
5. See Michael Barkun, *Disaster and the Millennium* (New Haven, Conn.: Yale University Press, 1974), passim.
6. *Norse Mythology: The Elder Edda in Prose Translation*, ed. Lawrence S. Thompson (Hamden, Conn.: Archon Books, 1974), pp. 16–17.
7. Ibid., pp. 17–18. Cf. the fuller twelfth-century account in Snorri Sturluson, *The Prose Edda*, tr. Jean I. Young (Berkeley and Los Angeles: University of California Press, 1966), pp. 86–93.
8. See Lawrence S. Thompson in *Norse Mythology*, p. 14.
9. See R. H. Charles, *Eschatology: The Doctrine of a Future Life in Israel, Judaism and Christianity* [1899] (New York: Schocken, 1963), p. 108 and fn 2.
10. Friedrich Engels, "On the History of Early Christianity" [1894], in Lewis S. Feuer, ed., *Marx and Engels: Basic Writings on Politics and Philosophy* (Garden City, N.Y.: Doubleday, 1959), p. 168.
11. See C. H. Dodd, *History and the Gospel* (New York: Scribner's, 1938); and

Rudolf Bultmann, *History and Eschatology* (Edinburgh: Edinburgh University Press, 1957). Cf. Oscar Cullmann, *Christ and Time: The Primitive Christian Conception of Time and History,* tr. Floyd V. Filson (Philadelphia: Westminster, 1950).

12. See Albert Schweitzer, *The Quest of the Historical Jesus: A Critical Study of Its Progress from Reimarus to Wrede,* tr. W. Montgomery (New York: Macmillan, 1922).

13. R. H. Charles, *Eschatology,* ch. 11, "The Pauline Eschatology in Its Four Stages."

Chapter Six

1. See Theodor E. Mommsen, "St. Augustine and the Christian Idea of Progress," *Journal of the History of Ideas,* 12:3 (June, 1951), 346–74.

2. Augustine, *The City of God,* tr. Marcus Dods (New York: Modern Library, 1950), p. 867; cf. p. 720.

3. Ibid., p. 762.

4. See Norman Cohn, *The Pursuit of the Millennium,* rev. ed. (New York: Oxford University Press, 1970).

5. Bernard McGinn, *Visions of the End: Apocalyptic Traditions in the Middle Ages* (New York: Columbia University Press, 1979), p. 32.

6. Quoted in Paul Vulliaud, *La fin du monde* (Paris: Payot, 1952), p. 129.

7. See James P. Martin, *The Last Judgment in Protestant Theology from Orthodoxy to Ritschl* (Grand Rapids, Mich.: Eerdmans, 1963); and Jakob Taubes, *Abendländische Eschatologie* (Bern: Francke, 1947), Books 3–4.

8. Perry Miller, *Errand into the Wilderness* (New York: Harper and Row, 1964), p. 218.

9. Ernest Lee Tuveson, *Millennium and Utopia,* chs. 3–4. See also Paul Vulliaud, *La fin du monde,* pp. 207–09, and cf. Victor Harris, *All Coherence Gone* (Chicago: University of Chicago Press, 1949), a close analysis of the debate between two earlier seventeenth-century eschatologists, Godfrey Goodman and George Hakewill.

10. See Franklin L. Baumer, *Religion and the Rise of Scepticism* (New York: Harcourt, Brace, 1960); and Owen Chadwick, *The Secularization of the European Mind in the Nineteenth Century* (Cambridge: Cambridge University Press, 1975).

11. Emil Brunner, *Christianity and Civilisation,* 2 vols. (New York: Scribner's, 1948–49), 1:55. See also Ludwig Edelstein, *The Idea of Progress,* pp. xi–xxi; W. Warren Wagar, "Modern Views of the Origins of the Idea of Progress," *Journal of the History of Ideas,* 28:1 (January-March, 1967), 55–70; and Wagar, *Good Tidings,* pp. 11–18.

Chapter Seven

1. Alfred Bester, "Adam and No Eve" [1941], in *Starburst* (New York: Signet, 1958), pp. 28–29.

2. Ibid., p. 37.

Chapter Eight

1. Martha Wolfenstein, *Disaster: A Psychological Essay* (Glencoe, Ill.: Free Press, 1957), pp. 189–98.

2. Allen H. Barton, *Communities in Disaster: A Sociological Analysis of Collective Stress Situations* (Garden City, N.Y.: Doubleday, 1969), p. 326.

3. Martha Wolfenstein, *Disaster*, p. 8.

4. Susan Sontag, "The Imagination of Disaster," in *Against Interpretation* (New York: Farrar, 1965), p. 215.

5. Martha Wolfenstein, *Disaster*, p. 9.

6. Ibid., p. 10.

7. Bruno Bettelheim, *The Uses of Enchantment: The Meaning and Importance of Fairy Tales* (New York: Knopf, 1976), passim.

8. Maurice Valency, *The End of the World: An Introduction to Contemporary Drama* (New York: Oxford University Press, 1980), p. 435.

9. R. C. Sherriff, *The Hopkins Manuscript* [1939] (New York: Macmillan, 1963), p. 205.

10. Edmund Cooper, *All Fools' Day* (London: Hodder and Stoughton, 1966), p. 192.

11. Richard Matheson, "The Last Day" [1953], in *The Shores of Space* (New York: Bantam, 1957), p. 154.

12. George Allan England, *Darkness and Dawn* (Boston: Small, Maynard, 1914), pp. 12 and 261.

13. Brian Aldiss, *Greybeard* (New York: Signet, 1965), p. 40.

14. Thomas Hood, "The Last Man" [1826], in *The Complete Poetical Works of Thomas Hood*, ed. Walter Jerrold (London: Oxford University Press, 1911), p. 41.

15. Ibid., pp. 42–43.

16. M. P. Shiel, *The Purple Cloud* [1901] (New York: Warner, 1963), p. 137.

17. Quoted by Brian Stableford in Peter Nicholls, ed., *The Science Fiction Encyclopedia*, p. 16.

18. See Peter Loewenberg, "The Unsuccessful Adolescence of Heinrich Himmler," *American Historical Review*, 76:3 (June, 1971), 612–41.

19. James Gould Cozzens, *Castaway* [1934] (New York: Harcourt, Brace, 1967), pp. 74 and 115.

20. Michael Moorcock, *The Black Corridor* (New York: Ace, 1969), p. 183.

21. Ballard in "An Interview with J. G. Ballard," in James Goddard and David Pringle, eds., *J. G. Ballard: The First Twenty Years* (Hayes, Middlesex: Bran's Head Books, 1976), pp. 25–26.

22. See J. G. Ballard, "Myth-Maker of the 20th Century," *New Worlds SF*, No. 142 (May-June, 1964), 121–27.

23. J. G. Ballard, *The Drowned World* [1962] (New York: Berkley, 1966), p. 22.

24. Ibid., p. 14.

25. Ibid., pp. 76 and 64.

26. Ibid., p. 158.

27. Ballard in "An Interview with J. G. Ballard," p. 24.

28. Anna Kavan, *Ice* [1967] (Garden City, N.Y.: Doubleday, 1970), p. 176.

Chapter Nine

1. Marquis de Sade, *L'histoire de Juliette* [1797], tr. Austryn Wainhouse (New York: Grove, 1968), p. 67.

2. Ibid., p. 98.

3. Marquis de Sade, *The 120 Days of Sodom* [1785], tr. Austryn Wainhouse and Richard Seaver (New York: Grove, 1966), p. 364.

4. Marquis de Sade, *La nouvelle Justine* [1797], 4 vols. (Sceaux: Pauvert, 1953), 1:152.

5. Brian Aldiss, "Introduction," in Kavan, *Ice*, p. 9.

6. Thomas Henry Huxley, "Prolegomena" [1894], in Huxley and Julian Huxley, *Touchstone for Ethics* (New York: Harper, 1947), p. 67.

7. Bertrand Russell, "A Free Man's Worship" [1903], in *Mysticism and Logic* (New York: Norton, 1929), p. 57.

8. H. G. Wells, *Men Like Gods* [1923], in *The Works of H. G. Wells*, Atlantic Edition, 28 vols. (London: Unwin and New York: Scribner's, 1924–27), 28:107.

9. William Hope Hodgson, *The Night Land* (London: Nash, 1912), p. 521.

10. Joe De Bolt and John R. Pfeiffer in Neil Barron, ed., *Anatomy of Wonder: Science Fiction* (New York: Bowker, 1976), p. 132.

11. Brian Aldiss, *The Long Afternoon of Earth* (title in U.K.: *Hothouse*) (New York: Signet, 1962), pp. 5, 44, 71, and 43.

12. H. G. Wells, "The Star" [1897], in *The Short Stories of H. G. Wells* (London: Benn, 1927), p. 648.

13. Garrett P. Serviss, *The Second Deluge* (New York: McBride, Nast, 1912), p. 397.

14. John Christopher, *The Long Winter* (title in U.K.: *The World in Winter*) (Greenwich, Conn.: Fawcett, 1962), p. 194.

15. George R. Stewart, *Earth Abides* (Boston: Houghton Mifflin, 1949), p. 15.

16. Ibid., p. 9.

17. J. J. Connington, *Nordenholt's Million* (London: Benn, 1923), p. 223.

18. Ibid., pp. 189 and 190.

19. For Garrett Hardin, see n. 5 in Chapter One.

20. John Christopher, *No Blade of Grass* (title in U.K.: *The Death of Grass*) (New York: Avon, 1967), p. 124.

21. H. G. Wells, *The War of the Worlds* [1898] in Wells, *Seven Famous Novels* (New York: Knopf, 1934), pp. 265–66.

22. Thomas M. Disch, *The Genocides* (New York: Berkley, 1965), pp. 70–71.

23. Ibid., pp. 31–32.

Chapter Ten

1. H. G. Wells, *The Croquet Player* (New York: Viking, 1937), pp. 89 and 94.

2. Ibid., p. 59.

3. Malcolm W. Browne, "Doomsday Debate: How Near Is the End?", *New York Times* (November 14, 1978), C1, C4; Isaac Asimov, *A Choice of Catastrophes* (New York: Simon and Schuster, 1979); and Kenneth Heuer, *The End of the World* (New York: Rinehart, 1953).

4. John Ames Mitchell, *The Last American* [1889] (New York: Stokes, 1902), unnumbered page in front matter.

5. George Griffith, *The Angel of the Revolution: A Tale of the Coming Terror* (London: Tower, 1893), p. 10.

6. Edward Shanks, *The People of the Ruins: A Story of the English Revolution and After* (New York: Stokes, 1920), p. 314.

7. Many others are listed in I. F. Clarke, *Tale of the Future;* and see Thomas D. Clareson, "The Emergence of the Scientific Romance: 1870–1926," in Neil Barron, ed., *Anatomy of Wonder,* pp. 37–38.

8. H. G. Wells, *The War in the Air* (New York: Macmillan, 1908), pp. 394–95.

9. I. F. Clarke, *The Pattern of Expectation* (London: Cape, 1979), p. 158.

10. Quoted in ibid., pp. 159–60.

11. M. P. Shiel, *The Yellow Danger* (London: Richards, 1898), p. 109. Shiel's life and work are sketched in Sam Moskowitz, *Explorers of the Infinite: Shapers of Science Fiction* (Cleveland: World, 1963), ch. 9, "The World, the Devil, and M. P. Shiel."

12. Sven Holm, *Termush* [1967], tr. Sylvia Clayton (London: Faber and Faber, 1969), p. 110.

13. J. G. Ballard, "The Terminal Beach" [1964], in *The Terminal Beach* (Harmondsworth, Middlesex: Penguin Books, 1966), p. 150.

Chapter Eleven

1. See W. Warren Wagar, *World Views: A Study in Comparative History* (Hinsdale, Ill.: Dryden, 1977).

2. Ibid., pp. 54–55.

3. Ibid., p. 98.

4. See H. Stuart Hughes, *Consciousness and Society: The Reorientation of European Social Thought, 1890–1930* (New York: Knopf, 1958), especially ch. 2, "The Decade of the 1890's: The Revolt against Positivism"; and Wagar, *World Views,* pp. 137–38.

5. *World Views,* p. 138.

6. Peter Nicholls in Nicholls, ed., *The Science Fiction Encyclopedia,* p. 556.

Chapter Twelve

1. Cicely Hamilton, *Lest Ye Die: A Story from the Past or of the Future* (New York: Scribner's, 1928), pp. ix–x.

2. Ibid., p. 221.

3. Edgar Allan Poe, "The Colloquy of Monos and Una" [1841], in *The Complete Works of Edgar Allan Poe,* ed. James A. Harrison, 17 vols. (New York: Crowell, 1902), 4:202–03.

4. Nathaniel Hawthorne, "The New Adam and Eve" [1842], in *The Complete Short Stories of Nathaniel Hawthorne* (Garden City, N.Y.: Hanover House, 1959), p. 337.

5. W. J. Keith argues that Felix is a thinly disguised version of the author. See Keith, *Richard Jefferies* (Toronto: University of Toronto Press, 1965), pp. 119–22.

6. J. Leslie Mitchell, *Gay Hunter* (London: Heinemann, 1934), p. 177.

7. Ibid., p. 268.

8. Ibid., "For Christopher Morley," unnumbered page in front matter.

9. Stephen Southwold [pseud. Neil Bell], *The Lord of Life* (Boston: Little, Brown, 1933), pp. 278–79.

10. Ray Bradbury, *The Martian Chronicles* (New York: Bantam, 1951), pp. 179–80.

11. Ray Bradbury, "The Highway" [1950], in *The Illustrated Man* (New York: Bantam, 1952), pp. 41–42.

12. Russell Hoban, *Riddley Walker* (New York: Summit Books, 1981), pp. 17–18.

13. Ibid., p. 197.

14. Czeslaw Milosz, "Science Fiction and the Coming of the Antichrist," tr. Richard Lourie, in Milosz, *Emperor of the Earth: Modes of Eccentric Vision* (Berkeley and Los Angeles: University of California Press, 1977), p. 29.

15. Ibid., pp. 28–29.

16. Among them, Robert Hugh Benson, *Lord of the World* (1907); Constancia Serjeant, *When the Saints Are Gone* (1908); and Sydney Watson, *The Mark of the Beast* (1911).

17. Benson, *Lord of the World* (New York: Dodd, Mead, 1908), p. 352.

18. See C. S. Lewis, *The Abolition of Man* (New York: Macmillan, 1947).

19. C. S. Lewis, *That Hideous Strength*, p. 37.

20. See Jacques Sadoul, *Histoire de la science fiction moderne*, Part II.

21. Charles-Ferdinand Ramuz, *The End of All Men* [*Présence de la mort*, 1922], tr. Allan Ross Macdougall (New York: Pantheon, 1944), p. 20.

22. Ibid., p. 223.

23. Quoted in Egon Gartenberg, *Mahler: The Man and His Music* (New York: Schirmer, 1978), p. 273.

24. Ibid., p. 266. Recent composers who have followed Mahler in offering their own interpretations of the Christian Last Days include Olivier Messiaen in his *Quatuor pour la fin du temps* and Carl Orff in his *De Temporum Fine Comoedia*.

Chapter Thirteen

1. F. W. J. Hemmings, *Emile Zola*, 2nd ed. (Oxford: Clarendon, 1966), p. 109.

2. Garrett P. Serviss, *The Second Deluge*, p. 76.

3. George Allan England, *Darkness and Dawn*, pp. 260 and 672.

4. John Wyndham, *The Kraken Wakes* [1953] (Harmondsworth, Middlesex: Penguin Books, 1955), p. 240.

5. Keith Roberts, *The Furies* (New York: Berkley, 1966), p. 191.

6. See Peter Nicholls, ed., *The Science Fiction Encyclopedia*, p. 406. The entry on Moorcock, pp. 405–07, is by John Clute.

7. Michael Moorcock, *An Alien Heat* (New York: Harper and Row, 1972), p. 11.

8. Moorcock, "Introduction," in *Dying for Tomorrow* (title in U.K.: *Moorcock's Book of Martyrs*) (New York: DAW Books, 1978), p. 9.

9. Isaac Asimov is one of the original fifty-eight signatories of the Secular Humanist Declaration of 1980, and the only writer of science fiction on the list. See *Free Inquiry*, 1:1 (Winter, 1980/81), 7.

10. James White, "Introduction: Reality in Science Fiction," in *Monsters and Medics* (New York: Ballantine, 1977), p. 7. *Second Ending* [1962] is reprinted on pp. 9–117 of this volume.

11. Ibid., p. 117.

12. John Wyndham, *Re-Birth* (title in U.K.: *The Chrysalids*) (New York: Ballantine, 1955), p. 38.

13. Edmund Cooper, *All Fools' Day*, p. 113.

14. Stephen Vincent Benét, "By the Waters of Babylon" [originally, "The Place of the Gods," 1937], in *Selected Works*, 2 vols. (New York: Farrar and Rinehart, 1942), 2:483.

15. Marvin Kaye and Parke Godwin, *The Masters of Solitude* (New York: Avon, 1979), p. 31.

16. D. Keith Mano, *The Bridge* (New York: Signet, 1974), pp. 40 and 53.

17. Ibid., pp. 26 and 189.

18. Ibid., p. 190.

19. Ibid., p. 12.

20. See E. F. Schumacher, *Small is Beautiful: Economics As If People Mattered* (New York: Harper and Row, 1973).

21. Sheila Sullivan, *The Calling of Bara* (title in U.K.: *Summer Rising*) (New York: Dutton, 1976), p. 11.

22. Ibid., pp. 198–99.

Chapter Fourteen

1. Karel Čapek, *The Absolute at Large* [1922] (New York: Macmillan, 1927), p. 220.

2. Kurt Vonnegut, *The Sirens of Titan* [1959] (New York: Dell, 1970), p. 8.

3. "There is an almost intolerable sentimentality beneath everything I write." Vonnegut, *Wampeters, Foma, and Granfalloons* (New York: Delta, 1975), p. xxv. See also James Lundquist, *Kurt Vonnegut* (New York: Ungar, 1977), pp. 12–13.

4. Darko Suvin in Peter Nicholls, ed., *Science Fiction Encyclopedia*, p. 351.

5. Ronald Duncan, *The Last Adam* (London: Dobson, 1952), p. 92.

6. Bernard Wolfe, *Limbo* (New York: Random House, 1952), pp. 316 and 413.

7. J. G. Ballard in Brian Ash, ed., *The Visual Encyclopedia of Science Fiction* (New York: Harmony Books, 1977), p. 130.

8. H. Bruce Franklin, "What Are We to Make of J. G. Ballard's Apocalypse?", in Thomas D. Clareson, ed., *Voices for the Future: Essays on Major Science Fiction Writers*, Vol. Two (Bowling Green, Ohio: Bowling Green University Popular Press, 1979), p. 90.

9. Ballard, *The Unlimited Dream Company* (New York: Holt, 1979), p. 238.

10. J.-P. Vernier, "The Science Fiction of J. H. Rosny the Elder," *Science-Fiction Studies*, 2:2 (July, 1975), 156–63.

11. Doris Lessing, *The Memoirs of a Survivor* (New York: Knopf, 1975), p. 213.

12. Roberta Rubenstein, *The Novelistic Vision of Doris Lessing: Breaking the Forms of Consciousness* (Champaign-Urbana, Ill.: University of Illinois Press, 1979), p. 237.

13. Robert Galbreath, "Problematic Gnosis: Hesse, Singer, Lessing, and the Limitations of Modern Gnosticism," *The Journal of Religion*, 61:1 (January, 1981), 20–36.

Chapter Fifteen

1. I. Bestuzhev-Lada and D. Yermolenko, "The Scientific Forecast of Interna-

tional Relations in the Light of Lenin's Teaching," *International Affairs*, No. 2–3 (February-March, 1970), 93.

2. Helen McCloy [pseud. Helen Clarkson], *The Last Day* (New York: Dodd, Mead, 1959), p. 183.

3. Ibid., p. 160.

4. Camille A. M. Caseleyr [pseud. Jack Danvers], *The End of It All* (London: Heinemann, 1962), p. 149.

5. Walter M. Miller, *A Canticle for Leibowitz* (Philadelphia: Lippincott, 1960), p. 255.

6. Robert Scholes and Eric S. Rabkin, *Science Fiction: History, Science, Vision* (New York: Oxford University Press, 1977), pp. 225–26.

7. *A Canticle for Leibowitz*, p. 235.

8. Jules Verne, *L'éternel Adam*, in *Hier et demain*, p. 263.

9. René Barjavel, *The Ice People* [*La nuit des temps*, 1968]), tr. Charles Lam Markmann (New York: Pyramid, 1973), p. 208.

10. James Blish, *Cities in Flight* [1955–62] (New York: Avon, 1970), pp. 82, 208, and 515; and see Richard D. Mullen, "Blish, van Vogt, and the Uses of Spengler," *Riverside Quarterly*, 3 (August, 1968), 172–86. A revised version, with sympathetic notes by Blish himself, appears as the Afterword, "The Earthmanist Culture: Cities in Flight as a Spenglerian History," in *Cities in Flight*, pp. 597–607. See also Blish's discussion of Spengler in Blish [pseud. William Atheling, Jr.], *The Issue at Hand* (Chicago: Advent, 1964), pp. 60–61.

11. *Cities in Flight*, p. 596. See also Blish's novels *The Seedling Stars* (1957) and *Midsummer Century* (1972), both with cyclical messages; and the Spenglerian and Toynbeean magazine stories discussed in Paul Carter, *The Creation of Tomorrow: Fifty Years of Magazine Science Fiction* (New York: Columbia University Press, 1977), pp. 221–27 and 254–55. Of special interest is the Jack Williamson story "Breakdown" (1942), which appeared in *Astounding Science-Fiction* just two years after L. Sprague de Camp published a factual article on Spengler, Toynbee, and other cyclical prophets in the same illustrious pulp.

12. James Thurber, *The Last Flower: A Parable in Pictures* [1939] (New York: Harper and Row, 1971), no pagination.

Chapter Sixteen

1. J. G. Ballard, "The Venus Hunters" [originally, "The Encounter," 1963], in *The Terminal Beach* (New York: Berkley, 1964), p. 107.

2. Thompson, *Darkness and Scattered Light*, p. 74.

3. I now seem to contradict myself. See my *Building the City of Man*, ch. 1, "The Great Explosion," where I give mankind poor odds of survival. But anyone who finishes the book will see that the first chapter is a kind of devil's advocacy, in which I avail myself of prophetic, if not poetic, license to overstate the case for doomsday in hopes of getting my readers awake.

4. See William Irwin Thompson, *At the Edge of History: Speculations on the Transformation of Culture* (New York: Harper and Row, 1971); Wagar, *Building the City of Man: Outlines of a World Civilization;* and Wagar, "At the Edge of Sanity: William Irwin Thompson and Planetary Culture," in *Alternative Futures: The Journal of Utopian Studies*, 1:3 (Fall, 1978), 72–80. My latest thoughts on these matters are summarized in "Technocracy as the Highest Stage of Capitalism," in Frank

Feather, ed., *Through the 80s: Thinking Globally, Acting Locally* (Washington: World Future Society, 1980), pp. 210–15.

5. See Wagar, "H. G. Wells and the Radicalism of Despair," *Studies in the Literary Imagination*, 6:2 (Fall, 1973), 1–10.

6. Wells, "The Story of the Last Trump" [1915], in *The Short Stories of H. G. Wells*, p. 604.

7. Wells, *The Food of the Gods* [1904], in *The Works of H. G. Wells*, 5:299 and 302.

8. Wells, "Preface to Volume V," in ibid., 5:ix.

9. J. G. Ballard, *The Drought* [1965] (Harmondsworth, Middlesex: Penguin Books, 1968), pp. 13 and 113.

10. Ibid., p. 176.

11. H. Bruce Franklin, "What Are We to Make of J. G. Ballard's Apocalypse?" p. 105.

SELECTED SOURCES

Listed below are the more than three hundred novels, stories, plays, and poems that comprise the primary source material for *Terminal Visions*. A few of these titles are only marginally eschatological, but the rest fully meet the criteria discussed in Chapter One. All have significance for a student of endtime fictions.

Although this is a more or less complete list of works consulted, it is far from a complete list of terminal visions in modern speculative literature. The entries in such a list would run into the thousands. One major category, wholly untouched, is the magazine short story not reprinted in anthologies or collected works. Because the magazines that publish genre fiction are difficult to locate, and because a representative sample of such material has been anthologized, no attempt is made below to indicate magazine sources.

A second sizeable group of terminal visions that I have largely, although in this case not entirely, ignored, are those originally published in languages other than English. A fair cross-section of French works appears, but only a scattering of German titles, and none at all from the Soviet Union, Japan, Italy, or the Spanish-speaking world. This is partly because, until recently, most of the world's science fiction was written by British, French, and American authors. The scarcity of entries from outside the Anglo-Franco-American heartland also reflects my own ignorance and biases, and the near impossibility of finding foreign-language genre fiction in American libraries. There is the further point that in so-called socialist countries, such as the Soviet Union, the production of world's end stories is officially discouraged for ideological reasons. I cannot use this excuse in the case of Japan, whose authors nowadays churn out large numbers of disaster tales, but I do not read a word of Japanese.

All the same, the list does include a considerable fraction of the most critically acclaimed and broadly influential works of eschatological literature published during the last one and three-quarters centuries. At least for students of the Western European and North American mind in the eras of mature and late capitalism, it furnishes a more than ample bibliographical introduction to its subject.

As a general rule, I have listed the first U.S. edition of a title, when one exists; otherwise, the first British, French, or German edition. For short stories, only one anthology or collected edition is cited, but it goes without saying that the same story may often be found in other volumes. Years in brackets refer to the first publication of a work whenever the entry supplies information only about a translated or reprinted edition.

Abel-Musgrave, Curt. *Der Bacillenkrieg.* Frankfurt: Impavidus, 1922.

Adam, R. J. See Paul MacTyre.

Aldiss, Brian. *Barefoot in the Head: A European Fantasia.* Garden City, N.Y.: Doubleday, 1970.

——. *The Canopy of Time* [title in U.S.: *Galaxies like Grains of Sand*]. New York: Signet, 1960.

——, ed. *Evil Earths* [1975]. New York: Avon, 1979.

——. *Greybeard.* New York: Harcourt, Brace, 1964.

——. "Heresies of the Huge God" [1966]: see Aldiss, ed., *Evil Earths*, pp. 280–91.

——. *Hothouse* [title in U.S.: *The Long Afternoon of Earth*]. New York: Signet, 1962.

Amery, Carl, pseud. [Christian Mayer]. *Der Untergang der Stadt Passau.* Munich: Heyne, 1975.

Anderson, Poul. *After Doomsday.* New York: Ballantine, 1962.

——. "Epilogue" [1962]: see Robert Silverberg, ed., *The Ends of Time*, pp. 128–80.

——. *Tau Zero.* Garden City, N.Y.: Doubleday, 1970.

Anthony, Piers, pseud. [Piers Anthony Jacob]. *Battle Circle* [trilogy composed of *Sos the Rope* (1968), *Var the Stick* (1972), and *Neq the Sword* (1975)]. New York: Avon, 1978.

——. *Rings of Ice.* New York: Avon, 1974.

Asimov, Isaac. *The Foundation Trilogy* [trilogy composed of *Foundation* (1951), *Foundation and Empire* (1952), and *Second Foundation* (1953)]. Garden City, N.Y.: Doubleday, 1964.

——. "The Last Question" [1956]. In Asimov, *Nine Tomorrows* [1959], pp. 170–83. New York: Fawcett, 1978.

Baker, Frank. *The Birds.* London: Davies, 1936.

Baldwin, Bee. *The Red Dust.* London: Hale, 1965.

Baldwin, Oliver. See Martin Hussingtree.

Ballard, J. G. "Build-Up" [also, "The Concentration City," 1957]. In Ballard, *Chronopolis*, pp. 218–40. New York: Berkley, 1972.

——. "Chronopolis" [1960]. In Ballard, *Chronopolis*, pp. 190–217.

——. *The Crystal World.* New York: Farrar, Straus, 1966.

——. "The Day of Forever." In Ballard, *The Impossible Man*, pp. 97–116. New York: Berkley, 1966.

——. "Deep End" [1961]. In Ballard, *The Voices of Time*, pp. 148–58. New York: Berkley, 1962.

——. *The Drought.* London: Cape, 1965. [A rewritten and expanded version of *The Burning World.* New York: Berkley, 1964.]

——. *The Drowned World.* New York: Berkley, 1962.

——. "The Garden of Time." In Ballard, *Billennium*, pp. 152–59. New York: Berkley, 1962.

——. "The Insane Ones." In Ballard, *Billennium*, pp. 21–30.

——. "Low-Flying Aircraft" [1975]. In Ballard, *Low-Flying Aircraft*, pp. 88–107. London: Cape, 1976.

——. "Mobile" [also, "Venus Smiles," 1957]. In Ballard, *Billennium*, pp. 104–17.

——. "A Place and a Time to Die" [1969]. In Ballard, *Low-Flying Aircraft*, pp. 155–64.

——. "The Reptile Enclosure" [also, "The Sherrington Theory," 1963]. In Ballard, *The Impossible Man*, pp. 19–31.

——. "Storm-Bird, Storm-Dreamer." In Ballard, *The Impossible Man*, pp. 50–69.

——. "The Ultimate City." In Ballard, *Low-Flying Aircraft*, pp. 7–87.

——. *The Unlimited Dream Company.* New York: Holt, 1979.

——. "The Voices of Time" [1960]. In Ballard, *The Voices of Time*, pp. 7–37.

——. *The Wind from Nowhere.* New York: Berkley, 1962.

Balmer, Edwin, and Philip Wylie. *After Worlds Collide.* New York: Stokes, 1934.

——. *When Worlds Collide.* New York: Stokes, 1933.

Barjavel, René. *Ashes, Ashes* [*Ravage*, 1943], tr. Damon Knight. Garden City, N.Y.: Doubleday, 1967.

——. *Le diable l'emporte.* Paris: Denoël, 1948.

——. *The Ice People* [*La nuit des temps*, 1968], tr. Charles Lam Markmann. New York: Morrow, 1971.

Beckett, Samuel. *Endgame* [*Fin de partie*], tr. Beckett. New York: Grove, 1958.

Bell, Neil, pseud. See Stephen Southwold.

Benét, Stephen Vincent. "By The Waters of Babylon" [also, "The Place of the Gods," 1937]. In Benét, *Selected Works*, 2 vols., 2:471–83. New York: Farrar and Rinehart, 1942.

Benford, Gregory. *Timescape.* New York: Simon and Schuster, 1980.

Bennett, Alfred Gordon. *The Demigods.* London: Jarrolds, 1939.

Benson, Robert Hugh. *Lord of the World.* New York: Dodd, Mead, 1908.

Berk, Howard. *The Sun Grows Cold.* New York: Delacorte, 1971.

Best, Herbert. *The Twenty-Fifth Hour.* New York: Random House, 1940.

Bester, Alfred. "Adam and No Eve" [1941]. In Bester, *Starburst*, pp. 24–37. New York: Signet, 1958.

Blish, James. *Cities in Flight* [tetralogy composed of *They Shall Have Stars* (1957), *A Life for the Stars* (1962), *Earthman, Come Home* (1955), and *The Triumph of Time* (1958)]. New York: Avon, 1970.

——. *Midsummer Century.* Garden City, N.Y.: Doubleday, 1972.

——. *The Seedling Stars.* New York: Gnome, 1957.

Boëx, Joseph-Henri. See J.-H. Rosny aîné.

Bowen, John. *After the Rain.* New York: Ballantine, 1959. [As a play, with the same title. New York: Random House, 1967.].

Brackett, Leigh. *The Long Tomorrow.* Garden City, N.Y.: Doubleday, 1955.

Bradbury, Ray. "The Highway" [1950]. In Bradbury, *The Illustrated Man*, pp. 39–42. New York: Bantam, 1952.

——. "The Last Night of the World." In Bradbury, *The Illustrated Man*, pp. 90–94.

——. *The Martian Chronicles.* Garden City, N.Y.: Doubleday, 1950.

Brunner, John. *Total Eclipse.* Garden City, N.Y.: Doubleday, 1974.

Bryant, Edward. "Among the Dead" [1971]. In Bryant, *Among the Dead: And Other Events Leading to the Apocalypse*, pp. 103–16. New York: Macmillan, 1973.

Bryant, Peter, pseud. See Peter George.

Bunch, David R. *Moderan.* New York: Avon, 1971.

Byron, George, 6th Baron. "Darkness" [1816]. In *The Works of Lord Byron*, 13 vols., 4:42–45. London: Murray, 1901–05.

Campbell, J. S. "Film of Death" [1948]: see Brian Aldiss, ed., *Evil Earths*, pp. 16–30.

Campbell, John W., Jr. [Don A. Stuart, pseud.]. "Night" [1935]: see Brian Aldiss, ed., *Evil Earths*, pp. 297–318.

——. [Don A. Stuart, pseud.]. "Twilight" [1934]: see Robert Silverberg, ed., *The Ends of Time*, pp. 51–73.

Campbell, Thomas. "The Last Man" [1823]. In *The Poetical Works of Thomas Campbell*, ed. W. A. Hill, pp. 128–30. Boston: Little, Brown, 1856.

Čapek, Karel. *The Absolute at Large* [*Továrna na Absolutno*, 1922]. New York: Macmillan, 1927; reprinted, Westport, Conn.: Hyperion, 1973.

——. *R.U.R.* [1921], tr. Paul Selver. Garden City, N.Y.: Doubleday, 1923.

——. *War with the Newts* [*Valka s Mloky*, 1936], tr. M. and R. Weatherall. New York: Putnam, 1937.

Carter, Angela. *Heroes and Villains*. New York: Simon and Schuster, 1969.

Caseleyr, Camille A. M. See Jack Danvers.

Charnas, Suzy McKee. *Walk to the End of the World*. New York: Ballantine, 1974.

Christopher, John, pseud. [Christopher Samuel Youd]. *The Death of Grass* [title in U.S.: *No Blade of Grass*]. New York: Simon and Schuster, 1957.

——. *The World in Winter* [title in U.S.: *The Long Winter*]. New York: Simon and Schuster, 1962.

——. *A Wrinkle in the Skin* [title in U.S.: *The Ragged Edge.*]. New York: Simon and Schuster, 1965.

Clarke, Arthur C. "All the Time in the World" [1952]. In Clarke, *The Other Side of the Sky*, pp. 97–108. New York: Signet, 1959.

——. "The Awakening" [1951]: see Robert Silverberg, ed., *The Ends of Time*, pp. 45–50.

——. *Childhood's End*. Boston: Houghton Mifflin, 1953.

——. "History Lesson" [1949]. In Clarke, *Expedition to Earth* [1953], pp. 81–91. New York: Harcourt, Brace, 1970.

——. "If I Forget Thee, Oh Earth . . ." [1951]: see Brian Aldiss, ed., *Evil Earths*, pp. 292–96.

——. "The Nine Billion Names of God" [1953]. In Clarke, *The Other Side of the Sky*, pp. 9–15.

——. "No Morning After" [1954]. In Clarke, *The Other Side of the Sky*, pp. 65–70.

——. "Rescue Party" [1946]: see Donald A. Wollheim, ed., *The End of the World*, pp. 87–121.

Clarkson, Helen, pseud. [Helen McCloy]. *The Last Day*. New York: Dodd, Mead, 1959.

Collier, John. *Tom's A-Cold* [title in U.S.: *Full Circle*]. New York: Appleton, 1933.

Compton, D. G. *The Silent Multitude*. London: Hodder and Stoughton, 1967.

Connington, J. J., pseud. [Alfred Walter Stewart]. *Nordenholt's Million*. London: Benn, 1923.

Cooper, Edmund. *All Fools' Day*. New York: Walker, 1966.

——. *The Cloud Walker*. New York: Ballantine, 1973.

——. "Judgment Day." In Cooper, *News from Elsewhere*, pp. 65–77. New York: Berkley, 1969.

——. *The Last Continent*. New York: Dell, 1969.

——. "The Menhir." In Cooper, *News from Elsewhere*, pp. 7–13.

——. *Seed of Light*. New York: Ballantine, 1959.

——. *The Slaves of Heaven*. New York: Putnam, 1974.

——. *The Tenth Planet*. New York: Putnam, 1973.

Coppel, Alfred. *Dark December*. Greenwich, Conn.: Fawcett, 1960.

——. "Last Night of Summer" [1954]: see Donald A. Wollheim, ed., *The End of the World*, pp. 53–66.

Cowper, Richard, pseud. [John Middleton Murry, Jr.]. *Kuldesak*. Garden City, N.Y.: Doubleday, 1972.

——. *Phoenix*. New York: Ballantine, 1967.

——. *Profundis* [1979]. New York: Pocket Books, 1981.

——. *The Road to Corlay*. New York: Pocket Books, 1979.

——. *The Twilight of Briareus*. New York: Day, 1974.

Cozzens, James Gould. *Castaway*. New York: Random House, 1934.

Cravens, Gwyneth, and John S. Marr. *The Black Death*. New York: Dutton, 1977.

Cromie, Robert. *The Crack of Doom*. London: Digby and Long, 1895.

Danvers, Jack, pseud. [Camille A. M. Caseleyr]. *The End of It All*. London: Heinemann, 1962.

Daudet, Léon. *Le Napus: Fléau de l'an 2227*. Paris: Flammarion, 1927.

Delany, Samuel R. *Dhalgren*. New York: Bantam, 1975.

Desmond, Shaw. *Chaos*. London: Hutchinson, 1938.

——. *Ragnarok*. London: Duckworth, 1926.

Dick, Philip K., and Roger Zelazny. *Deus Irae*. Garden City, N.Y.: Doubleday, 1976.

Dick, Philip K. *Dr. Bloodmoney (Or How We Got Along after the Bomb)*. New York: Ace, 1965.

Disch, Thomas M. *The Genocides*. New York: Berkley, 1965.

Dobraczyński, Jan. *To Drain the Sea* [*Wyczerpać Morze*, 1961], tr. H. C. Stevens. London: Heinemann, 1964.

Donnelly, Ignatius. *Caesar's Column: A Story of the Twentieth Century*. Chicago: Schulte, 1890; reprinted, Cambridge, Mass.: Harvard University Press, 1960.

Doyle, Arthur Conan. *The Poison Belt*. New York: Doran, 1913.

Duncan, Ronald. *The Last Adam*. London: Dobson, 1952.

Edmonds, Helen Woods. See Anna Kavan.

Ehrlich, Paul R. "Eco-Catastrophe!" [1969]: see Frederik Pohl, ed., *Nightmare Age*, pp. 3–18.

Ellison, Harlan. "A Boy and His Dog" [1969]. In Ellison, *The Beast That Shouted Love at the Heart of the World* [1969] pp. 217–54. New York: Signet, 1974.

——. "I Have No Mouth, and I Must Scream" [1967]. In Robert Silverberg, ed., *The Mirror of Infinity*, pp. 269–84. San Francisco: Canfield, 1970.

——. "The Wine Has Been Left Open Too Long and the Memory Has Gone Flat." In Terry Carr, ed., *Universe 6*, pp. 87–98. Garden City, N.Y.: Doubleday, 1976.

Elwood, Roger, and Virginia Kidd, eds. *Saving Worlds*. Garden City, N.Y.: Doubleday, 1973. [Also available as *The Wounded Planet*. New York: Bantam, 1974.]

England, George Allan. *Darkness and Dawn*. Boston: Small, Maynard, 1914; reprinted, Westport, Conn.: Hyperion, 1974.

Farjeon, J. Jefferson. *Death of a World*. London: Collins, 1948.

Federbush, Arnold. *Ice!* New York: Bantam, 1978.

Fitzgibbon, Constantine. *The Golden Age*. New York: Norton, 1975.

Flammarion, Camille. *Omega: The Last Days of the World* [*La fin du monde*, 1893]. New York: Cosmopolitan, 1894; reprinted, New York: Arno, 1975.

Flecker, James Elroy. "The Last Generation: A Story of the Future" [1908]. In Flecker, *Collected Prose*, pp. 3–32. London: Heinemann, 1922.

Forster, E. M. "The Machine Stops" [1909]. In Damon Knight, ed., *Cities of Wonder*, pp. 163–92. Garden City, N.Y.: Doubleday, 1966.

France, Anatole, pseud. [Anatole-François Thibault]. Penguin Island [*L'île des pingouins*, 1907], tr. A. W. Evans. New York: Dodd, Mead, 1909.

Frank, Pat. *Alas, Babylon*. Philadelphia: Lippincott, 1959.

Franke, Herbert W. *The Orchid Cage* [*Der Orchideenkäfig*, 1961], tr. Christine Priest. New York: DAW Books, 1973.

Galouye, Daniel F. *Dark Universe*. New York: Bantam, 1961.

George, Peter. *Commander-1*. New York: Delacorte, 1965.

——. *Dr. Strangelove, Or: How I Learned to Stop Worrying and Love the Bomb*. New York: Bantam, 1963.

——. [Peter Bryant, pseud.] *Two Hours to Doom* [title in U.S.: *Red Alert*]. New York: Ace, 1958.

Giffard, Hardinge Goulburn. See Halsbury.

Gobsch, Hanns. *Death Rattle* [*Wahn-Europa 1934*], tr. Ian F. D. Morrow. Boston: Little, Brown, 1932.

Godwin, Parke. See Marvin Kaye.

Golding, William. *Lord of the Flies*. New York: Coward-McCann, 1955.

Graham, P. Anderson. *The Collapse of Homo Sapiens*. New York: Putnam, 1923.

Grainville, J.-B. Cousin de. *The Last Man: Or, Omegarus and Syderia, a Romance in Futurity* [*Le dernier homme*, 1805]. London: Dutton, 1806; reprinted, New York: Arno, 1978.

Green, A. Lincoln. *The End of an Epoch: Being the Personal Narrative of Adam Godwin, the Survivor*. Edinburgh, Blackwood, 1901.

Gribbin, John. See Douglas Orgill.

Griffith, George. *The Angel of the Revolution: A Tale of the Coming Terror*. London: Tower, 1893; reprinted, Westport, Conn.: Hyperion, 1974.

——. *Olga Romanoff: Or, The Syren of the Skies*. London: Tower, 1894; reprinted, Westport, Conn.: Hyperion, 1974.

——. *The World Peril of 1910*. London: White, 1907.

Halsbury, 2nd Earl of, (Hardinge Goulburn Giffard). *1944*. London: Butterworth, 1926.

Hamilton, Cicely. *Lest Ye Die: A Story from the Past or of the Future*. New York: Scribner's, 1928. [A rewritten version of *Theodore Savage*. London: Parsons, 1922.]

Hamilton, Edmond. "After a Judgment Day" [1963]. In *The Best of Edmond Hamilton*, ed. Leigh Brackett, pp. 301–11. Garden City, N.Y.: Doubleday, 1977.

——. "Day of Judgment" [1946]. In *The Best of Edmond Hamilton*, pp. 226–38.

——. "In the World's Dusk" [1936]. In *The Best of Edmond Hamilton*, pp. 136–47.

——. "Requiem" [1962]. In *The Best of Edmond Hamilton*, pp. 284–300.

Harness, Charles L. *The Ring of Ritornel*. New York: Berkley, 1968.

——. *Wolfhead*. New York: Berkley, 1978.

Harris, John Beynon. See John Wyndham.

Harrison, M. John. *The Committed Men*. Garden City, N.Y.: Doubleday, 1971.

Hartley, L. P. *Facial Justice*. Garden City. N.Y.: Doubleday, 1961.

Hartridge, Jon. *Earthjacket.* New York; Walker, 1970.

Hawthorne, Nathaniel. "The New Adam and Eve" [1842]. In *The Complete Short Stories of Nathaniel Hawthorne,* pp. 327–38. Garden City, N.Y.: Hanover House, 1959.

Heinlein, Robert. "The Year of the Jackpot" [1952]: see Frederik Pohl, ed., *Nightmare Age,* pp. 273–312.

Henneberg, Nathalie and Charles. *The Green Gods* [*Les dieux verts,* 1961], tr. C. J. Cherryh. New York: DAW Books, 1980.

Hernaman-Johnson, Francis. *The Polyphemes.* London: Ward, Lock, 1906.

Herzog, Arthur. *Heat.* New York: Simon and Schuster, 1977.

——. *The Swarm.* New York: Simon and Schuster, 1974.

Hoban, Russell. *Riddley Walker.* New York: Summit Books, 1981.

Hodgson, William Hope. *The House on the Borderland.* London: Chapman and Hall, 1908; reprinted, Westport, Conn.: Hyperion, 1976.

——. *The Night Land.* London: Nash, 1912; reprinted, Westport, Conn.: Hyperion, 1976.

Holm, Sven. *Termush* [*Termush, Atlanterhavskysten,* 1967], tr. Sylvia Clayton. London: Faber and Faber, 1969.

Hood, Thomas. "The Last Man" [1826], in *The Complete Poetical Works of Thomas Hood,* ed. Walter Jerrold, pp. 41–43. London: Oxford University Press, 1911.

Horsnell, Horace. *Man Alone.* London: Hamish Hamilton, 1940.

Hoyle, Fred and Geoffrey. *The Inferno.* New York: Harper and Row, 1973.

Hubbard, L. Ron. *Final Blackout* [1940]. Providence: Hadley, 1948.

Hudson, William Henry. *A Crystal Age* [1887]. New York: Dutton, 1906.

Hussingtree, Martin, pseud. [Oliver Baldwin]. *Konyetz.* London: Hodder and Stoughton, 1924.

Huxley, Aldous. *Ape and Essence.* New York: Harper, 1948.

Ionesco, Eugène. *A Stroll in the Air* [*Le piéton de l'air,* 1963]. In *A Stroll in the Air and Frenzy for Two, or More,* tr. Donald Watson, pp. 7–117. New York: Grove, 1968.

Jacob, Piers Anthony. See Piers Anthony.

Jefferies, Richard. *After London; Or, Wild England.* London and New York: Cassell, 1885; reprinted, New York: Arno, 1974.

Kaul, Fedor. *Contagion to this World* [*Die Welt ohne Gedächtnis,* 1930], tr. Winifred Ray. London: Bles, 1933.

Kavan, Anna, pseud. [Helen Woods Edmonds]. *Ice* [1967]. Garden City, N.Y.: Doubleday, 1970.

Kaye, Marvin, and Parke Godwin. *The Masters of Solitude.* Garden City, N.Y.: Doubleday, 1978.

Kidd, Virginia. See Roger Elwood.

King, Stephen. *The Stand.* Garden City, N.Y.: Doubleday, 1978.

Kingsmill, Hugh, pseud. [Hugh Kingsmill Lunn]. "The End of the World." In Kingsmill, *The Dawn's Delay* [1924], pp. 9–55. London: Eyre and Spottiswoode, 1948.

Kirst, Hans Helmut. *The Seventh Day* [*Keiner kommt davon,* 1957], tr. Richard Graves. Garden City, N.Y.: Doubleday, 1959.

Klass, Philip. See William Tenn.
Kornbluth, C. M. "Shark Ship" [also, "Reap the Dark Tide," 1958]: see Robert Silverberg, ed., *Dark Stars*, pp. 1–36.
——. *The Syndic.* Garden City, N.Y.: Doubleday, 1953.
Kurland, Michael. *Pluribus.* Garden City, N.Y.: Doubleday, 1975.
Kuttner, Henry. See C. L. Moore.

Lamb, William. *The World Ends.* London: Dent, 1937.
Lamszus, Wilhelm. *The Human Slaughterhouse: Scenes from the War That Is Sure to Come [Das Menschenschlachthaus,* 1912], tr. Oakley Williams. New York: Stokes, 1913.
Lanier, Sterling E. *Hiero's Journey: A Romance of the Future.* Radnor, Pa.: Chilton, 1973.
Laumer, Keith. *Catastrophe Planet.* New York: Berkley, 1966.
Leiber, Fritz. "Last" [1957]: see Robert Silverberg, ed., *The Ends of Time*, pp. 187–88.
——. "Later Than You Think" [1950]: see Brian Aldiss, ed., *Evil Earths*, pp. 145–52.
——. "The Moon Is Green." In Everett F. Bleiler and T. E. Dikty, eds., *The Best Science-Fiction Stories: 1953*, pp. 111–27. New York: Fell, 1953.
——. "A Pail of Air" [1951]. In Leiber, *A Pail of Air*, pp. 9–24. New York: Ballantine, 1964.
——. *The Wanderer.* New York: Ballantine, 1964.
——. "When the Last Gods Die" [1951]: see Robert Silverberg, ed., *The Ends of Time*, pp. 181–86.
——. "The Wolf Pair" [also, "The Night of the Long Knives," 1960]. In Leiber, *The Night of the Wolf*, pp. 56–137. New York: Ballantine, 1966.
Lem, Stanislaw. *The Futurological Congress [Kongres Futurologiczny,* 1971], tr. Michael Kandel. New York: Seabury, 1974.
Lessing, Doris. *The Four-Gated City.* New York: Knopf, 1969.
——. *The Memoirs of a Survivor.* New York: Knopf, 1975.
——. *Shikasta: Re: Colonised Planet 5.* New York: Knopf, 1979.
  Lewis, Charles. *The Cain Factor.* London: Harwood-Smart, 1975.
Lewis, C. S. *That Hideous Strength.* New York: Macmillan, 1946.
Ley, Robert Arthur. See Arthur Sellings.
Llewellyn, Alun. *The Strange Invaders.* London: Bell, 1934.
Logsdon, Syd. *A Fond Farewell to Dying.* New York: Pocket Books, 1981.
London, Jack. "The Scarlet Plague" [1912]. In *Curious Fragments: Jack London's Tales of Fantasy Fiction*, ed. Dale L. Walker, pp. 155–97. Port Washington, N.Y.: Kennikat, 1975.
——. "The Unparalleled Invasion" [1910], in *Curious Fragments*, pp. 109–20.
Long, Amelia Reynolds. "Omega" [1932]: see Donald A. Wollheim, ed., *The End of the World*, pp. 123–41.
Long, Doug. See Vic Mayhew.
Lunn, Hugh Kingsmill. See Hugh Kingsmill.
Luther, Otto Jens. See Jens Rehn.

Macauley, Robie. *A Secret History of Time to Come.* New York: Knopf, 1979.
McCloy, Helen. See Helen Clarkson.

MacGregor, James Murdoch. See J. T. McIntosh.

McIlwain, David. See Charles Eric Maine.

McIntosh, J. T., pseud. [James Murdoch MacGregor]. *The Fittest*. Garden City, N.Y.: Doubleday, 1955.

——. *One in Three Hundred*. Garden City, N.Y.: Doubleday, 1954.

MacTyre, Paul, pseud. [R. J. Adam]. *Midge* [title in U.S.: *Doomsday, 1999*]. New York: Ace, 1962.

Maine, Charles Eric, pseud. [David McIlwain]. *The Darkest of Nights* [1962; title in U.S.: *Survival Margin*]. Greenwich, Conn.: Fawcett, 1968.

——. *The Tide Went Out*. New York: Ballantine, 1959.

Mano, D. Keith. *The Bridge*. Garden City, N.Y.: Doubleday, 1973.

Marr, John S. See Gwyneth Cravens.

Matheson, Richard. *I Am Legend*. New York: Fawcett, 1954.

——. "The Last Day" [1953]. In Matheson, *The Shores of Space*, pp. 149–64. New York: Bantam, 1957.

Mayer, Christian. See Carl Amery.

Mayhew, Vic, and Doug Long. *Fireball*. New York: Signet, 1979.

Merle, Robert. *Malevil* [*Malevil*, 1972], tr. Derek Coltman. New York: Simon and Schuster, 1973.

Miles, pseud. See Stephen Southwold.

Miller, Walter M., Jr. "Big Joe and the Nth Generation" [also, "It Takes a Thief," 1952]. In *The Science Fiction Stories of Walter M. Miller, Jr.*, pp. 155–73. Boston: Gregg, 1978.

——. *A Canticle for Leibowitz*. Philadelphia: Lippincott, 1960.

Mitchell, J. Leslie. *Gay Hunter*. London: Heinemann, 1934.

Mitchell, John Ames. *The Last American*. New York: Stokes, 1889; reprinted, Boston: Gregg, 1970.

Moorcock, Michael. *An Alien Heat* [*Dancers at the End of Time*, Vol. One]. New York: Harper and Row, 1972.

——. *The Black Corridor*. New York: Ace, 1969.

——. *Breakfast in the Ruins*. New York: Random House, 1971.

——. *The End of All Songs* [*Dancers at the End of Time*, Vol. Three]. New York: Harper and Row, 1976.

——. *The Hollow Lands* [*Dancers at the End of Time*, Vol. Two]. New York: Harper and Row, 1974.

——. *The Ice Schooner*. New York: Berkley, 1969.

——. *Legends from the End of Time*. New York: Harper and Row, 1976.

——. *The Shores of Death* [1966; title in U.S.: *The Twilight Man*]. New York: Berkley, 1970.

——. *The Transformation of Miss Mavis Ming* [title in U.S.: *A Messiah at the End of Time*]. New York: DAW Books, 1978.

——. "Waiting for the End of Time" [1970]. In Moorcock, *Moorcock's Book of Martyrs* [title in U.S.: *Dying for Tomorrow*], pp. 180–92. New York: DAW Books, 1978.

Moore, C. L., and Henry Kuttner. *Earth's Last Citadel* [1943]. New York: Ace, 1964.

Moore, Ward. *Greener Than You Think*. New York: Sloane, 1947.

Morris, William. *New from Nowhere; or, An Epoch of Rest*. Boston: Roberts, 1890; reprinted, London and Boston: Routledge, 1970.

Moxley, F. Wright. *Red Snow*. New York: Simon and Schuster, 1930.
Murry, John Middleton, Jr. See Richard Cowper.

Nation, Terry. *Survivors*. New York: Coward-McCann, 1976.
Nicolson, Harold. *Public Faces*. Boston: Houghton Mifflin, 1933.
Niven, Larry. "At the Core" [1966]. In Niven, *Neutron Star*, pp. 51–72. New York: Ballantine, 1968.
——, and Jerry Pournelle. *Lucifer's Hammer*. Chicago: Playboy, 1977.
Norway, Nevil Shute. See Nevil Shute.
Nowlan, Philip Francis. *Armageddon 2419 A.D.* [1928–29]. New York: Bouregy, 1962.
Noyes, Alfred. *The Last Man* [title in U.S.: *No Other Man*]. New York: Stokes, 1940.

O'Neill, Joseph. *Day of Wrath*. London: Gollancz, 1936.
Orgill, Douglas, and John Gribbin. *The Sixth Winter*. New York: Simon and Schuster, 1979.

Pangborn, Edgar. *The Company of Glory*. New York: Pyramid, 1975.
——. *Davy*. New York: St. Martin's, 1964.
——. *The Judgment of Eve*. New York: Simon and Schuster, 1966.
Phillpotts, Eden. *The Owl of Athene*. London: Hutchinson, 1936.
Piserchia, Doris. *A Billion Days of Earth*. New York: Bantam, 1976.
Poe, Edgar Allan. "The Colloquy of Monos and Una" [1841]. In *The Complete Works of Edgar Allan Poe*, ed. James A. Harrison, 17 vols., 4:200–12. New York: Crowell, 1902.
——. "The Conversation of Eiros and Charmion" [1839]. In *The Complete Works*, 4:1–8.
——. "The Masque of the Red Death" [1842]. In *The Complete Works*, 4:250–58.
Pohl, Frederik. *Jem*. New York: St. Martin's, 1979.
——, ed. *Nightmare Age*. New York: Ballantine, 1970.
Pournelle, Jerry. See Larry Niven.
Priest, Christopher. *Fugue for a Darkening Island* [title in U.S.: *Darkening Island*]. New York: Harper and Row, 1972.
Priestley, J. B. *The Doomsday Men*. New York: Harper, 1938.

Ramuz, Charles-Ferdinand. *The End of All Men* [*Présence de la mort*, 1922], tr. Allan Ross Macdougall. New York: Pantheon, 1944.
Rash, Dora. See Doreen Wallace.
Rehn, Jens, pseud. [Otto Jens Luther]. *Die Kinder des Saturn*. Darmstadt: Luchterhand, 1959.
Rein, Harold. *Few Were Left*. New York: Day, 1955.
Roberts, Keith. *The Chalk Giants*. London: Hutchinson, 1974; abr. ed. New York: Putnam, 1976.
——. *The Furies*. New York: Berkley, 1966.
Roshwald, Mordecai. *Level 7*. New York: McGraw-Hill, 1959.
Rosny aîné, J.-H., pseud. [Joseph-Henri Boëx]. *The Death of the Earth* [*La mort de la terre*, 1912], tr. George Edgar Slusser. In Rosny, *The Xipehuz and The Death of the Earth*, pp. 51–183. New York: Arno, 1978.

Scortia, Thomas N. *Earthwreck!* Greenwich, Conn.: Fawcett, 1974.

Sellings, Arthur, pseud. [Robert Arthur Ley]. *Junk Day*. London: Dobson, 1970.

Serviss, Garrett P. *The Second Deluge*. New York: McBride, Nast, 1912; reprinted, Westport, Conn.: Hyperion, 1974.

Shanks, Edward. *The People of the Ruins: A Story of the English Revolution and After*. New York: Stokes, 1920.

Shelley, Mary. *The Last Man*. London: Colburn, 1826; reprinted, Lincoln, Neb.: University of Nebraska Press, 1965.

Sherriff, R. C. *The Hopkins Manuscript*. New York: Macmillan, 1939.

Shiel, M. P. *The Dragon*. London: Richards, 1913.

——. *The Purple Cloud*. London: Chatto and Windus, 1901; reprinted, New York: Warner, 1963.

——. *The Yellow Danger*. New York: Fenno, 1899.

——. *The Yellow Wave*. London: Ward, Lock, 1905.

Shute, Nevil, pseud. [Nevil Shute Norway]. *On the Beach*. New York: Morrow, 1957.

Sibson, Francis H. *Unthinkable*. New York: Smith and Haas, 1933.

Silverberg, Robert, ed. *Dark Stars*. New York: Ballantine, 1969.

——, ed. *The Ends of Time*. New York: Award Books, 1970.

——. "Road to Nightfall" [1958]: see Silverberg, ed., *Dark Stars*, pp. 137–62.

——. "When We Went to See the End of the World." In Silverberg, *Unfamiliar Territory*, pp. 138–46. New York: Scribner's, 1973.

——. "The Wind and the Rain": see Roger Elwood and Virginia Kidd, eds., *Saving Worlds*, pp. 225–35.

Simak, Clifford D. *City*. New York: Gnome, 1952.

Slater, Henry J. *Ship of Destiny*. New York: Crowell, 1951.

Solovyov, Vladimir. *War and Christianity* [*Tri Razgovora*, 1900], tr. Edward Cazalet, et al. New York: Putnam, 1915.

Southwold, Stephen. [Miles, pseud.]. *The Gas War of 1940*. London: Partridge, 1931.

——. [Neil Bell, pseud.]. *The Lord of Life*. Boston: Little, Brown, 1933.

——. [Miles, pseud.]. *The Seventh Bowl*. London: Partridge, 1930.

Spitz, Jacques. *La guerre des mouches*. Paris: Gallimard, 1938.

——. *Sever the Earth* [*L'agonie du globe*, 1935], tr. Margaret Mitchiner. London: Bodley Head, 1936.

Stableford, Brian. *The Blind Worm*. New York: Ace, 1970.

——. *Cradle of the Sun*. New York: Ace, 1969.

Stapledon, Olaf. *Darkness and the Light*. London: Methuen, 1942; reprinted, Westport, Conn.: Hyperion, 1974.

——. *Last and First Men: A Story of the Near and Far Future* [1930]. New York: Cape and Smith, 1931; reprinted, New York: Dover, 1968.

——. *Last Men in London*. London: Methuen, 1932.

——. *Star Maker*. London: Methuen, 1937; reprinted, New York: Dover, 1968.

Stevenson, Dorothy Emily. *The Empty World: A Romance of the Future*. London: Jenkins, 1936.

Stewart, Alfred Walter. See J. J. Connington.

Stewart, George R. *Earth Abides*. Boston: Houghton Mifflin, 1949.

Stone, George. *Blizzard*. New York: Grosset and Dunlap, 1977.

Stuart, Don. A., pseud. See John W. Campbell, Jr.

Sucharitkul, Somtow. *Starship & Haiku.* New York: Pocket Books, 1981.

Sullivan, Sheila. *Summer Rising* [title in U.S.: *The Calling of Bara*]. New York: Dutton, 1976.

Sutphen, Van Tassel. *The Doomsman.* New York: Harper, 1906; reprinted, Boston: Gregg, 1975.

Tarde, Gabriel. *Underground Man* [*Fragment d'histoire future*, 1904], tr. Cloudesley Brereton. London: Duckworth, 1905; reprinted, Westport, Conn.: Hyperion, 1974.

Tenn, William, pseud. [Philip Klass]. "The Custodian" [1953]. In Tenn, *Of All Possible Worlds*, pp. 138–59. New York: Ballantine, 1955.

——. "Generation of Noah" [1951]. In Tenn, *The Wooden Star*, pp. 11–25. New York: Ballantine, 1968.

Thibault, Anatole-François. See Anatole France.

Thurber, James. *The Last Flower: A Parable in Pictures.* New York: Harper, 1939.

Toynbee, Polly. *Leftovers.* London: Weidenfeld and Nicolson, 1966.

Tucker, Wilson. *The Long Loud Silence.* New York: Rinehart, 1952.

Vance, Jack. *The Dying Earth.* New York: Lancer, 1950.

Van Zeller, Claude Hubert. See Hugh Venning.

Venning, Hugh, pseud. [Claude Hubert Van Zeller]. *The End: A Projection, Not a Prophecy.* Buffalo: Desmond and Stapleton, 1948.

Verne, Jules. "L'éternel Adam." In Verne, *Hier et demain: Contes et nouvelles*, pp. 213–63. Paris: Hetzel, 1910.

Vidal, Gore. *Kalki.* New York: Random House, 1978.

——. *Messiah.* New York: Dutton, 1954.

Vonnegut, Kurt, Jr. *Cat's Cradle.* New York: Holt, 1963.

Walker, David. *The Lord's Pink Ocean.* Boston: Houghton Mifflin, 1972.

Wallace, Doreen, pseud. [Dora Rash]. *Forty Years On.* London: Collins, 1958.

Wandrei, Donald. "On the Threshold of Eternity." In Wandrei, *The Eye and the Finger*, pp. 339–44. Sauk City, Wis.: Arkham House, 1944.

——. "The Red Brain" [1927]. In Wandrei, *The Eye and the Finger*, pp. 328–38.

Waterloo, Stanley. *Armageddon.* Chicago: Rand, McNally, 1898; reprinted, Boston: Gregg, 1976.

Weinbaum, Stanley G. *The Black Flame* [1939]. Reading, Pa.: Fantasy Press, 1948.

Wells, H. G. *All Aboard for Ararat.* New York: Alliance, 1941.

——. "The Culminating Man." From the manuscript in the Wells Archive, University of Illinois, in W. Warren Wagar, ed., *H. G. Wells: Journalism and Prophecy, 1893–1946*, pp. 441–42. Boston: Houghton Mifflin, 1964.

——. "A Dream of Armageddon" [1901]. In *The Complete Short Stories of H. G. Wells*, pp. 1010–38. New York: St. Martin's, 1970.

——. "The Empire of the Ants" [1905]. In *The Complete Short Stories*, pp. 92–108.

——. *In the Days of the Comet.* New York: Century, 1906.

——. "The Man of the Year Million" [1893]. In Wagar, ed., *H. G. Wells: Journalism and Prophecy*, pp. 3–9.

——. *The Shape of Things to Come.* New York: Macmillan, 1933.

——. "The Star" [1897]. In *The Complete Short Stories*, pp. 644–55.

———. "The Story of the Last Trump" [1915]. In *The Complete Short Stories,* pp. 587–604.

———. *Things to Come.* New York: Macmillan, 1935.

———. *The Time Machine* [1895]. In *The Complete Short Stories,* pp. 9–91.

———. "A Vision of Judgment" [1899]. In *The Complete Short Stories,* pp. 109–14.

———. *The War in the Air.* New York: Macmillan, 1908.

———. *The War of the Worlds.* New York: Harper, 1898.

———. *The World Set Free.* New York: Dutton, 1914.

Wheatley, Dennis. *Sixty Days to Live.* London: Hutchinson, 1939.

White, James. *The Dream Millennium.* New York: Ballantine, 1974.

———. *Second Ending.* New York: Ace, 1962.

Wilhelm, Kate. *Where Late the Sweet Birds Sang.* New York: Harper and Row, 1976.

Wilson, Steve. *The Lost Traveller.* New York: St. Martins's, 1977.

Wolfe, Bernard. *Limbo.* New York: Random House, 1952.

Wollheim, Donald A., ed. *The End of the World.* New York: Ace, 1956.

Wright, S. Fowler. *The Adventure of Wyndham Smith.* London: Jenkins, 1938.

———. *The Amphibians: A Romance of 500,000 Years Hence.* London: Merton, 1925; reprinted, New York: World, 1951.

———. *Dawn.* New York: Cosmopolitan, 1929; reprinted, New York: Arno, 1975.

———. *Deluge.* New York: Cosmopolitan, 1928; reprinted, New York: Arno, 1975.

Wylie, Philip. *Tomorrow.* New York: Holt, 1954.

———. *Triumph.* Garden City, N.Y.: Doubleday, 1962.

———. See Edwin Balmer.

Wyndham, John, pseud. [John Beynon Harris]. *The Chrysalids* [title in U.S.: *Re-Birth*]. New York: Ballantine, 1955.

———. *The Day of the Triffids.* Garden City, N.Y.: Doubleday, 1951.

———. *The Kraken Wakes* [title in U.S.: *Out of the Deeps*]. New York: Ballantine, 1953.

Youd, Christopher Samuel. See John Christopher.

Zebrowski, George. *Macrolife.* New York: Harper and Row, 1979.

Zelazny, Roger. *Damnation Alley.* New York: Putnam, 1969.

——— See Philip K. Dick.

INDEX

235